THE DESCENDANTS

of

JOHANN ADAM FORNEY

1557 - 1963

by **HOWARD G. FORNEY**

> ## Notice
>
> In many older books, foxing (or discoloration) occurs and, in some instances, print lightens with wear and age. Reprinted books, such as this, often duplicate these flaws, notwithstanding efforts to reduce or eliminate them. The pages of this reprint have been digitally enhanced and, where possible, the flaws eliminated in order to provide clarity of content and a pleasant reading experience.

The Descendants of Johann Adam Forney 1557-1963.

Originally published
1963

Reprinted by:

Janaway Publishing, Inc.
732 Kelsey Ct.
Santa Maria, California 93454
(805) 925-1038
www.JanawayGenealogy.com

2013

ISBN: 978-1-59641-306-1

Made in the United States of America

SHIELD: Azure, (blue) In chief three stras (3) Argent, (silver) issuing from base three (3) ferns or (gold) out of mount Gules, red. Helmet, of proper color, lined Gules, (red).

WREATH: of alternate colors of Azure and or (blue and gold).

CREST: one (1) wing of Gules, (red), surmounted by one (1) fern of or (gold).

MANTLING: left side Gules, (red) or (gold) and Argent, (silver); right side of Azure, (blue) or (gold) and Argent, (argent). Under 1510 a small shield of Gules (red) there on a tower of Argent, silver or white under which is a mount of Argent, (silver).

MEANING of COLORS: (Azure, blue, air, summer, childhood, justice, hopeful, sapphire, Jupiter). (Ar., Argent, silver, white, morning, infancy, hope, pearl, Luna). (or, gold, yellow moon, fortitude, topaz, Sol). (Gu., Gules, red, fire, autumn, charity, jewels, ruby, Mars). (Ppr., proper color or the color of nature).

STARS: The five (5) pointed star Guillim states is a falling or fallen star, not supposed to be fallen from its high estate, but to denote some Divine quality bestowed from above, whereby men shine in virtue, learning and works of piety like bright stars on the earth.

FERNS: were worn at weddings, festivals and feast in that spring time of the world, the ancient classic times. The wreath was often worn around the neck in order that the scent might be fully enjoyed. It was the emblem of "Joy." The fern represents some splendid service, possibly in behalf of the House of Feeney. This lovely graceful fern lent origin to the name spelled in various ways. (French: Ferney); (Switzerland: Fahrni); (Germany: Farny); (America: Forney).

MANTLING: is a cloth suspended from a point on the top of the helmet. Its purpose in real warfare was to save the armour from rust; to absorb the heat of the sun playing upon the metal armour; and entangle the sword of an adversary. Originally it was of hood or cape shape. It was torn during battle and Heraldry holds no set rules as to its design. However, it usually takes its colors from the shield.

WREATH: is a skein of silk with a gold or silver cord twisted round it. It is drawn as six (6) alternate links of metal and color. Originally it was drawn of twelve (12) alternate links and was used to hide the joining of the crest to the helmet.

CREST: was made of light wood or leather. It was taken off during battle. It is the ornament which surmounts the helmet. Only those families which were of tournament rank were entitled to crest.

HELMET: is that of an Esquire, is in profile; of metal and lined with red velvet.

WING: denotes a higher life.

CASTLE: on small shield just under 1510 denotes one who has faithfully held one for his king, or who has captured one by force or stratagem. There may also be a scriptural reference intended. The castle or tower is the emblem of grandeur and solidity.

PREFACE

This name, so honorably known in America, emanates from several emigrant heads, all undoubtedly traceable to the ancestral family seat at Ferney, a town in the Department of Ain, on the border of France, near the City of Geneva. The name occurs prominently in French History. Some of this name of the Huguenot faith forsook their native land, because of the religious persecutions, and located in Switzerland and the Palatinate immediately adjacent; from whence they came to America. It is a significant fact that nearly all the immigrants of this name came in the company of Huguenots. While we are not prepared to say that all of the Forney immigrants were of Huguenot antecedents, it is established beyond a doubt that Peter Forney, Sr., who came to Lancaster County prior to 1733, must be designated as one. He is known to have come from the borders of France, near Geneva, which would incline to the belief that his home was at or near the town from which the family took its name. The date of his arrival is not certainly known. In 1733 he obtained a warrant for land on Cocalico, where he died intestate in 1749, leaving five children and a considerable estate. It is a significant fact that his minor child, Anna, choose as her guardian "Christian Farnoy" who probably was an uncle and who arrived in 1734. The descendants of Peter Forney preserve many traditions of their Huguenot antecedents. The late Colonel John W. Forney, during a visit to France in 1875, had the pleasure of meeting several distinguished personages of his name who claimed kinship. Among the descendants of Peter Forney were Colonel John W. Forney, Colonel Wien Forney, both of whom were born in Lancaster County.

The Father of Jacob Forney (1721-1806) fled from France to the Palatinate, from whence the Son came to Lancaster County, in Pennsylvania. He married Maria Bergner, and in 1754 moved to Lincoln County, North Carolina; in Wheeler's History of that State, we learn that they were Huguenots. He and his sons, Jacob, Peter and Abraham, became very prominent. The son, Gen. Peter Forney (1756-1834), served in the Revolution and was one of the foremost men of the State; he was a member of Congress 1813-1815. His brother Abraham (1758-1849), also served in the Revolution and greatly distinguished himself at the battle of King's Mountain.

Generals John H. Forney and William H. Forney of the Confederate Army were descendents of Jacob Forney (see "Forney Forever" and "The Swope Family").

Johann Adam Forney, son of Christian and Madle Frick Forney, no doubt was born at or near the village of Fahrni, Switzerland. Records show he was an apprentice tailor at Steffisburg, Switzerland. During this writer's trip (1963) and search of the records of the archives in the town of Wachenheim, Germany, it was found that Johann Adam owned large vineyards of #1 quality. (There are five grades of quality in this area, where the finest wine grapes in the world are grown). His brothers, Christian, a vinedresser, and Felix, who was six years younger and also a tailor by trade, lived at Wachenheim.

Johann Adam Forney and his wife, Elizabeth Lowisa, with their four children arrived at Philadelphia on October 16, 1721. The name then was spelled "Farney," and his wife was listed as "Lowisa Farnison." Their first ten years were spent in Philadelphia County, after which the family located in 1734 in Conewago Settlement, or, as is sometimes called "Diggs' Choice." Today this is known as Hanover, York County, Pa.

There is an early tradition that three Forney Brothers came together to America, but all the geneologists deny the statement; however, with all the traditions and statistics gathered from many, many Forney families in various countries, it should be proof beyond doubt that Peter, Jacob and Johann Adam Forney were very closely related and that they all were Huguenots.

FORWARD

Authentic written history supplies one of the chief wants of the highest civilization, and the character and culture of the people of a nation are in no small degree measured by their published records.

Local history stimulates local pride, which is a bond of sympathy in the smaller communities, the surest safeguard of liberty and the staunchest champion of right and justice.

The following is a list of people who undertook the responsibility of recording Forney History:

"Tracings of the Ancestral Lines"
   by *Mrs. Annie Forney Bush*

"Forneys of Hanover, Pennsylvania"
   by *Lucy Forney Bittinger,* published in
   1893, a private edition and very scarce
   now.

"Sketches of the Forney Family"
   by *H. O. F.,* privately published in 1911.

"The Forney Family from Lancaster County, Pa."
   printed in 1926 by *John K. Forney* of Abilene,
   Kansas.

"Forney's Five Family Records"
   by *Charles William Forney,* Thurman, Iowa.

"Forney Forever"
   by *Mrs. Webb Crawford, Jr.,* Birmingham, Alabama.

H.G.F.

Forney

The Forney Coat of Arms as shown in *"The Colonial and Revolutionary Lineages of America,"* Vol. 1, opp. page 40.

Forney Coat of Arms: (Spelled also Forneys or Fornens). Co., Norfolk. **SHIELD:** Sa., a pile engr., Ar., **CREST:** a wheel Az. This information found on page 367 in General Armory by Burke in the Library of Congress.

MOTTO: A Deo lux nostra. (Our light is from God).

MEANING OF COLORS: (Sa., sable, black, earth, winter, night, death, prudence, discreet, Saturn). (Ar., argent, silver, white, water, infancy, hope, diamond, Luna). (Az., azure, blue, air, summer, childhood, justice, hopeful, ardent, dragon's head, sapphire, Jupiter). (Gu., gules, red, fire, autumn, manhood, charity, fiery, ruby, jewels, Mars). (Or., gold, yellow, light, moon, fortitude, topaz, Sol).

PILE: representing a pile used in the erection of military bridges, should contain, if borne plain, one-third of the chief in breadth, and when charged, two-thirds; it issues from the chief and tapers to a point, like a wedge, toward the base. It is also one of the Heraldic honorable Ordinaries, which is a piece of steel bolted to the shield to render added strength.

ENGRAILED: is a line of partition. An in and out line of semicircles touching in points or points outward.

THE WHEEL: a circular frame or structure capable of turning on a central axle. The wheel is the symbol of progress. Civilization advanced slowly until the invention of the wheel; up until this time drags were used to transport articles. The invention of the wheel took place about 6000 years ago, revolutionizing locomation on land, replacing ox drawn sledges. At first a round disc was used, which gradually gave way to spokes.

Fleur-de-lis

The flower of a plant of the genus; also the plant. The heraldic lily; the royal arms of France; hence the French Royal Family, the French flag (before 1789), hence the French royal arms of France; the French Nation or Government.

HUGUENOT

Huguenots - the name was given about the middle of the 16th Century to the Protestants of France; the word is a nickname. A monk in a sermon declared that Lutherans ought to be called Huguenots, as kinsmen of King Hugo.

The Huguenots were routed at the battle of Moncontour in France. The date was Oct. 3, 1569.

French Huguenots in America date back as far as the Mayflower. Priscilla Mullins, who married John Alden in Henry Wadsworth Longfellow's tale of "*The Courtship of Miles Standish,*" no doubt was one of the first to reach American soil. She was supposed to be English, but historians now know she was a French Huguenot who had spent only a few days on British soil while waiting for the Mayflower to sail. Other well-known Huguenot names have appeared in America; such as, Paul Revere, Marquis de Lafayette, of Revolutionary War fame, Charles L'Enfant, who designed the Great Seal of the United States with its symbolic eagle, French-American John C. Garand who invented The Garand Rifle that was used in World War 11. Presidents of the United States of Huguenot Ancestry were: Garfield, Tyler and both Roosevelts. The name du Pont is a powerful one in American industry. Many American cities acquired French names.

French culinary is responsible for many words in the American vocabulary; such as, bouillon, omelette, puree', mayonnaise, hors d'oeuvre, consomme', filet mignon, and saute'.

Bartholdi's Statue of Liberty, erected on the tiny Island in New York Harbor, was given to us by a nation whose immigrant sons have contributed so much and in so many ways to the making of a great America.

FERNEY-VOLTAIRE, CHATEAU

This estate is situated in the district of Gex in France, just over the Swiss frontier, close to Geneva. Voltaire said, here, he had his front legs in Switzerland and his hind legs in France, and *"so happy that he was ashamed of it."*

Ferney, France is no doubt the birthplace of the Forney family. Some of this name fled to Switzerland during the Huguenot religious persecutions and settled in what is now Fahrni, Switzerland; later on some went to the Palatinate along the Rhine in Germany. From this area is where Johann Adam Forney left for America in 1721.

HEREDITY

I've tried to trace our family name -
Not because I want acclaim,
But 'cause we Forneys all should be
Sharers in our heredity.

'Tis a very proud name we bear
So our children should be taught to care,
As our kinfolks' traits oft appear
In many of our mannerisms queer.

I fervently hope in years to come
Someone may benefit from the work I've done,
And carry on our Forney history;
For me that would be a victory.

If any mistakes you happen to see,
In past or present pedigree,
This hasn't been an easy task,
So "bear with me" is all I ask.

                Written for
                Howard G. Forney
                      by
                His Wife, Mary Louise

THE STORY OF STEFFISBURG IN SWITZERLAND

Formerly the name of this place was written as Stevensburg, Stesansburg, and Staffisburg. In the year 1133 this place was mentioned in a document for the first time. The old knight family names were Von Steffisburg, Von Schwarzenegg, Von Kyburg, and Von Buchegg. The land belonged to the Government of Bern; its capitol was Thun. Originally the country was property of some monasteries; for instance, Interlaken.

Steffisburg was the seat of the Courts to which other places belonged; like Fahrni, Schwarzenegg, Eriz, Teufental, Langenegg, Horrenbach, Hofstetten, Heimburg, Goldiwil and Sigriswil. These villages are situated mainly in the north of Lake Thun, where the country "rises with its rugged, uncouth precipitous rocks to wooded hills which compete courageously with giants and Stockhorn."

In war, the citizens of Steffisburg fought under the flag of Thun. During the Peasant War of 1641 and 1653, many people from Steffisburg played their part, e. g. the "Weibel" (military rank at that time); for example, Christen Zimmermann.

The reformation was introduced in 1528; the church was altered in 1681. The Emigration was caused by economical, political, and religious causes, partly; just as well by the love for migrating. An example is the people of Bern - most of them emigrated secretly, individually, and others in groups. They settled in waste and rarely populated places in the Pfalz, so forming the basic roots for a new population. They also wandered to other German provinces, and to Holland, America, and the Cape. Vice versa, citizens from the Pfalz moved to Switzerland. Therefore, about the year 1650 teachers lived in Steffisburg who originated in the Pfalz. After the Emigration Period was over - the emigration taking place from 1650 until 1750 - Steffisburg counted 900 inhabitants.

STEFFISBURG OF TODAY

The village lies on the road Bern and Thun and is almost grown together with the latter. The widespread settlement changes from farm country to smaller cities, separated by gardens and meadows, as well as by wooded areas. Around the church in the upper village is the heart, so to speak; the center lies 600 meters above sea level. Beautiful houses with bent and triangular-shaped gabled roofs are predominant; from the windows, cornices and fountains greet red flowers.

Since 1760 the population grew. About 1800 there were 1,500; by 1850 - 3,200; and by 1900 - 4,800 citizens. That was the time when Steffisburg developed its industry. Equipment, textile and furniture factories moved in, and by 1957, the small city exceeded 10,000. Many family names are well known to the people living in the Pfalz. But none of the names appear as often as the name Farni.

Here also many names can be traced back to places, as for example the Burgdorfer, Frutiger, Opliger, Reutiger, as well as the name Frick for the village Frick near Aargau, and Farni from the 3 kilometers which in clerical matters belongs to Steffisburg. We find in 1559 a Christian von Farne, a Nicolaus and Hansen von Farne, a Uli von Farnir and in 1557 an Agens von Farne. After 1600, the name is also written Varni and Varny. In the course of time, the most common form is FARNI, but among all these different ways of writing appears also FORNI. Certain families seemed to prefer the "o" way of writing; sometimes it seems to be just a habit of writing. The children from the marriage between Christen FARNI and Cahrin ULI are partly written with an "a," partly with an "o."

In 1650 we have a marriage of FORNI and FARNI and in 1627 an Anna FORNY. The emigrated Farnis often in their new settlements acquired entirely new names, according to the pronunciation or way of writing in their new home places. The emigrated Farnis near Durkheim and Pfalz are spelled FARNE and FARNY. The latter form of writing is common to the present time. The greatest change occurs with Christian Farni, who moved from Switzerland to Wachenheim near Durkheim about 1680. His name becomes FORNICH, also FORNICK and VORNICK, even FORNICK-ER. The ones who remained in Switzerland, generally spell the name FAHRNI. Around the whole environs north from Lake Thun and in Thun itself, live numerous Fahrnis; also in Steffisburg, and in farther distant places of the land Bern.

Baptisms of children whose fathers' name were Farni:
(In Switzerland)

Many emigrants were baptized by the Pastor Johannes Jacob Freudenreich, and also married by him. His tombstone is in the church yard in Steffisburg and the text reads: *Johannes Jacob Freudenrych, born 1639, Pastor in Damlingen 1664, came to Steffisburg 1670. Deacon of the Class Thun 1705, died Oct. 21, 1717.* He did the registering with a beautiful and legible hand writing.

          1560 *Hans*, son of Hansen Farne and Dichtla Meyteler.
9 Apr. 1559 *Elsbeth,* dau. of Nicolausen Farne and Maria Schluen.

15 Jan. 1559 *Steffan,* son of Christanus Farne and Barblen Mathisen.
      1557 *Christina,* dau. of Christan Farnir and Barbara Mathisen.
11 July 1557 *Lucia,* dau. of Peter Zunor? and Agnesen Farni.
20   1557 *Peter,* son of Clauri Farnir and Maria Widmann.
15   1559 *Dichtla,* dau. of Uli Farnir and Barbli Tustherr.
        1642 *Uli Farni.*
19 Dec. 1641 *Agathe,* dau. of Michel Farni and Margret Roth.
10 Oct. 1661 *Christen,* son of Christen Farni and Christine Roth;
             Godparents - Christen Roth, Nicolaus Fucher,
             Vernena Gerber.
        1641 *Anni,* dau. of Steffan Forny and Madlen Glauren.
        1641 *Uli,* son of Peter Farni and Cathri.
27 Dec. 1640 *Anna,* dau. of Clauri Farni and Anna Gissler.
 9 Jan. 1640 *Maria,* dau. of Steffan Farni and Mari Gurther;
             Godparents - Christine and Verena Farnin.
14 Jan. 1658 *Hans,* son of Hans Farni and Elsbeth Mettler;
             Godparents - Hans Oppliger, Hans Pirri? Barb.
             Maasovis?
20 June 1658 *Christen,* son of Steffanus Farni and Barbara Reuber;
             Godparents - Peter Dummermuth   Molitor Rotach.
19 Sept. 1658 *Uli,* son of Hans Farni and Madelen Gerber;
             Godmother - Mari Farni.
16 Jan. 1659 *Hans,* son of Steffan Farni and Baby Reusser;
             Godfather - Hans Farni.
16 Jan. 1659 *Hans,* son of Christen Farni and Madelena Frick;
             Godparents - Peter Gerber, Hans Buhler, Maria
             Dachseggerin.
    Jan. 1660 *Adam,* son of Hans Farni and Madle Gerber.
25 Aug. 1661 *Hans,* son of Steffan Farni and Babi Reusser;
             Godparents - Hans Farni, Steffen's son in Eriz,
             Hans Farni, Peter's son.
 8 Sept. 1661 *Christen,* son of Christen Farni and Madel Frick;
             Godparents - Uli Zimmermann, Hans Kolb,
             Christen Wertmuller.
19 Oct. 1662 *Hans,* son of Peter Farni and ?
             Godparents - Hans Farni in Horrenbach,
             Christen Weib, Cathie.
26 July 1663 *Christen,* son of Adam Farni and Cathie Ruxegger;
             Godparents - Christen Wertmuller, Christien
             Zimmermann, Anne Schreiber, Hansen Tochter.
15 Oct. 1663 *Michel,* son of Uli Farni and Elsbeth Roth;
             Godparents - Peter Farni, Uli's son, Uli Russer,
             Cathie.
 2 Nov. 1663 *Hans,* son of Hans Farni and Madle Gerber;

	Godparents - Hans Farni, and Hans Farni in Eriz and Baby Russer.
1664	*Benedicta,* dau. of Hans Farni and Trini Gerger.
25 Sept. 1664	*Christen,* son of Hans Farni and Eva Usinger; Godparents - Hans Reuber, Uli, Peter Farni's son.
6 Nov. 1664	*Uli,* son of Peter Farni and Margret Rupp; Godparents - Hans Farni in Horrenbach, Uli Farni.
11 Dec. 1664	*Hans,* son of Christen Forni and Cathie Uli.
1664	*Christen,* son of Steffan Farni, Uli's son and Baby Reusser; Godparents - Uli Farni, Peter's son Uli Stucker, Madle Gerber.
5 Mar. 1665	*Michel,* son of Uli Farni and Elsi Roth.
30 Apr. 1665	*Uli,* son of Hans Farni and Elsi Schwaar in Eriz; Godparents - Uli Gerber, Hans Zimmermann, Babi Farni.
22 Oct. 1665	*Hans,* son of Christen Farni and Madlen Frick.
1665	*Uli,* son of Christen Farni and Cathrie Farni.
14 Jan. 1666	*Peter,* son of Hans Farni and Cathrie Gerber; Godparents - Peter Farni, Uli Farni, Josef Reuber, Cath.
14 Jan. 1666	*Anna,* dau. of Michel Forni and Anna Zimmermann; Godfather - Christ.
11 Mar. 1666	*Mattys,* son of Peter Farni and Froni Roth; Godparents - Hans Farni, Cathrin Farni, Peter Tochter.
11 Nov. 1666	*Uli,* son of Steffan Farni and Babi Reusser; Godfather - Uli Farni.
24 Feb. 1667	*Peter,* son of Peter Farni and Margret Rupp.
31 Mar. 1667	*Peter,* son of Uli Farni and Elisabeth; Godparents - Peter Farni, Uli Gerber in Eriz and Buler.
10 Mar. 1667	*Peter,* son of Christen Forni and Froni Schneeberg; Godfather - Peter Ruxegger.
21 Apr. 1667	*Nicolaus,* son of Christen Farni and Madle Frick; Godparents - Hans Ruxegger, Christine Zongg, Matthys Zonggs Weib.
26 May 1667	*Hans,* son of Hans Farni and Elsi Schwaar in Eriz.
22 Sept. 1667	*Hansen,* son of Nicol Farni, from Durren and Lucia; Godfather - Hans Farni.
1668	*Abraham,* son of Stefan Farni and Barb. Russer.
4 Oct. 1668	*Nicolaus,* son of Adam Farni and Cathrin Ruxegger.
4 Oct. 1668	*Uli,* son of Uli Farni and Elsi Roth.
1668	*Nicolaus,* son of Hans Farni and Elsbeth Schwaar.

15 Aug. 1669 *Hans,* son of Christen Forni and Cathrin Uli.
24 Nov. 1669 *Steffan,* son of Steffan Farni and Babi Reusser.
29 May 1670 *Michel,* son of Uli Farni and Elsi Roth.
23 Oct. 1670 *Hans,* son of Michel Forni and Anna Frey.
        1671 *Barbara,* dau. of Christen Farni and Cathrie Uli.
 7 Apr. 1671 *Hans,* son of Hans Farni, in Eriz and Elsbeth
            Schwaar; Godparents - Christen Farni, Barb. Farni.
19 Mar. 1671 *Hans,* son of Adam Farni and Cath. Ruxegger;
            Godfather - Peter Farni.
 2 July 1671 *Hans,* son of Nicolaus Farni, in Durren.
19 Nov. 1671 *Nickel,* son of Steffan Farni and Barbara
            Reusser; Godparents - Michel Buler and
            Elsbeth Krafft.
24 Sept. 1671 *Matthys,* son of Christen Farni and Magdalena Frick;
            Godparents - Uli Gerber, Matthaus Uli, Anna Sterno?
 6 Mar. 1681 *Hans,* son of Uli Forni and Barbara Schenk.
        1681 *Ulrich,* son of Peter Farni, in Horrenbach,
            and Elsbeth Egli.
 2 Oct. 1681 *Christen,* son of Steffan Farni and Maria Hagg.
30 Oct. 1681 *Anna,* dau. of Christen Forni and Cathrin Uli.
30 Oct. 1681 *Hans,* son of Christ. Forni and Anna Forni.
        1682 *Verena,* dau. of Michel Forni and Anna Frey.
12 Nov. 1682 *Child,* of Ulrich Farni, from Kiesen and
            Verena Muller.
12 Nov. 1682 *Cathrin,* dau. of Michel Farni and Anna Schneiter.
 1 July 1683 *Christen,* son of Christen Forni and Anna Forni.
28 Oct. 1683 *Anna,* dau. of Peter Farni and Elsbeth Egli.
17 Feb. 1684 *Anna,* dau. of Hans Farni and Anna.
        1684 *Johannes,* son of Peter Farni, of Eriz, and
            Magdalena Starr.
13 July 1684 *Abraham,* son of Steffan Farni and Mari Hegg;
            Godfather - Christen Farni.
15 Feb. 1685 *Christen,* son of Christen Farni and Cathrin Farni;
            Godmother - Maria.
25 Oct. 1685 *Christen,* son of Christen Farni and Cathrin Uli.
 6 Dec. 1685 *Jakob,* son of Peter Farni and Magdalena Starr.
 3 Jan. 1686 *Jakob,* son of Christen Farni and Anna Farni.
18 Aug. 1686 *Christen,* son of Ulrich Farni and Elsbeth Reusser;
            Godfather - Ulrich Farni.
12 Sept. 1686 *Elsbeth,* dau. of Peter Farni and Elsbeth Egli;
            Godfather - Ulrich Farni.
12 Sept. 1686 *Elsbeth,* dau. of Christen Farni and Cathrin;
            Godfather - Peter Farni.
 7 Aug. 1687 *Verena,* dau. of Ulrich, Peter's son, and
            Magdalena Zimmermann.

13 Nov. 1687 *Peter,* son of Ulrich Farni, Christen's son, and Elsbeth; Godfather - Peter Farni.

27 Nov. 1687 *Barbara,* dau. of Christen Farni and Verena; Godmother - Cathr. Farni.

1688 *Verena,* dau. of Christen Farni and Cathrin.

3 Feb. 1689 *Verena,* dau. of Ulrich Farni and Cathr.

27 ? 1689 *Christen,* son of Peter Farni, of Eriz, and Magdalena Starr.

9 June 1689 *Magdalena,* dau. of Elsbeth Engel, Peter Farni, of Horrenbach; Godfather - Peter Farni.

1689 *Cathrin,* dau. of Ulrich Farni, the young son of Christen, and Elsbeth Reusser.

16 Nov. 1689 *Hans,* son of Hans Farni and Anna; Godfather - Christen Farni.

9 Mar. 1690 *Barbara,* dau. of Christen Farni and Cathrin.

15 May 1690 *Cathrin,* dau of Ulrich Farni, Steffan's son from Dachsegg and Elsbeth Farni.

1690 *Hans,* son of Hans Farni the miller, Cathrin Rupp.

3 Aug. 1690 *Ulrich,* son of Ulrich, Christen Farni's son and Elesbeth Reusser; Godfather - Ulrich, Peters son.

? ? ? *Hans,* son of Ulrich Farni, Steffan's son in Dachsegg and Elsbeth Farni.

12 July 1691 *Anna,* dau. of Christen Farni, Steffan's son and Cathrin.

24 Apr. 1692 *Peter,* son of Peter Farni and Elsbeth Egli.

? ? ? *Anna,* dau. of Michel Farni and Anna Buler; Godmother - Cathrin Farni.

6 Dec. 1692 *Cathrin,* dau. of Ulrich Farni and Elsbeth Reusser; Godmother - Barb. Farni.

1695 - 94 *Magdalena,* dau. of Peter Farni, Steffan's son from Eriz, and Magdalena Starr.

1696 - 95 *Barbara,* dau. of Peter Farni.

1697 *Barbara,* dau. of Abraham Farni, of Eriz and Anna Carli.

1697 *Magdalena,* dau. of Hans Farni and Anna.

16 Apr. 1699 *Verena,* dau. of Peter Farni, of Eriz.

9 June 1700 *Peter,* son of Hans Farni and Anna; Godmother - Barbara Farni.

17 Feb. 1701 *Peter,* son of Ulrich Farni and Christine Rupp.

Marriages
(The husband's name is Farni)

7 Oct. 1611 *Stefan Farni* and Madlen Mettler.

22 Jan. 1619 *Hans Varni* and Christiana Luscher.

26	?	1621	*Jacob Forni* and Cathrin Mettler.
11	July	1631	*Hans Varni* and Margaretha Wenger.
28	Jan.	1631	*Nicolaus Farni* and Anna Stutzmann.
6	June	1631	*Peter Forni* and Anna.
25	June	1631	*Steffan Farni* and Maria Gurtner.
18	Sept.	1637	*Steffan Farni* and Anna Jenner?
18	Sept.	1637	*Christen Forni* and Christina Rot.
17	May	1639	*Michel Forni* and Margret Rot.
27	Apr.	1646	*Hans Farne* and Eva Uziger.
29	Mar.	1647	*Steffan Farni* and Barb. Russer.
9	Mar.	1648	*Uli Farni* and ? Schoni.
15	Mar.	1650	*Hans Forni* and Catharina Farni.
5	Dec.	1651	*Steffan Farni* and Barb. Russer.
7	Nov.	1653	*Hans Forni* and Elsbeth Metler.
27	Oct.	1654	*Steffan Forni* and Anna Zuomin.
19	Oct.	1654	*Christen Farni* and Madle Frick.
25	May	1657	*Hans Farni* and Magdalena Gerber.
25	May	1657	*Peter Farni* and Verena Roht.
4	Sept.	1659	*Uli Farni* and Elsbeth Roth.
18	Nov.	1659	*Hans Farni* and Elsbeth Schwaar.
7	Nov.	1662	*Peter Farni* from Eriz and Barbara Isti?
23	June	1663	*Christen Forni* and Cathrie Uli.
23	June	1666	*Hans Farni* and Anni Schmid.
			Christen Forni and Froni Schneeberg.
11	Nov.	1670	*Hans Farni* from Eriz and Verena Stauffer.
30	Jan.	1670	*Christen Forni* and Anna Forni.
9	Feb.	1672	*Hans Forni* and Anna Sutterin from Emmendingden belonging to Margraviate Hochberg, from which they showed a Lutheran Document.
10	Oct.	1672	*Michel Forni* and Anna Wenger from Diesbach.
18	Oct.	1672	*Peter Farni* and Elsbeth Egli.
21	Apr.	1673	*Hans Farni* from Eriz and Anna Schenk.
31	May	1675	*Christen Forni* and Verena Muller.
22	June	1677	*Steffan Farni* and Maria Hagg.
4	Oct.	1678	*Hans Forni* and ? Schonenberg.
20	June	1679	*Peter Farni* and Anna Tschiner.
24	Oct.	1679	*Ulrich Forni* and Barbara Schenk.
25	Feb.	1681	*Ulrich Farni* and Anna Brendli.
5	Feb.	1682	*Peter Farni* and Magdal. Starr.
8	June	1683	*Hans Farni* and Anna.
2	Nov.	1683	*Steffan Farni* and Margret Willener.
2	Nov.	1683	*Ulrich Farni* and Elsbeth Tschiener.
6	Mar.	1685	*Christen Farni* and Verena.
18	June	1685	*Ulrich Farni* and Elsbeth Reusser.

2 Oct. 1685 *Peter Farni* and Barbara Murer.
15 Oct. 1686 *Christen Farni* and Cathrin.
 3 Dec. 1686 *Ulrich Farni* and Änna Bankmann.
24 Feb. 1688 *Hans Farni* and Cathrin Rupp.
15 Aug. 1690 *Hans Farni* and Barbara Byland.
 6 June 1692 *Michel Farni* and Anna Buler.

Marriages
(The Wife's name is Farni)

        1611 Vincentz Stauffer and *Christina Farni.*
10 Oct. 1616 Hans Gurtner and *Verena Varni.*
22 Jan. 1619 Uli Rot and *Anna Varny.*
18 May 1627 Uli Gerber(?) and *Barbli Farni.*
25 June 1627 Christen Murer and *Anna Forny.*
    1627-30 Peter and *Margareta Forni.*
 2 Apr. 1638 Wolfgang Blank and *Margret Forni.*
25 May 1646 Fenner Weibel and *Barbli Forni.*
13 June 1646 Christen Schneiter and *Barbli Forni.*
21 Feb. 1653 Valentin Gerber and *Verena Farni.*
 2 May 1656 Christen Stauffer and *Verena Farni.*
13 June 1656 Abraham Hofstetter and *Madle Farni.*
16 Jan. 1657 Peter Burki and *Verena Forni.*
23 Jan. 1657 Peter Zimmermann and *Verena Farni.*
25 May 1657 Hans Stutzmann and *Anna Farni.*
 5 Feb. 1658 Michel Meier and *Baby Farni from Eriz.*
 8 Nov. 1661 Hans Wittwer and *Anna Forni.*
 7 Aug. 1663 Hans Lemann and *Anni Farni.*
15 Jan. 1664 Christen F? and *Cathrie Farnie in Eriz.*
 7 Dec. 1666 Niehaus Galli and *Anna Farni.*
 1 Feb. 1667 Hans Sutor and *Agathe Farni.*
 5 Oct. 1668 Christen Wyss and *Anna Farni from Eriz.*
              Peter Buchsel and *Mari Farni from Eriz.*
30 Sept. 1672 Ulrich Steiner and *Barbara Farni.*
18 Nov. 1672 Uli Sterno? and *Elsbeth Farni.*
27 June 1673 Andreas Hiesing and *Elsbeth Farni.*
 4 Dec. 1674 Christen Lemann and *Cathrin Farni.*
24 Jan. 1676 Matthys Zuber and *Christina Farni.*
        1676 Christen Gurtner and *Verena Farni.*
22 June 1677 Hans Rupp and *Ana Farni.*
16 July 1680 Hans Finger and *Cathrin Farni.*
21 Jan. 1681 Christen Ruchti and *Anna Farni.*
11 Feb. 1681 Adam Blank and *Anna Farni.*
28 Oct. 1681 Josef Reusser and *Benedikta Farni.*
15 Dec. 1682 Hans Frey and *Cathrin Forni.*
 2 Nov. 1683 Michel Meier and *Barbara Farni.*

11 Dec. 1685 Ulrich Reusser and *Barbara Farni*.
14 Jan. 1687 Adam Kaufmann and *Barb. Farni*.
10 Jan. 1689 Jacob Stutz and *Christina Farni*.
28 Mar. 1690 Hans Kraff and *Elsbeth Farni*.
18 Nov. 1692 Christen Schneiter and *Verena Farni*.
9 Dec. 1692 Hans Sempach and *Barb. Farni*.
9 Dec. 1692 Christoffel Meier from Hilterfingen and *Anna Farni*.
30 June 1693 Jacob and *Christina Farni*.
17 Feb. 1696 Ulrich Hempeler and *Barb. Farni*.
20 Mar. 1705 Ulrich Gerber and *Elsbeth Farni, from Schwarzenegg*.
21 Jan. 1707 Nicolaus Gerber and *Magdalena Farni, from Schwarzenegg*.
25 Oct. 1709 Jacob Bapben from Spiez and *Anna Farni from Schwarzenegg*.

THE FORNEY FAMILY*
(In Germany)

"In reply to your letter we did investigations concerning the family Forney and hereby are able to confirm and certify the following Extract Copies from the Reformed Church-Book of Wachenheim 1700/70:-

"Under the Family Name: Forny, Vornick, Fornick, Fornich, Fornig, and Farnir we found the following statements:-

"1. On Nov. 7, 1700 **Christian Vornick** and his wife Christina had baptized their daughter Elisabeth. Her Godmother was Elisabetha Johannis Oberly, here citizen and Midwife and married wife (1st marriage).

"2. On Sept. 3, 1702 **Christian Forneick,** and his wife Christina had baptized their daughter Rosina Margaretha. Godmother and Godfather were Rosina Margaretha and Peter Zimmermanns, citizens here and married wife. The child died on March 22, 1703.

"3. On Dec. 7, 1704 **Christian Forny** and his wife Christina baptized a daughter Rosina Margaretha. The Godmother was Rosina Margaretha, wife of Peter Zimmermann.

"4. On March 7, 1705 was **burried Anna Christina**, wife of the **Christian Fornig.**

"5. Note 1705: **New Communicants** during Whitsun-Time have been: (10 names, hereunder twice Fornig) **Hans Adam Fornick** (Hans Adam Fornick was possibly in 1705 14 years old, consequently must have been born about 1691).

Maria ? (not readable Fornickin).

"6. On Aug. 26, 1705 **Christian Fornick** citizen here, was married with Apollonia, widow of Mattias Hasslers, former at Turckheim.
(2nd Marriage)

"7. On Jan. 25, 1713 Hans Georg Fili and **Maria Christina Fornick,** daughter of Christian Fornick, here, were married in **Seebach.**

"8. On Apr. 18, 1713 Rosina Margaretha, daughter of **Christian Fornick,** citizen here and his late wife Christina, was **burried** at the age of 9 years.

"9. On Nov. 10, 1713 Marx, son of **Johann Adam Fornick,** citizen and

Tailor here, and his wife Elisabeth Louisa, was baptized. Godfather was Marx Oberle, citizen and practitioner in curing and his wife, Godmother. (The Godfather died 1714, 23 years of age).

"10. On July 7, 1715 Niclas, son of Johann Adam Fornick, citizen and Tailor here, and his wife Elisabeth Louisa, was baptized. Godfather: Nickl Fornick, Grave-Digger at Durkheim, and his wife, Godmother.

"11. On April 26, 1718 Louisa Charlotte, daughter of Johann Adam Fornick and his wife Louisa, was baptized. Godmothers were: the two noble Fraulein von Blarer and Geiersberg. (Compare with the Wachenheimer History Sheets, Part 1).

"12. **Baptized** on Jan. 8, 1721 was Maria Eva, daughter of **Johann Adam Farnier** and Elisabetha, his wife. Godmother was Maria Eva, legal daughter of Matthias Hassler.

"13. On Dec. 1, 1722 have been married Christian Fornich, citizen here, and Anna, the widow of the late Hans Gayger.

(3rd Marriage)

"14. On Jan. 2, 1725 have been married **Christian Fornick,** citizen here, and Dorothea, the widow of the late Engelhardt Buhl. (Engelhardt Buhl has been a locksmith).

(4th Marriage)

"15. On Aug. 13, 1724 was burried the wife of Christian Fornick. (See No. 13 Gayger).

"16. On March 4, 1734 was burried Christian Fornick, 71 years of age, (therefore born in 1663). (The Church Books at Wachenheim start with the year 1700 only).

"17. On July 22, 1746 was burried the wife of the former citizen **Christian Fornich.** Her age is not stated since she died in poverty and was burried with the help of alms, and nobody knew anything about her age. (Widow Buhl).

"There are many ways of writing the names in the Church Books at Wachenheim - often you encounter two different ways of spelling a name on one page. We may assume that the name "Farny," which is common around Bad Durkheim, is the same as the Wachenheim name "Forny," which has become "Forney" in English."

*Note: The above is a translated letter, dated February 26, 1958, received from the Mayor of Wachenheim - Town Administration, **Das Bergermeistermat,** of the town Wachenheim a. d. Weinstr.*

Fornich Christian in the year of 1721
Register of Assessment 1721 11 No. 97

The house owned in the Lauer-District again registered, but then cancelled with remark: *Sold.* (The conclusion is drawn that this happened at this time).
Newly registered is:
One house in the Holzgasse, South Georg Peter Rettinger, North Jakob Zimmerman.
The house owned was about 1 Ar = 100 Square Meters, large. Of the Vineyards the one near the Red Tower is already sold, one "auf der Hoh" (½ Logel = barrel Treber-Wine Stift = Foundation Limburg) and also the other vineyards are sold. The acres are sold, 2 grass-lands (meadows) are still there, the one at Durkheimer Weg and a new one at the Schafweg, bearing an interest of 45 Kr (Kreuzer = German Coin at that time) from the University of Heidelberg. Fornich here again states, as his trade, Vinedresser; his age 65; for his wife, 59; his son, who for the time lived out of the country, he gives an age of 23; and the daughter, 19. Remark of the Council: In the assessment register as "70 year old man" taxed with 75 fl. (florins = old coin of that time). The age data are often contradicting; it is often presumed that they themselves did not know their age exactly enough. Johann Adam Forney, and his family are not any more registered in 1721. At this time he may not have lived here anymore. In 1721 he immigrated to America. In a book about the Maryland-Germans, published in English, he is nominated as one of the first immigrants. In thick books are the Assessment-Registers of 1718 bound, which are taxation lists, in which the citizen states his property and his earnings, and the town estimates the tax he has to pay to the town after quality and quantity. Either the inhabitants made out these lists by themselves or had sombody else do it for them. The lists of Christian Fornic and of Hans Adam Fornick are written in the same handwriting; possibly they were not very good at it. Both lists are signed with the name of "Fornich." Very likely that was the way the name was pronounced in Wachenheim. In Durkheim, the name is always written "Farni" or "Farne."

The lists of both the Fornichs show the numbers 92 and 93.

Christian Fornich States:

1. Buildings

One house in the Lauer-Viertel, towards the woods = (West) Pleikard Parish, toward the Rhine (= East) the Townwall, Up-Town (= South) the Gass, Down-Town (= North) the Townwall.

Bearing an interest to the Foundation Limburg 1 fl Pension (= Annual Due).

2. Vineyards

The half of one ½ Quarter "auf dem Graben" (at the trench) behind the Red Tower, interest: 1 Quarter 1 Mass (certain quantity of that time) of Wine to Limburg bordered with 95 Posts, today vineyards are bordered of or fenced in by wire, in those days the posts were bound to the grape-roots, and the size of the vineyard was estimated after the number of posts.

1 Quarter at the Red Tower is owned and contains 130 posts.

1 Quarter in the Brummersmorgen, let to the Junker von Dienheim, 2 Mass very good Wine, contains 163 posts.

1¾ Quarters "auf der Hoh", let to the Foundation Limburg, 2 Quarter 2 Schoppen of Wine, (Quarters and Schoppen are pots of a certain quanity) containing 270 Posts.

3. Acreages

1 Quarter on the Dalweg, owned, in 1719 it has been cultivated for the use of a vineyard.

1 Quarter on the Dalweg near the Chestnut-Forest (toward the South Hans Adam Fornich).

1 Quarter in "Hägel" (toward the South Hans Adam Fornich).

1½ Quarter in Oderstal, let to the "Kollektur" 7½.

½ Quarter in Königswingert.

4. Grassland

2 Quarters at the Dürkheimer Weg, let to the Kollektur 36 Kr.

My business and trade is Vinedresser, I am 60 years of age, my wife is 55 years of age. I have 2 children, 1 son, 20 years old 1 daughter, 17 years old. Wachenheim, May 25, 1718.

Signed: Christian Fornich

xxxxxxxxxxxxxxxxxxxxxxxxxxxxx

The Town estimates the Income and Property with 75 Gulden (of which the house itself is taxed with 15 Florins).

xxxxxxxxxxxxxxxxxxxxxxxxxxxxxx

In another Assessment Register of the year 1721 "**Fornich** does not live anymore in the **Lauerviertel**, but **Theobalth Mayer**, a tailor, it may be the son-in-law, at whom Fornich lives. The house now is taxed double as much, it could well be that it has been partly rebuilt and renovated. Mr. Fornich later on lived in the Holzgasse, 1733, next to Peter Rettinger, a man from Switzerland, who came from Obersimmental.

Fornich bought the house in the Lauer-Viertel (today Entengasse, Manz Jakob) on May 13, 1799 from the town for 12 Gulden (today's value about 300 German Marks), concluding from remarks noted, it should have been a "bad" house in poor shape, in 1689 it was burnt down and had no owner. The town sold the houses for little money, to encourage new citizens to settle down here."

The following is a copy of a letter (in part) from Hans Farny to the writer.

21 Sept. 1960
Beuel Bei Bonn,
Germany

Dear Sir:

Since a certain time I pursue vigorously the history of my family. This history will also be of interest to you, because we have the same family tree.

Mr. Spangenberger and myself have been 6 weeks ago in Switzerland at Steffisburg (Lake of Thun) and searched for our ancestors. We were very well satisfied with the results of our efforts. We had found the parents of Christian Farni in Wachenheim and of Niclas Farni in Durkheim. The two were cousins. Their fathers were brothers. The parents of your ancestor Christian were: Adam Farni and Cathie Ruxegger. Christian was baptized on 26th July 1663, his brother Niclas on the 4th October 1688 and his brother John on 19 March 1671. The godfathers of Christian were: Christian Wertmuller and Christian Zimmermann of Steffisburg. Niclas Farni in Durkheim (Palatinate) was *my* ancestor who emigrated from Switzerland to the Palatinate. His parents were: Christian Farni and Madle Frick of Steffisburg. My searching for our ancestors further backward will be continued. I shall start again as soon as possible to the Oberland of Bern where is the native country of all our ancestors. There is also the village "Farni" near Steffisburg. The historical and biografical dictionary of Switzerland reports on this village that this place before his settling was grown with fern (in German: Farn). This is the base of formation of our name. Farmers told me in Farni that the escutcheon of this village shows a fern.

Will you kindly excuse my not very sufficient knowledge of English, but I think you understand me. I hope you will be interested in a mutual correspondence about our family tree and I would be glad to hear from you soon.

I remain,

Yours truly

/s/ Hans Farny

Der Standesbeamte in Bad Dürkheim Mar. 6, 1959
Subject: Family History Farny/Farni/Farne.

1. Farni Nikolaus born 1666 in ? died Feb. 27, 1745. Married with Christina Apollonia (Maiden name not known) (no date) born about 1671 in ? died Dec. 16, 1703.

Children From 1st Marriage:
1689 Aug. 20 - Maria Salome
1690 Aug. 17 - Anna Elisabetha died Aug. 13, 1695
1693 Feb. 10 - Dau. without Christian name, died one hour after birth
1697 Feb. 13 - Anna Sophia
1699 Nov. 20 - Anna Elisabetha
1703 Apr.   4 - Maria Elisabetha died Jan. 11, 1704.

Married on May 30, 1704 with Anna Margaretha Zolikhoffer born 1680 in Weinheim a. d. Bergstrasse died De. 17, 1732.

Children From 2nd Marriage:
1705 Feb.   1 - Sybilla Philippina
1707 Jan. 16 - Maria Katharina
1710 June 18 - Hans Georg, married on Apr. 22, 1738
             (See Paragraph 11)

Married on Nov. 30, 1734 with Barbara Elisabetha. Widow - name Bockmeyer born ? died ? no children from 3rd marriage.

Nikolaus Farni died 1745 in the age of 79. He was 50 years long grave digger in Dürkheim. The first marriage did not take place in Dürkheim. The family presumably immigrated, first mentioned in Dürkheim 1689 according to Records in the Lutheran and Reformed Church Books.

11. Farny Joh. Georg (See above the ninth child of Nikolaus) born June 18, 1710 died Mar. 4, 1779. Married on Apr. 22, 1738 with Maria Magdalena Hamsch. Born about 1711 in ? Died Nov. 28, 1775.

Children

1739 Mar. 16 - Catharina Margaretha
1742 May 20 - Johann Jakob
1743 Aug. 18 - Maria Anna

lll. Farne Matthäus Married on Jan. 9, 1700 with Währung Anna Eva, born about 1671 presumably in Steffensburg died Oct. 5, 1749. The date of birth and death of Mrs. Farne is not known.

Children

1700 Oct. 20 - Susanna Catharina

Writing Styles of the Name: Farne and Farny

The way of writing Farne is according to the dialect, which is still the same as it was at that time. The official way of writing used today is Farny. Mattäus Farne was a son of Christian Farne from Steffensburg, Switzerland, District Bern. Matth. Farny died as a temporary gravedigger in Durkheim. Supposedly he took over this office from Nikolaus Farny, who presumably were brothers, or the children of two brothers, who immigrated from Switzerland.

xxxxxxxxxxxxxxxxxxx

Where no remarks are made, all birth, marriage and death dates refer to Dürkheim.

(Official Stamp
of
Der Standesbeamte
in Bad Dürkheim).

Der Standesbeamte
I. V.
Signed: Buchert

EXTRACT

from Daily Newspaper "Die Rheinpfalz"
(Wednesday April 8, 1959)
(TRANSLATION)

SWISS FAMILY IMMIGRATED HERE

(History of the Family Farny in Dürkheim and Wachenheim)
30 Kilometers south east of Bern, near Lake Thun, is Steffisburg, amidst

a district, from where 300 years ago thousands of Swiss people emigrated to find a new home place in the Pfalz. Amongst them are quite a few members of a family Forny of Farni, who deduce their name from the village Fahrni near Steffisburg.

1687 Christian Fornich is mentioned as a cowherd in Wachenheim. He immigrated as a young man with his wife to this town, which was destroyed by fire in 1674 and was almost rebuilt at the time he immigrated. In the "Lauer-Quarter" he acquired a ruin-place, which he called "A housing built up auxiliary." Two of his neighbors were also Swiss people, one Peter Zimmermann, had come from Steffisburg too. Christian Fornich acquired during the next years wineyards and acres, and all the 50 years through living in Wachenheim, he was called "Shepherd and Vine-dresser." The Wachenheim people changed his Swiss-sounding name right away into Fornich. Besides of that you can find many ways of writing this name, for instance Fornig, Vornick and Farnir.

The Swiss Immigration history teaches us, that often whole family groups settled down in the same district. In 1689 in Dürkheim for the first time Nickel Farni is mentioned. He was somewhat younger than the Wachenheim Fornich, also married, became a grave-digger and stayed that all his life long. Another name-cousin, Mattüas Farne, was married in Dürkheim in 1700, where as the father of the bridegroom Christian Farne from Steffisburg is stated. Presumably these 3 Farne Sons were the three sons of Christian F., Steffisburg. (Amongst the 70 Swiss Immigrants, who are mentioned in the Wachenheim History Booklets, are several from Steffisburg).

Furthermore we will mention the next generation, as far as the Male breed is concerned: Christian Fornich of Wachenheim had one son: Johannes Adam. He was a tailor, lived with his father, but did not own any property. The godfather of the grandchild Marx was the practitioner Marx Oberli, at the Nickel - the Grave-Digger of Dürkheim, at the daughter Luise Charlotte - "the two high-born (Right Honorable) Fräulein von Blarer von Geiersberg," and at the Baptism of Eva - the wife of Matthias Hässler in Dürkheim. In 1721 Johann Adam Fornich immigrated with his wife and four children to "the New Country Amerika." For so many Swiss people the Pfalz was nothing but a transit-station to America, particularly so with the Mennonites. Howard G. Forney, who lives in Warren, Ohio, puts a great effort in the search for his ancesters, and as far as we know, is a descendant of Johannes Adam.

Nickel Farni in Dürkheim had amongst 9 children one son Johann Georg, and his son was Johann Jakob. The male descendants of the Dürkheim

Farni are the still living Farny-Members.

It is not astonishing that the name Farny is spelled so many ways. Often the people were not able to write, and the officials of the town wrote the name of the family down after the sound only. And even though the people were able to write, it happened often that they spelled their names in different ways, whereas it was one and the same name. This happened to many Swiss Families, what the history registers show.

The following example will show this clearly:-
In Wachenheim the name Muhrer is widely spread. The first one of this name was the carpenter Hans Jerg Muhrer. We find his signature often on bills and receipts. In most cases he signs with Morrer, sometimes just Morr, but also Murrer and Murr. Morrer was formerly the way the name was pronounced. The form Muhrer developed later as the officially used one in writing and signing. It was similar with the names of places and villages. We find for instance the Steffisburg, the home place of the Forney family, spelled: Stefansburg or Bäffisburg.

Today Steffisburg is a wide spread village with more than 10,000 inhabitants; the village Farni is a parochial community with somewhat more than 700 people, its church is an underparochial church of Steffisburg. The names Farny and Zimmermann are still existent, and the family lines of the Pfalz people can be searched back further, because the Registers at the Standesamt Steffisburg lead back to the year 1557.

Airview of Steffisburg

View to the North: In the foreground at the left - two schoolhouses (Grammer Schools). *The River:* The Zulg, to the right the buildings of the Oil Company Astaa, in the background at the left hand the Church of Steffisburg. In the background at the hill: The Farmhouses of the Fahrni Family. The arrow shows the underparochial church of Fahrni.

ADVERTISEMENT

(The Country's First "War Loan" Advertisement)

"Notice is hereby given to all who have contracted to send wagons and teams or single horses from York County to the Army at Wills Creek, that David M. Conaugby and Micheal Schwoope of said county, Gentlemen, will attend on my behalf at York Town on Friday next, and at Philip Forney's on Saturday, to value or appraise all such wagons, teams and horses, as shall appear at those places on the said days for that purpose; and such as do not appear must be values at Wills Creek. The wagons that are valued at York and Forneys are to set out immediately after valuation from thence to Wills Creek, under the Conduct and Direction of persons I shall appoint for the purpose. The owner or owners of each wagon or set of horses should bring with them to the Place of Valuation and deliver to the appraisers, a paper containing a description of their several horses in writing, with their several marks natural and artificial; which paper is to be annexed to the contract. Each wagon should be furnished with a cover, that the goods laden therein may be kept from damage by the rain, and the health of the drivers preserved, who are to lodge in the wagons. And each cover should be marked with the contractor's name in large characters. Each wagon, and every horse driver, should also be furnished with a hook or sickle, fit to cut long grass that grows in the country beyond the mountains. As all the wagons are oblidged to carry a load of oats, or Indian corn, persons who have such grain to dispose of are desired to be cautious how they hinder the Kings Service, by demanding an extravagant price on this occasion."

B. FRANKLIN

Ben Franklin, at Lancaster, Pennsylvania, on May 6, 1775, caused to be written what is termed the country's first war loan advertisement. Franklin warned his readers against inflationary prices lest they "hinder the King's Service." The document was written in German as well as English. This was a loan of materials and not dollars.

GETTYSBURG NATIONAL MILITARY PARK
ETERNAL LIGHT PEACE MONUMENT
(John S. Forney "Farm")

Eternal Light Peace Monument - Gettysburg, Pa.

The Gettysburg National Military Park was established by Act of Congress and approved Feb. 11, 1895. The Secretary of War appointed, for the Gettysburg National Park Commission, Col. John P. Nicholson, Pa., Chairman; John B. Bachelder, Mass., and Brigadier General William H. Forney, Ala. Colonel E.B. Cope was selected as Topographical Engineer.

The area of Gettysburg National Military Park is nearly 40 square miles. The part surrounding Gettysburg covers about 24 square miles, and was the scene of the principal engagements on July 1, 2 and 3, 1863. The Government owns a total of 2441 acres; the remainder is held by private owners. John S. Forney, a "Forty-niner" who crossed the Western Plains in 1849 and, after a ten-year stay in California, came east again to Gettysburg. Holes through eight joists were caused by passage of a shell that struck the second-story floor of the Forney house, which was located on the scene of the first day's battle at Gettysburg. A section of the Forney house is now in the Gettysburg National Museum. The Forney buildings were removed late in 1937 by W.A. Kelly as part of the landscape work in the immediate front of the Nation's Eternal Light Peace Memorial.

JOHN W. FORNEY

*Secretary of the Senate of the United States
Proprietor and Editor of the
"Philadelphia Press" and "Washington Chronicle"*

The town of Forney, Texas was named for this gentleman

COL. JOHN WEIN FORNEY

John Wein Forney, an American Journalist and politician was born at Lancaster, Pennsylvania, on Sept. 30, 1817. Mr. Forney left school at the age of thirteen to work in a store. He was apprenticed to a printer in Lancaster, Pennsylvania in 1833, and later became an editor in 1836; in 1840 he published the Intelligencer and Journal of that city, a democratic paper and in 1845 (by virtue of an appointment by President Polk), he became surveyor of the port of Philadelphia; 1845 to 1851 was editor of the Pennsylvanian, a paper published in Philadelphia. From 1851 to 1855 he was clerk of the house of Representatives at Washington, D.C., and in 1856 was elected chairman of the Pennsylvania Democratic state committee, and a candidate for the United States Senate in 1857. In 1859 he was again elected clerk of the House of Representatives and in 1861 became secretary of the United States Senate. In 1871 - 72 he became collector of the city of Philadelphia. He was editor of the Washington Union in 1851, of the Philadelphia Press in 1857, of Washington Chronicle in 1859, and of Progress, a weekly journal published in Philadelphia, in 1879. He died in Philadelphia December 9, 1881. He and his wife, Elizabeth M. are buried in Laurel Hill Cemetery, Philadelphia, Pennsylvania. He is mentioned on pages 34-35 in the book, "The Day Lincoln Was Shot," by Jim Bishop, published by Harper and Brothers, New York.

This writer wishes to thank *Mr. Felton M. Johnston* Secretary of the United States Senate, (Mar. 3, 1958) for valuable information.

FORNEY, TEXAS

Col. Forney was employed by Jay Gould, and other eastern capitalists, to help promote the construction of the Texas and Pacific Railway. This was in the early 1870's. The present town was then located about one mile south of its present location and was known by the name of Brooklyn. There was considerable interest shown as to just how the line would be constructed through this particular territory. Finally the civil engineers decided the most practical way was to miss Brooklyn by about one mile, and the Texas and Pacific was given several acres of land to develop into business and residential property.

When the application was made for a post office by the name of Brooklyn, it was discovered that Texas already had a town by that name; since Col. Forney was credited with bringing the railway to Texas, at a mass meeting of the citizens of the community, the town was given the name of Forney. Col. Forney was one of the original directors of the Southern Pacific Railway. He died in the historical Forney Mansion 618 South Washington St., Philadelphia, Pennsylvania.

Forney, Kaufman County, Texas had a population of 2500 in 1958, and boasts it is a small town with all city conveniences. The first settlers in Kaufman Co. arrived in 1840 in an ox train made up at Holly Springs, Mississippi, by William P. King. They claimed land near the present site of Kaufman for script they had purchased from the new Republic of Texas. Here they built Kings Fort, which offered protection from Indians, and was an inducement to new settlers. Among the early settlers were John H. Regan and David Spangler Kaufman, for whom the town of Kaufman and the County were to be named. The new area, under Reagan's leadership, was separated from Henderson County in 1848 and organized as Kaufman County with Kaufman a raw, new village, as its county seat.

This writer wishes to thank, *Walter D. Adams*, owner of The Adams Drug Company, Forney, Texas for valuable information.

1st Generation

AN ATTESTED CERTIFICATE

Johann Adam Forney brought with him to this country a certificate, which stated:

"We Magistrates, burgomasters and council of the city of Wachenheim-in-the-Haardt, certify herewith that before us came the worthy Johann Adam Forney, citizen and tailor here, the legitimate son of the worthy Christian Forney, also a citizen here, and informed us that he, with his wedded wife, Elizabetha Lowisa, have firmly resolved to set out with their four children and effects, on the journey to the island of Pennsylvania and to settle there; but he stands in need of an attested certificate of how he behaves with us and why he departed, such as he can show at the place of his settlement. Which we gave him according to his reasonable desire and truthfully: moreover because we believed it would be required in order that no one could calumniate our citizen or citizen's Children; although we have indeed sought diligently and earnestly to disuade him from such departure, yet he remains of his first intention, therefore after steadfast perseverance we have given the said Johann Adam Forney this certificate: That as long as we have known him he has behaved himself honorably, piously and honestly, as well becomes a good citizen and artisan, and, moreover, showed himself so neighborly that no one has had any complaint to make of him; he also is bound to no compulsory service or serfdom; he will not be unwilling to give, to show with all readiness to those of his intended residence all affection and kindness.

To this true certificate, we, the authorities have affixed our city council's great seal to this statement which is given at Wachenheim-in-the-Haardt, the 7th of May, 1721."

(I) JOHANN ADAM FORNEY

Son of Christian and Madle Frick Forney. b. 1690, m. Elizabetha Lowisa, Jan. 1713, d. 1752.

Johann Adam Forney, a tailor, and his wife, Elizabetha Lowisa, with their four children arrived at Philadelphia on 16 October 1721. The name was then spelled Farny, and his wife was listed as Lowisa Farnison. Their first ten years were spent in Philadelphia County, after which the family located in Conewago Settlement, or as is sometimes called "Digges' Choice." This is today known as Hanover, York County, Pennsylvania.

(The following was copied from the family bible of Johann Adam Forney)

"In the year 1721 on the 16th October, I, Johann Adam Forney and wife Louisa with four children arrived at Philadelphia in Penn., having lived at Wachenheim-on-the-Hart (Mountain) in the Palatinate. Johann Adam Forney to him belongs this Bible, and love it, and bought it for four gulden at Wachenheim-on-the-Hart (Mountain) on the 10th of May. In the year 1713, I married my dear wife Elizabeth Louisa. On the 6th of October 1713 my first child, a son, was born at 10 o'clock at night, in the sign of the Crab, and his sponsor was the Honorable Marx Oberle. On the first of July 1715 my second child, a son, was born in the night, at four o'clock in the sign of the Virgin, and his sponsor was the Honorable Nicholas Forney of Durkheim-on-the-Hart (Mountain). January 1717, my third child, a daughter, was born dead. April 24th 1718 my 4th child, a daughter, was born and her Godmother was Lady Bloon from Wachenheim, her name Louisa Harbater. On the 6th of January 1721 my fifth child was born, and her Godmother was my step sister Maria Bertha. On the 29th of September 1724 my sixth child was born in Pennsylvania - his name Frederick (Philip) Forney. On the 16th of February 1728 my seventh child was born in Pennsylvania - her name is Clara."

Johann Adam Forney, a burger, lived ten miles west of Mannheim at Wachenheim-in-the-Haardt, in the Palatinate of the Rhine, in Germany.

He was settled in the neighborhood of what is now Hanover, York County, Pa., in 1734. It was then known as the "Conewago Settlements," or "Digges' Choice." The latter name it got from John Digges, who some years before had taken up some land there on a Maryland warrant; had it surveyed for him by a Maryland surveyor; and sold some of it to Forney and others, whose lives were "made miserable for years by the turmoils arising out of disputes between Digges and other settlers, which were aggravated by the conflicting claims of Penn. and Baltimore to the proprietorship. For many years the region was known as the 'disputed land,' and there naturally was much lawlessness."

Thomas Cookson, surveyor of Lancaster County, was sent by the Pennsylvania authorities to read the Royal Order to Digges in the spring of 1746. This Royal Order was designed to settle the vexed question of the boundary between the provinces, and in this case it bore upon Digges' right to take up vacant land in Pennsylvania on his Maryland warrant. But this invocation of the Majesty of the law was without effect, as we see from the following letter with its quaint German idioms, "Adam Forne to Thomas Cookson:

"Worshipful Sir:

May it please your worship we cannot but acquaint your worship what has happened here since your departure from us. Yesterday as the 24th of April, Mr. Digges sent a Deputy Sheriff out of Maryland for to arrest Matthew Ulrich and Nicholas Forne he took them two until my house where I asked the Sheriff by what authority he rested those men, if they owed any money. If they owed money I would be bound for their appearance at court, but if he could not tell me no more cause as this, viz.: that those men should give their bonds to Digges for the land or depart from the land. The two people have taken up their lands these five years ago from the Hon'r Propr's land office in Philadelphia and it was surveyed for the same. I ordered upon this them two men as Matthias Ulrich and Nicholas Forne to return to their habitation, whereupon the Sheriff and Digges' son made resistance and the Sheriff drew his sword upon me and we then drew our swords and was a-going in upon them, whereupon they fled to their horses and so ran away and so was the way that we got ridden of our new guests. Now is our humble request to you for to come up speedily and to look into the matter and settle it that we may have rest and live in peace and quietness as his Majesty's Subjects and not be troubled forever. For if this matter is not rectified and we do not get help speedily we must help ourselves and should it be with our last drop of blood, for I am well assured that we will not be put upon by no Digges that ever lived under the sun. So wishing that you may soon come over, I have no more to add but remain your

Humble & Ob't Servant

/s/ *Adam Forne*

Little Canowako,
April 25, 1746.

P.S. Sir: - Digges also troubled many more in short all them that lives in his resurveyed additional lines and was going to have them arrested, but some sent him a-packing in the striving, and yesterday I heard that he should have said that he had made up with your worship, and if you did not come in ten days you would not come in ten years more."

MASON DIXON LINE

In 1763, surveyors Charles Mason and Jeremiah Dixon landed at Philadelphia to begin running their line establishing the border between Pennsylvania and Delaware, Maryland and Virginia. This border was later to become a symbol of the border between north and south.

Above, Leroy Forney, a brother of the author, holding the Forney Sword.

"This sword came to America with the founder of the Forney family from Wachenheim-in-the-Haardt on October 16th, 1721.

The sword has been handed down from the family founder, Johann Adam Forney, to his son Marx, who in turn gave it to his son John Adam, who in turn passed it to my Grandfather, John Adam Forney, through whom it has come to me, John Adam Melsheimer.

The sword was used in frequent fights in the settlement of the Maryland-Pennsylvania line; was carried by a Forney in 1776 and in the 1812 War by my Grandfather at the battle of North Point. He was there in his 23rd year."

by John Adam Melsheimer

The above information was given to this writer by the daughter of John Adam Melsheimer,*Mrs. C. F. (Amelia) Ehrehart. Mrs. Ehrehart put the Forney sword in The Hanover Public Library Historical Section for safekeeping and also so it will stay in Hanover, Pennsylvania.

*John Adam Melsheimer was a medical doctor who practiced for many years in and around Hanover.

AN OBLIGATION

Know all men by these presents, that I, John Diggs, of Prince George's County, in the Province of Maryland, Gent, am held and firmly bound unto Adam Faurney (Forney), of Philadelphia County, in the Province of Pennsylvania, Farmer and Tailor, in the full and just sum of Sixty pounds current money of Maryland, to which payment well and truly to be made and done, I bind myself, my Heirs Executors, and Administrators, firmly by these presents. Sealed with my seal and dated this fifth day of October, Anno Domino, 1731.

The condition of the above obligation is such that if the above bound John Diggs, his Heirs, Executors or Administrators, shall and will at the reasonable request of the above Adam Faurney, make and order by sufficient conveyance according to the custom and common usage of the Province of Maryland a certain parcell of land containing one hundred and fifty acres, already marked out by the above named Adam Faurney, near a place known by the name of Robert Owing's Spring, and on the same tract of land where the said Robert Owing now dwells in the Province of Maryland, then this obligation to be void, otherwise to remain in full force and virtue in Law.

JOHN DIGGS,

Sealed and Delivered in the Presence of us,

GEORGE DOUGLASS
JOHANN PETER ZARICH

FORNEY HOMESTEAD

This home was built (about 1810) by Samuel Forney, son of Philip Forney, on the original homestead of Johann Adam Forney, and was called a "Colonial Mansion." The buildings have been torn down to make way for a modern Super Market located on the corner of Forney Avenue and Frederick Street, Hanover, Pa. Samuel Forney built the brick house on the old Forney farm near the site of the "long log house" which stood under willow trees at a chain of springs in the "little meadow." The original stable stood on the rising ground to the west. There was an old pear tree that stood at the back porch, said to have been brought from Germany. In the spring at the edge of the grove, in the large meadow, the Indian mothers were said to have bathed their papooses.

Samuel Forney was the last person in York County who owned a slave; this latest survivor of slavery in this section - "old Uncle Sam" - died in 1814. There were small houses on the Westminister road, just before it entered the Frederick road, that were originally built as slave quarters.

LILAC FARM

The Lilac Farm is located at 9 Beck Mill Road, Hanover, Penna. This home is on the tract of land originally purchased from Wm. Penn; it was then known as the "Conewago Settlements," or "Digges' Choice."

In 1850 there were trees that measured twenty-one feet in circumference on these farms. Today this home is owned by Mr. and Mrs. Robert D. Kauffman. Mrs. Kauffman is a direct descendent of the original owner of the land, Johann Adam Forney. They have worked hard restoring the old home and now have a comfortable home, as well as a beautiful landmark.

2nd Generation

Headstone of Phillip Forney - 1724-1783

This marker is located in The Emanuel Reformed and Lutheran Church Cemetery, Locust Street, Hanover, Pa.

MARX FORNEY

Son of Johann Adam and Elizabetha Lowisa Forney
b. 6 Oct. 1713   m. Barbel 16 Feb. 1745   d. 1800

CHILDREN

Eva, A Daughter, Christian George, Catherine, Anna Margaret, John Adam, Marx, and Daniel.

Marx Forney was born in Germany and brought up in Penna. Record shows his wife's name as "Barbel," or Barbara. The family bible says Marx was joined in wedlock with Camdell.

In 1750 when York County was set off from Lancaster, "Marx Forney" was the first supervisor of Manheim Township. Three years later he was naturalized, a step rarely taken in those days. Tradition says that Marx was wealthy, a statement born out by his will, dated April 30, 1800.

(Taken from family bible records - - "Marx Forney to him belongs this bible & received it from my father Hans Adam Forney 27 July 1750)

"On the 25th of May 1746 Marx Forney's oldest child, a daughter was born into this deplorable world in the sign of the Ram, her name is Eva. On the 9th of Feb. 1748 my second child, a daughter, was born and immediately died. On the 26th of Mar. 1749 my third born child, a son, at ten o'clock came into the world between the Ram and Bull. His name is Christian George Forney. On the 3rd of May 1752 my fourth child, a daughter, was born in the sign of the Twins at five o'clock p.m. Her name is Anna Margaret. She died 23 Feb. 1775. On the 15th of Feb. 1757 my sixth child, a son, was born at 2 p.m. between the sign of the Balance and Scorpion on the third day of the new moon. His name is John A. Forney. On the 6th of April 1760 my seventh child, a son, was born in the sign of the Ram. His name is Marx Forney. On the 17th of Aug. 1762 my eighth child, a son, was born in the sign of Twins. His name is Daniel Forney."

NICHOLAUS FORNEY

Son of Johann Adam and Elizabetha Lowisa Forney
b. 1 July 1715   m. Mary Magdalena 1742   d. 1774

CHILDREN

Sophia, Johann Adam, Heinrich (Henry), Abraham, Margarethe, Philip, Lewis, Ester, and Johann Nicholaus.

Nicholaus Forney, the emigrant's second son, was born 1 July 1715 in Wachenheim; his sponsor was the worthy Nickel Forney of Durkheim, a larger town a few miles from Wachenheim. He was one of the four children with the parents in their emigration, being six years old when taken to Pennsylvania. He was brought up in the back woods "across Susquehanna," surrounded by the trials and hardships of pioneer life. In 1745 Nicholaus Forney was arrested by Maryland officers sent by John Diggs, for trespassing on the latter's land and cutting timber there; probably his father had given him a part of his own land, as the young man was now setting up a home of his own, and Nicholaus cut down the trees to clear it. His father, Johann Adam Forney, gives this account of his dealings with Digges: "That sundry Germans, together with the deponent, having agreed for the purchase of some lands from John Diggs, lying at Conewago, after some time, finding that Mr. Digges' claim was of great extent, and did not appear at all ascertained. At first he told Mr. Forney he had 14,000 acres in the tract; at another time, 11,000, and at another time, 10,000." Nicholaus did not have his family baptized in infancy; perhaps he believed with the opinions on infant baptism held by the Mennonites who were so numerous among the German settlers of Pennsylvania, but afterwards changing his views, had his family baptised. He must have become interested in the Reformed Church, for we find his family followed the Reformed and Lutheran Churches, for a number of generations.

In 1772 "Nicholaus Forney of Manheim Township was naturalised." At some time, Marx, his older brother, sold him a part of the land which their father had taken up on his Pennsylvania Warrant.

LOWISA CHARLOTTE FORNEY

Daughter of Johann Adam and Elizabetha Lowisa Forney
b. 24 Apr. 1718   m. Abraham Sell March 11, 1742.

Lowisa Charlotte Forney was born in Wachenheim. It is believed that she did not live long after her marriage, or that she left any children; the Christ Church records show Mr. Sell's name with another wife in 1751.

MARIA EVA FORNEY

Daughter of Johann Adam and Elizabetha Lowisa Forney
b. 6 January 1721

Maria Eva Forney was born in Wachenheim. Johann Adam Forney recorded in his bible that his stepsister Maria Bertha was Maria Eva's Godmother.

The last we know of her was that she was at home when her father was arrested in 1747.

PHILIP FORNEY

Son of Johann Adam and Elizabetha Lowisa Forney
b. 29 Sept. 1724; m. Elizabeth Sherz; d. 3 Feb. 1783

Philip Forney continued to live on the family homestead, which had been purchased from William Penn. Here he raised a large family.

(The following was taken from the family bible:)

"Philip Forney married Elizabeth Forney 8 May 1753. 15 June was born my first son Adam Forney. 17 Sept. 1755 was born my first daughter Marie Forney. 26 ? 1757 was born my second daughter Lovice Forney. 4 Oct. 1758 was born my third daughter Elizabeth Forney. 7 July 1760 was born my second son Philip Forney. 23 Apr. 1762 was born my third son Samuel Forney. 7 Nov. 1763 was born my fourth son Peter Forney. 27 Mar. 1767 was born my fourth daughter Hanna Forney. 12 Oct. 1770 was born my sixth son Jacob Forney. 8 Oct. 1773 was born my fifth daughter Susana Forney. 20 Feb. 1776 was born my sixth daughter Sally Forney. Philip Forney b. 29 Sept. 1724, buried Feb. 1783, aged 58 years and seven months. Elizabeth, his wife, b. 1732, d. 8 Aug. 1794, buried August 10th, aged 62 years and 6 months."

Philip Forney, the youngest son of the emigrant, was the first of the family born in America. Other records show Philip and Elizabeth Sherz Forney had twelve children: Adam, Maria, Lovice, Elizabeth, Philip, Samuel, David, Peter, Hannah, Jacob, Susanna, and Salome.

Philip Forney also owned land near Reistertown, Md., adjoining that of Marx Forney's son Daniel; this land he willed to furnish doweries for each of his daughters who were single at the time of his death. Philip Forney and his wife are interred in the old Reformed graveyard at Hanover, Pennsylvania.

CLORA FORNEY

Daughter of Johann Adam and Elizabetha Lowisa Forney
b. 16 Feb. 1728 (no records)

1765 York
Mark Turner
In right of Adam
Swaney

112 " 22 [illegible]

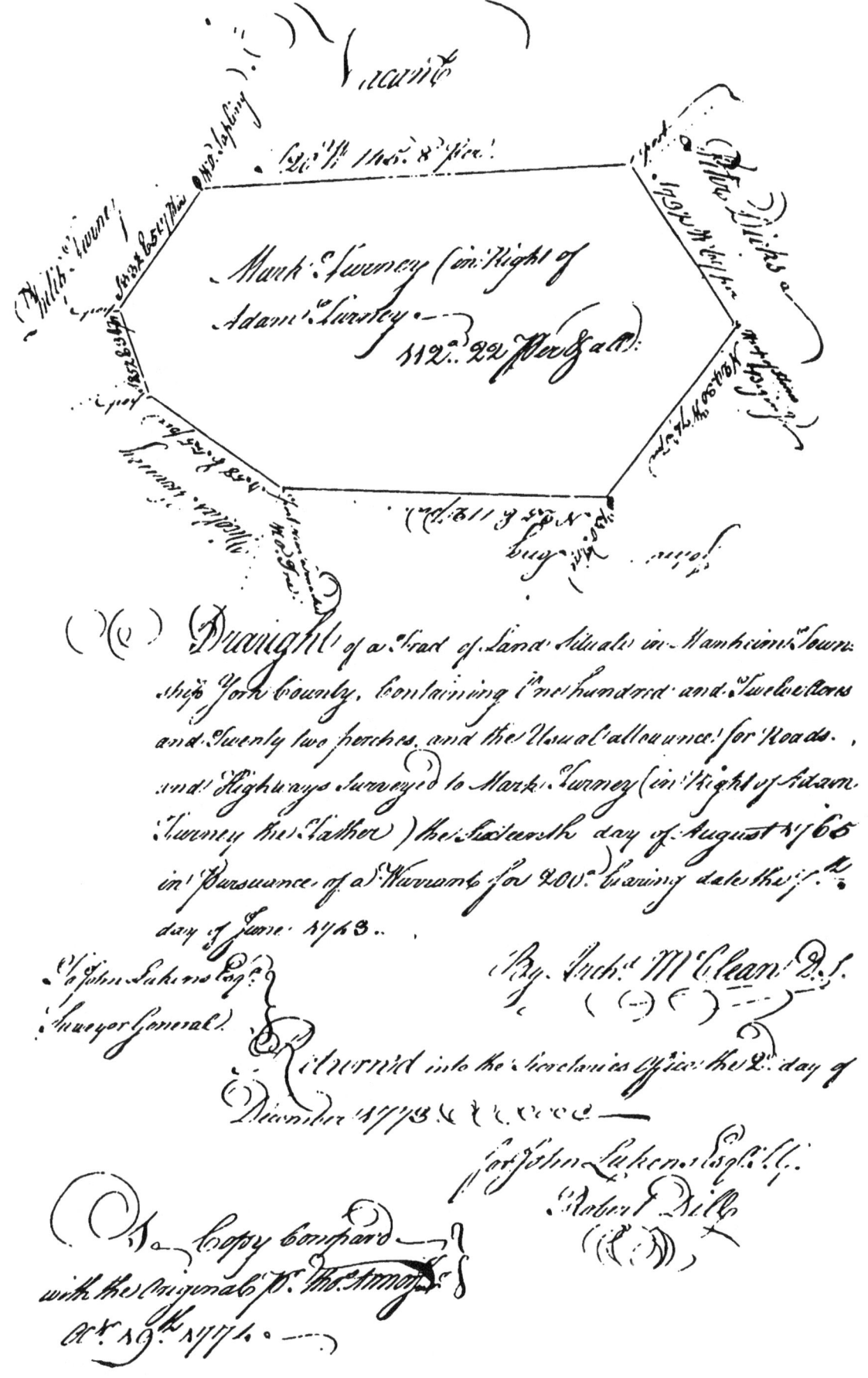

Draught of a Tract of Land situate in Manheim Township York County, Containing One hundred and Twelve acres and Twenty two perches, and the Usual allowances for Roads and Highways Surveyed to Mark Turney (in Right of Adam Turney the Father) the Sixteenth day of August 1765 in Pursuance of a Warrant for 200 a. bearing date the 1st day of June 1763.

To John Lukens Esq.
Surveyor General

By. Arch.d McClean D.S.

Return'd into the Secretaries Office the 2d day of December 1773

for John Lukens Esq. S.G.
Robert Dill

A Copy Compar'd with the Original p. Tho. Armor
Oct.r 19. 1774.

Draught

Adam Murray Junr

as 146 & 128 ft

And Allowance

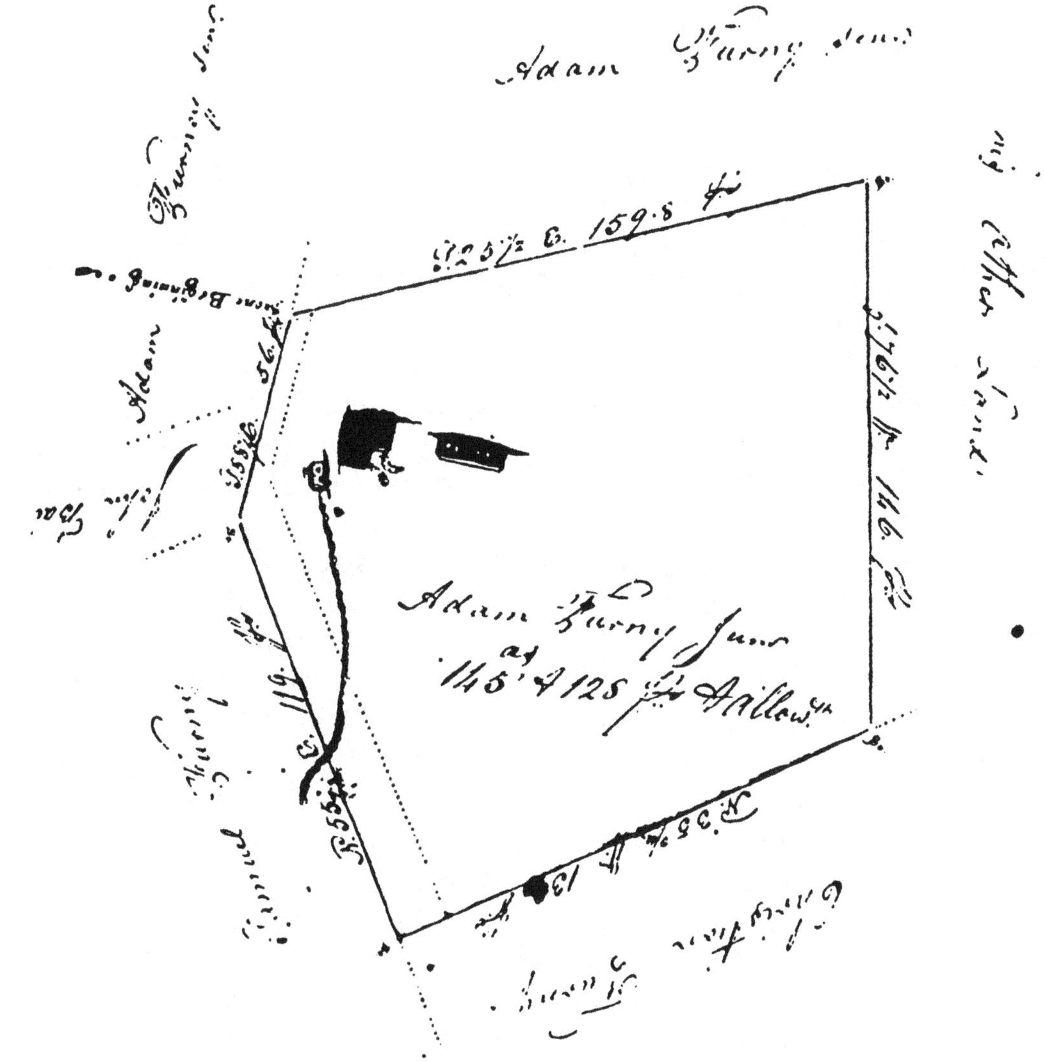

Drawght of two Contegious Larger tracts of land situate in Heidleberg township York County Resurvey and laid off from said larger tracts at the request of Adam Zurny Senr for his son Adam Zurny the 1st day of February A.D. 1821.

per John T. Kinkle

The following is an excerpt of the deed given to Mark Furney, Lancaster County, Pennsylvania. (deed shown on page 53):

JOHN PENN, THOMAS PENN and RICHARD PENN

"BEGINNING at a marked white oak in a line of Adam Furney's land and extending thence by the same north thirty degrees west one hundred and twenty-four perches to a post; thence by John Diggs' land north sixty degrees east one hundred and eighteen perches to a marked Spanish oak and south eighty-five degrees east one hundred and thirty-six perches to a marked white oak; thence by Andrew Flekingar's land south one hundred and fifty-four perches to a marked white oak; thence by vacant land west one hundred and twenty-six perches to the place of beginning containing one hundred and ninety acres, and the allowance of six acres per cent for road and highways. As in and by the survey thereof remaining in our surveyor general's office and from thence certified into our secretary's office. YIELDING AND PAYING therefore yearly to us our heirs and succesors at the town of Lancaster in the said county, upon the first day of March in every year from the first day of March last past, one-half penny sterling for every acre of the same or value thereof in coin current according as the exchange then between our said province and the city of London to such person or persons as shall from time to time be appointed to receive the same AND in case of no payment thereof within ninety days next after the same shall become due, then it shall and may be lawful for our heirs and succesors and their receiver or receivers into and upon the hereby granted land premises to rescind and the same to hold and until the said quit rent and all arrears thereof together with the charges accruing by means of such nonpayment and rentry be fully paid and discharged. WITNESS George Thomas Esq., Lieutenant Governor of the said province, who in pursuance and by virtue of certain powers and authorities to him for this purpose granted by the said proprietors hath hereunto set his hand and caused the great seal of the said province to be therefore affixed at Philadelphia this twentyeth day of November in the year of our Lord one thousand seven hundred and forty-five the nineteenth year of the reign of King George the second."

/s/ Geo. Thomas

3rd Generation

MARIA EVA FORNEY

Daughter of Marx and Barbel - - - - Forney
b. 26 May 1746 m. Georg Carl Gelwicks d. 1770
CHILDREN
Eva Cathrine b. 29 March 1767

Maria Eva Forney married Georg Carl Gelwicks 2 July 1765. He was a member of a family then prominent in Hanover, Pennsylvania, and was an innkeeper. Georg Carl Gelwicks was born 16 Sept. 1741.

CHRISTIAN GEORGE FORNEY

Son of Marx and Barbel - - - - Forney
b. 26 Mar. 1749 m. two times d. 11 Aug. 1824
CHILDREN

First marriage:	Second marriage:
Elizabeth	Rebecca
John Daniel	
John Christian	
Jacob (Bush Jake)	
Matthias	

Christian George Forney was a farmer. The name of his first wife is not known. His second wife was a widow, Mrs. Miller, who had several children by her first marriage.

MARIA CATARINA FORNEY

Daughter of Marx and Barbel - - - - Forney
b. 3 May 1752 m. Nicholas Kiefauber
CHILDREN
Johann Nicolaus, Maria Catarina, and Peter

Maria Catarina Forney was married to Nicholas Kiefauber, who lived in the neighborhood of Littles-town. He was the son of Conrad and Anna Margaretha Kiefauber, and a twin brother of Eva Dorthea, married to Col. Henry Slagle.

ANNA MARGARETHA FORNEY

Daughter of Marx and Barbel - - - - Forney
b. 11 May 1755

Anna Margaretha Forney died in her twentieth year.

JOHANN ADAM FORNEY

Son of Marx and Barbel - - - - Forney
b. 15 Feb. 1756 m. Maria Hoffman d. 21 June 1834
CHILDREN

Catharine, Mary Christina, Elizabeth, John Adam, Lydia, Juliana, Anna Margaret, and Susanna.

John Adam Forney married Maria Christina, daughter of Henry and Christina Hoffman. They built the house afterwards known as the Pleasant Hill Hotel, but died in the small brick residence in which their three single daughters lived and died.

MARX FORNEY

Son of Marx and Barbel - - - - Forney
b. 6 Apr. 1760 m. Elizabeth Ziegler d. 5 Aug. 1844
CHILDREN

George, Margaret, Elizabeth, Marks, Jacob, Magdalena, Salome, Susan, Eva, Daniel and Emanuel.

Of Marx Forney little is known. He lived at Marsh Creek, west of Gettysburg, where his wife is buried, though he himself is interred in the old graveyard of the Reformed Church at Hanover, Pennsylvania.

DANIEL FORNEY

Son of Marx and Barbel - - - - Forney
b. 17 Aug. 1762 m. Sabina Smyser d. 4 Oct. 1846
CHILDREN

Michael, Anna Mary, Sarah, Susanna, Elizabeth, Margaret, Jacob S., Daniel Smyser, and John.

Daniel and Sabina Forney settled in Reisterstown, Md., in 1791, where for many years they kept a stage tavern of well-known excellence on the Baltimore Pike.

SOPHIA FORNEY

Daughter of Nicholaus and Maria Magdalena Forney
b. ? m. - - - - Meyer
CHILDREN
Anna Margarethe - Baptized 31 May 1762

VALUABLE PROPERTY
FOR SALE.

The subscriber offers at Private Sale,
That elegant and well known PLANTATION and
..TAVERN STAND..

Situate within the limits of the borough of Hanover, York county, Pennsylvania, on a beautiful rising ground, overlooking the town, and called "*Pleasant Hill*," on the Turnpike road leading to the city of Baltimore, containing about
100 Acres of Limestone Land.

About 60 acres clear, 12 acres of which excellent meadow, and the remainder covered with good timber. The arable land being of the first quality for grain and grass, is laid off in 8 convenient fields, with the meadow in the centre, and adjoining the Turnpike, and the woodland consists of young thriving and heavy timber of all sorts. The cultivated land runs along the Turnpike 253 perches, and from the door of the tavern a view may be had of the whole, with the exception of the woodland. It is under good fences, many of them put up with chesnut rails. The house is built of brick, two-story, large and convenient, 43 by 33 feet; it contains 9 rooms, with a brick back building thereto attached, 42 feet; the kitchen is 25 feet square, a cellar under the whole house, 8 feet deep, and a well of excellent water with a pump near the kitchen door; a spring house, granary, and smoke house, all covered with cedar shingles, a good garden, inclosed with a paling 7 feet high, a brick barn, and other necessary outhouses. The Tavern stand is one of the handsomest situations between Hanover and Baltimore, and has fine advantages for drovers and other travellers. It is thought unnecessary to say any thing more respecting the above valuable property, as those inclined to purchase, will no doubt first view the premises. Possession can be had on the 1st of April, 1834, and an indisputable title will be given to the purchaser.

ALSO:
A new one-story brick Dwelling House,

Lately finished, with a Lot of Ground, nearly opposite the above described Tavern stand. The house has two rooms, and a kitchen. There is also a new Blacksmith shop, and a new stable on this lot. If this house is not sold before the first of November next, it will then be rented, and possession given immediately.

Persons wishing to view the above described property, will please apply to the subscriber, living near it, who will shew the same, and make known the terms of sale.

ADAM FORNEY, senr.

September 13, 1833.

Schätzbares Eigenthum zum Verkauf.

Der Unterschriebene bietet durch Privathandel zum Verkauf an:
Jene vortrefliche und wohlbekannte Plantasche und Wirthshaus,

Gelegen innerhalb den Grenzen der Stadt Hannover, York Caunty, Pennsylvanien, auf einer schönen Anhöhe, von welcher man die Stadt übersieht, genannt "Pleasant Hill," an der nach der Stadt Baltimore führenden Turnpeikstrasse, enthaltend ungefehr
100 Acker Kalkstein-Land.

Etwa 60 Acker sind geklart, wovon 12 Acker vortrefliche Wiesen, und der Ueberrest mit gutem Holze bewachsen. Das Bauland, welches von der ersten Güte für Getreide und Gras, ist in 8 bequeme Felder getheilt, die Wiese im Mittelpunkt, und an die Turnpeikstrasse stossend, und das Holzland besteht aus jungen wachsenden und schweren Baumen von allen Arten. Das angebaute Land läuft 253 Ruthen dem Turnpeik entlang, und von der Thür des Wirthshauses kann man, mit Ausnahme des Holzlandes, das Ganze übersehen. Es ist unter guten Fensen, wovon viele mit Kastanienriegel gemacht sind. Das Haus ist gross und bequem, von Backsteinen erbaut, zweistöckig, und 43 bey 33 Fuss: es enthält 9 Stuben, mit einem daran gebauten backsteinernen Hintergebäude, 42 Fuss; die Küche ist 25 Fuss viereckig, ein Keller unter dem ganzen Hause, 8 Fuss tief, nebst einem Brunnen mit vortreflichem Wasser und einer Pumpe nahe bey der Küchenthür; ein Springhaus, Fruchtkammer, und Rauchhaus, in guter Garten, mit einer 7 Fuss hohen Fens umgeben, eine backsteinerne Scheuer, und andere nöthige Nebengebäude. Das Wirthshaus hat eine der schönsten Lagen zwischen Hannover und Baltimore, und schöne Bequemlichkeiten für Viehtreiber, und andere Reisende. Es wird für überflüssig gehalten mehr über das obige schätzbare Eigenthum zu sagen, indem Kauflustige es vorher erst besehen werden. Besitz kann am 1sten April, 1834 gegeben, und dem Käufer ein unstreitiges Recht ertheilt werden.

Ferner:
Ein neues einstöckiges backsteinernes Wohnhaus,

Erst kürzlich fertig gemacht, beynahe dem obenbeschriebenen Wirthshause gegenüber. Das Haus hat zwey Stuben, und eine Küche. Auch befindet sich ein neuer Schmidtschop, und ein Stall auf dieser Lot. Wenn dies Haus nicht vor dem 1sten nächsten November verkauft seyn sollte, so wird es alsdann verlehnt, und sogleich Besitz gegeben werden.

Kauflustige, welche das obenbeschriebene Eigenthum zu besehen wünschen, belieben sich bey dem Unterschriebenen zu melden, welcher nahe dabey wohnt, der dasselbe zeigen, und die Bedingungen sagen wird.

Adam Forney, senr.

Den 13ten September, 1833.

HANOVER, Pa.) Printed by Daniel Philip Lange.

JOHANN ADAM FORNEY

Son of Nicholaus and Maria Magdalene Forney
b. 1740   m. Barbara - - - -
CHILDREN
Maria Margarethe, Abraham, Johann Adam, Anna Maria, and Anna Catrina

Johann Adam Forney is believed to be the ancestor of Charles William Forney, author of "Forney's Five Family Records," printed by Standard Printing Co., Boone, Iowa, although there is no legal proof of this. Charles W. Forney speaks of births in Pennsylvania and Maryland, which tie in with the same trouble that arose from the "Disputed Land," between the Penn. and Maryland Line. Charles also states the oldest Forney of his branch that he could locate was Johannes Forney, whose wife was Barbara Gautschin.

JACKSON TOWNSHIP
Stark Co., Ohio

Jackson Township was at first included in Plain, the latter being one of the original five townships into which the county of Stark was divided. In 1811 Jackson became part of Green Township, the latter being taken to help form Summit County. In March 1815 Jackson was separated from Green, and included Lawrence then, and for about a year later, until the latter was set off by itself. The names of Jacob Ettleman and John Forney were included in the list of early settlers of Jackson Township, Forney was spelled "Fauney" in the old records. The foregoing list must have been made some time near the year 1815. There was a new list made in 1827 containing many new names. McDonaldsville is the only village in Jackson Twp. that has been laid out, plotted and recorded. This was done as early as 1829 by John Clapper and Abrahm Routan, the surveyer being Henry Beard (Mr. Beard married Catherine Forney, Ref., Forney's Five Family Records). The village is located on sections 9 and 10; and twenty-four lots were laid out.

HEINRICH or HENRY FORNEY

Son of Nicholaus and Maria Magdalena Forney
b. 22 Oct. 1747   m. Mary Magdalena   d. 21 Aug. 1831
CHILDREN
Johan, John Peter, Andrew, Henry Jr., Adam, and Nicholas

Henry Forney served as a second lieutenant in the Seventh Company of the Fourth Battalion of The York County Militia. Henry and his brother, Johann Adam, were two of the founders and benefactors of the building of The Emanuel Reformed and Lutheran Church, one mile northwest of Hanover, Pa., (1764-5).

Mary Forney died 1 Apr. 1817, aged 73 years 45 days. Henry Forney purchased section 10 in Unity Township, Columbiana County, Ohio, in 1802. He had six sons, among whom his land was divided. In 1879 the middle part of the section was still the property of a Forney, Benjamin Forney, son of Adam, and included the place where Henry Forney built his log cabin; the family meanwhile lived under a large grape vine. On the southwest corner of Henry Forney's Section 10 was erected a log meeting house; today it is known as The Salem Evangelical and Reformed Church, where Henry and his wife Mary are buried. This Cemetery has been known for many years as the "Old Forney Cemetery." Henry Forney had the first public house (tavern) before 1820 on the southeast corner of the Square, Unity, Ohio, in a small brick house with a frame lean-to. The Fourth Census of the U.S. (1820), Ohio, Vol. 6 lists Henry Forney as a "Manufacturer," this no doubt was due to the fact that along with farming he was engaged in the manufacture of bricks; there was a deposit of clay on Section #10.

Reference to the "Revolutionary War" Military Record of *Henry Forney* (b. 22 Oct. 1747, d. 21 Aug. 1831) of York County, Pennsylvania.

See Index to 6th Series in Vol. 2 - 7th Series.

xxxxxxxxxxxxxxxxxxxx

"Pennsylvania Archives" - 6th Series, Vol. 2
Pages 503-504-505-506: "York Associations"

FOURTH BATTALION

Colonel	John Andrew	Apr. 5, 1778
Lt. Colonel	William Walker	Apr. 5, 1778
Major	Simon Vanarsdale	Apr. 5, 1778

SEVENTH COMPANY

Captain	Samuel Erwin	Apr. 5, 1778
1st Lieut.	William Haughelin	Apr. 5, 1778

2nd Lieut. .... **Henry Forney** ....Apr. 5, 1778
Ensign .... William Read .... Apr. 5, 1778

(Rank & File - 79 Men)

1st Company	(Rank & File - 58 Men)	Apr. 5, 1778
2nd "	(" - 64 ")	Apr. 5, 1778
3rd "	(" - 67 ")	" " "
4th "	(" - 64 ")	" " "
5th "	(" - 74 ")	" " "
6th "	(" - 64 ")	" " "
8th "	(" - 59 ")	" " "

Names of Captains, 1st & 2nd Lieutenants, and Ensigns are listed in Volume 2, Series 6.

Note: On Page 503, same Series, Vol. 2, there appears the framework of the Fourth Battalion under date of 1775.

SALEM EVANGELICAL AND REFORMED CHURCH
Unity, Ohio

Some time in 1802 or 1803 a log cabin meeting house, about 30 feet square, was erected on the southwest corner of what is known as the

Forney Section, No. 10. This is the site of the present church and here the Reformed settlers worshipped with the Lutheran congregation for several years. It is possible that this hilltop may have been selected as a burial ground (Old Forney Cemetery) before the first church was erected, for there are old fieldstone markers in the cemetery adjacent to the present building with dates so eroded by time that they are completely lost. The oldest decipherable gravestone found to date bears the date 1810 and the initials "J.M."

In 1823 with their combined leadership, the Lutheran and Reformed congregations labored together to tear down the unfinished log church and erect a two-story edifice. This church took the name *Salem or Union Church*. The new edifice faced south and was the pride of the township with its high pulpit and gallery.

In 1861 the Salem Lutherans and Reformed again cooperatively worked to complete the task of tearing down the old brick church and building the present red brick church. Some of the old materials were utilized in constructing the new church. This fact was verified by the present consistory, while working in the loft of the church to make needed repairs. They noticed that some of the beams differed greatly from the others and seemed more worn.

Since 1900, Salem Church has undergone a series of projects toward modernization. Electric lights replaced hanging oil lamps; a furnace outmoded two coal stoves; a central entrance, exemplifying equality and democracy, has removed the two doors (one for men and one for women) and the divided pews; a modern parking lot has supplanted the old hitching rails and dilapidated buggy shed.

COLUMBIANA COUNTY, OHIO

After the County organization had been established in 1803, numerous men from this area were active in its affairs. The first Session of the Common Pleas Court, which met that year at Mathias Lower's house (because it was in the center of the county) included Moses Blackburn, Joshua Dixon, James Andrews, William Hurrah, and Henry Forney. For their services they were paid $1.10 each.

The first session of the Probate Court was held also at the Lower home in 1803. A resident of the immediate area brought before it the first case. Docket 1, Page 1, Case 1, states that Sara Piper, wife of William of Section 26, (The East Palestine Section), asked for administrators to be appointed to settle her husband's estate. Henry Forney of Section 10, and Jacob Liebert of Section 14 having been appointed, thereby, became the first men in the County to administer an estate.

A road was laid out from the State line to Peter Musser's mill in 1803, by William Heald, Surveyor, and James Taylor, Henry Forney, and Jacob Rudysill, viewers, for which the court allowed them "in full compensation" the sum of four dollars Sept. 9th of that year. The road was laid thirty-three feet wide, and confirmed by the court Dec. 1, 1803.

ABRAHAM FORNEY SR.

Son of Nicholaus and Maria Magdalena Forney
b. 1758   m. Susanna   d. 27 Aug. 1842   84 yrs.
CHILDREN
John, Abraham, Frederick, Mary (Polly), Susanna, and Sophia

In 1801 Abraham Forney arrived in Harrison County, Ohio, on a tract now adjoining the city of Cadiz. He was a man of strong convictions and sound judgment, traces of which can now be seen in his descendents. Mr. & Mrs. Forney are buried in an old graveyard at Cadiz; the headstones were removed by the W.P.A. Works Program, to make way for a Shrine, but this was never completed.

HARRISON COUNTY WILLS

Abraham Forney, Cadiz Township; Date of Will, July 26, 1822; date of probate, Oct. 11, 1842. Wife Susann; Children, John, Abraham, Frederick, Polly, Susan, and Sophia; Execs., Sons John Forney and Abraham Forney; Wits., Walter B. Beebe, John Pritchard, J. Harris. Susanna Forney, Harrison County: Date of Will, July 14, 1834; date of probate, June 28, 1842. Children Polly Timmons, Susannah Rabe; Friend, John Maholm. Exec.; John Maholm; Wits., Walter Beebe, James Smylie. Susanna Forney b. 1752 d. 28 May 1842, 90 yrs.

MARGARETHE FORNEY

Daughter of Nicholaus and Maria Magdalena Forney
m. Heinrich Bayer
CHILDREN
Johann Nicholaus

PHILIP FORNEY

Son of Nicholaus and Maria Magdalena Forney
(no records)

LEWIS FORNEY

Son of Nicholaus and Maria Magdalena Forney

19 Mar. 1808 Lewis Forney, Unity Township, was given a license to open a tavern at $4.50 tax per year. 1803 - 1820 Treasurer's book of Columbiana County.

ESTER FORNEY
Daughter of Nicholaus and Maria Magdalena Forney
(no records)

JOHANN NICHOLAUS FORNEY

(no records)

ADAM FORNEY

Son of Philip and Elizabeth Sherz Forney
b. 15 June 1754 m. Rachel Shriver d. 29 June 1822
CHILDREN
Lydia, David Shriver, Samuel, Anna Maria (Polly), Rebecca, Jacob, Susannah, Peter, Lewis S., and Sarah

Rachel Forney was the daughter of David and Rebecca (Farree) Shriver. She was a member of the family which was the next, after the Forneys, to settle in the neighborhood of what is now Hanover. Tradition tells how the Forneys, on their first settlement at "Conewago," supposed themselves to be the only white people there, until one day they found a pig in the woods, and by the presence of a domestic animal knew that they had civilized neighbors, who afterwards proved to be the Shrivers. Adam Forney was engaged in the business of tanning. Mr. and Mrs. Adam Forney and daughter, Maria, are buried in The Emanuel Reformed Lutheran Church Cemetery, Locust Street, Hanover, Pennsylvania. They have a beautiful marker that lays flat and covers the grave.

MARIA FORNEY

Daughter of Philip and Elizabeth Sherz Forney
b. 17 Sept. 1755 m. Ludwig Shriver

Mr. and Mrs. Shriver died within two days of each other. They have a double gravestone in the old graveyard of Hanover with the inscription, *"They were lovely in their lives and in their death were not parted."*

LOVICE FORNEY

Daughter of Philip and Elizabeth Sherz Forney
b. 26 Apr. 1757   m. Leonard Lease

As far as is known they had only one child, a son, George Lease, who was a merchant in Carlisle, Pennsylvania.

ELIZABETH FORNEY

Daughter of Philip and Elizabeth Sherz Forney
b. 4 Oct. 1758   m. Daniel Lammot   d. 24 Sept. 1803
CHILDREN
Elizabeth, and Daniel

Elizabeth Forney, who is said to have been a very elegant, lady-like woman, was married to Daniel LaMotte, the second son of Jean Henri LaMotte, a French Protestant who, after he came to America, became a Mennonite. He never would tell his children anything about his family, saying they were proud enough without knowing anything about it, but adding: *"If you do not disgrace your family, it will never disgrace you."* We do not have any idea as to where Elizabeth Forney Lammot is buried.

Her son, Daniel, married Susanna Beck, from a very well known family in Philadelphia. Elizabeth Forney's granddaughter, Margaretta Elizabeth Lammot, married Alfred Victor du Pont, eldest son of Eleuthere Irenee du Pont, founder of E. I. du Pont deNemours and Co., that started in 1802 in a small mill on Brandywine Creek, near Wilmington, Delaware, and grew into the giant industry it is today. Margaretta Elizabeth Lammot du Pont is buried in the du Pont family cemetery near Christ Church, just outside of Wilmington, Delaware.

This writer wishes to thank Pierre S. du Pont, 3rd, for valuable information.

PHILIP FORNEY

Son of Philip and Elizabeth Sherz Forney
b. 7 July 1760

Philip Forney is believed to have died young, as there is no further mention of him.

DAVID FORNEY

Son of Philip and Elizabeth Sherz Forney
b. 7 Nov. 1763   m. Louisa Nace   d. 6 Mar. 1826
CHILDREN
Elizabeth, Louisa, Matthias, Susan, Anna Maria, and David

David Forney married Louisa, daughter of Matthias and Elizabeth Bowman Nace. David Forney and his wife moved to Baltimore, about 1791, and always resided there. He owned and operated a tannery.

PETER FORNEY

Son of Philip and Elizabeth Sherz Forney
b. 20 Oct. 1765   d. 29 Apr. 1840
(no records)

HANNAH FORNEY

Daughter of Philip and Elizabeth Sherz Forney
b. 27 Mar. 1767   m. John Henry LaMotte   d. 1794
CHILDREN
John

Hannah Forney is said to have married John Henry LaMotte, a brother of Elizabeth Forney's husband. They lived in Baltimore; there her husband died and she soon followed him, dying, it is said, of a broken heart. They had but one son, John, who left Baltimore about 1810, going either to Mississippi or Missouri, where sight of him was lost.

JACOB FORNEY

Son of Philip and Elizabeth Sherz Forney
b. 12 Oct. 1770   d. 5 Oct. 1796

Jacob Forney died young, in Baltimore, on the day he was to have been married to "a very lovely young woman, Catherine Myers"; he was buried in his wedding suit. He seems to have been much beloved in his family; several persons, including Jacob Forney, of Hanover, son of Adam, were named for him.

SUSANNA FORNEY

Daughter of Philip and Elizabeth Sherz Forney
b. 5 Oct. 1773   m. George Decker   d. 3 Jan. 1854

CHILDREN
Jacob Forney, Salome, and Lydia

Susanna Forney was married to George Decker, a Revolutionary Soldier, who entered mercantile life in Baltimore about 1786.

SALOME FORNEY

Daughter of Philip and Elizabeth Sherz Forney
b. 20 Feb. 1776   m. Stephen Grove   d. 22 Apr. 1859
CHILDREN
Elizabeth Margaretta, Catharine Susanna, and Jacob Forney

Salome Forney was commonly called "Sally," and her name has been given as Sarah. She married Stephen Grove, like herself a native of York County, but after their marriage they lived on Green Street, Baltimore, near David Forney's home. She was early left a widow.

SAMUEL FORNEY

Son of Philip and Elizabeth Sherz Forney
b. 23 Apr. 1762   m. Susanna Karle   d. about 1844
CHILDREN
George, John (who died young), Elizabeth, Jesse (who also died in youth), Helena (who died in infancy), and Karle

Samuel Forney lived on the old Forney homestead where he built the fine brick house (picture on page 41). Samuel was the last person in York County who owned a slave; this latest survivor of slavery in this section-"Old Uncle Sam"-died in 1814.

There were small houses on the Westminister Road, just before it entered the Frederick Road, that were originally built as slave quarters. Samuel Forney lost his sight from an injury caused by a nail striking him in the eye, on March 21, 1832; he lived after this misfortune about twelve years. His wife was Susanna, daughter of George Adam Karle. Susanna Karle Forney b. 14 Apr. 1767 d. 20 Aug. 1843.

4th Generation

JOHAN FORNEY

Son of Heinrich and Maria Magdalena Forney
b. 1774   m. Christine Rohrbach   d. 1836, 62 yrs., 7 mo.
CHILDREN
Andrew, Henry, and Alexander

Johan Forney was born and raised in York County, Pa. He came to Ohio in 1802 and spent the rest of his life on Forney Section #10, Unity Township, Columbiana County. Johan and Christine Forney are buried in the Salem Evangelical and Reformed Church (Old Forney) Cemetery, Unity, Ohio.

(War of 1812 - Columbiana County)

Forney, John — Roll Call of Capt. John Ramsey's Co.
    Served Aug. 24th until Nov. 30, 1812

Forney, John — Roll Call of Martin Sittler's Co.
    (Records incomplete)

Forney, John — Roll Call of Capt. Geo. Shemmell's Co.
    Served Aug. 7, 1813 until ?

Forney, John — First Regiment Second Brigade Fourth Division Ohio Militia, organized 8 May 1806 in Columbiana, Ohio. Captain John Nichol's Company.

(John Forney — Will 1836)

"I, John Forney of the County of Columbiana in the State of Ohio, do make and publish this my last will and testament in manner and form following, that is to say:

First, it is my will that my funeral expense and all my just debts be fully paid. *Second,* I give, devise and bequeath to my beloved wife, Christina Forney, the Plantation on which we now reside, situate and being in Columbiana County and State of Ohio; it being a part of southwest quarter of Section No. 10, in Township Eight, Range One, containing one hundred acres, during her natural life, and one horse, beast, her choice of the team, three cows, twenty sheep and ten head of hogs now owned and all the increase of the above mentioned, also all the household furniture and items not particularly named and otherwise disposed of in the will by settling of to my Son, Alexander Forney; one bed and bedding during her natural life as aforesaid. She, however, first disposing of a suffiency thereof to pay my just debts as aforesaid and that at the death of my said wife all the property hereby devised or bequeathed to her as aforesaid, or so much thereof as may there remain unexpended, to my three Sons Andrew Forney, Henry Forney now deceased, and Alexander Forney, and to their heirs and assigns forever. *Third,* I give and devise to my eldest son, Andrew Forney, the sum of one dollar. *Fourth,* I give and devise to my son, Henry Forney deceased, to his heirs the sum of forty dollars to be paid as follows, which is to pay ten dollars to Christina Forney, my granddaughter, and ten dollars to John Forney, my grandson, and ten dollars to Elias Forney my grandson, and ten dollars to M---- Forney my granddaughter, all of which payments are to be made when the above-mentioned children become of age. *Fifth,* I give and devise to my third son, Alexander Forney, the farm on which we now reside on situate and being in the County of Columbiana and State of Ohio, being part of the southwest quarter of Section No. Ten, Range One, Township Eight, containing one hundred acres; and to his heirs and assigns forever, not to get full possession of the above mentioned farm until the death of the above mentioned Christina Forney and three horses, wagon and geers and all the farm contents. *Sixthly,* I give and devise to my grandson, Daniel Forney, one bay mare. *Lastly,* I hereby constitute and appoint my son, Alexander Forney, and James Early to be the Executors for this my last will and testament, severing and annulling all former wills by me made and ratifying and confirming this and no other to be my last will and testament whereof I have hereunto set my hand and seal this twenty sixth day of October one thousand eight hundred and thirty six."

           John Forney   Seal

(The above will was copied from book #9, page 180, in Columbiana County Court House, Lisbon, Ohio.)

JOHN PETER FORNEY

Son of Heinrich and Maria Magdalena Forney
b. 29 Apr. 1776   m. Fanny Gundy
CHILDREN
John Peter Jr.

John Peter Forney — mostly known as Peter because his first name was so similar to his Brother's first name. Peter Forney and Fanny Gundy were married 20 Mar. 1823 by Rev. John Crom. The story has been told that it was Peter who was influential in his father purchasing Section #10 in Unity, Ohio, as he had been there with a covered wagon train, bringing live stock to Ohio, and fell in love with that part of the country.

Headstone of Andrew Forney

ANDREW FORNEY

Son of Heinrich and Maria Magdalena Forney
b. 1778 m. Catherine d. 24 Jan. 1851, 73 yrs., 29 days
CHILDREN
Andrew, Joseph, and Elizabeth

Andrew Forney was born and raised in York County, Pa. He was a very well educated man for his day; some of his school papers are still in the possession of his great-grandson, Frank Forney, Niles, Ohio. Mr. Forney is buried in the Salem Evangelical and Reformed Church (Old Forney) Cemetery, Unity, Ohio.

Andrew Forney – First Regiment, Second Brigade, Fourth Division Ohio Militia, organized 8 May 1806 in Columbiana County, Ohio. Capt. John Nichols' Company.

HENRY FORNEY, JR.

Son of Heinrich and Maria Magdalena Forney
b. 1768 m. Susanna Shriver

Henry Forney, Jr. was born and raised in York County, Pa., and is buried in the Salem Evangelical and Reformed Church (Old Forney) Cemetery, Unity, Ohio.

Henry Forney — First Regiment, Second Brigade, Fourth Division Ohio Militia, organized 8 May 1806 in Columbiana County, Ohio. Capt. John Nichols' Company.

ADAM FORNEY

Son of Heinrich and Maria Magdalena Forney
b. 1780   m. Sarah May   d. 3 Oct. 1861

CHILDREN

Benjamin, Mary, Samuel, Sophia, David, Anne, Sarah, Moses, Levi, Hannah, Sarah P., Adam, Anjaline, and Morris Lewis

Adam Forney was born and raised in York County, Pa. Sarah, wife of Adam Forney, was born 14 Nov. 1790 at Adams County, Pa.; died 27 Mar. 1868 Unity, Ohio. Adam and Sarah May Forney are buried in the Salem Evangelical and Reformed Church (Old Forney) Cemetery. They were married 31 Jan. 1811 by Rev. John Stough (L) Minister.

Adam Forney — First Regiment, Second Brigade, Fourth Division Ohio Militia, organized 8 May 1806 in Columbiana County, Ohio. Capt. John Nichols' Company.

NICHOLAS FORNEY

Son of Heinrich and Maria Magdalena Forney
b. 1780 m. Elizabeth Sponsailer d. 17 July 1857, 77 yrs., 2 mo. & 10 day

CHILDREN

Fredrick, Samuel, George, Isaac, Eli, Susan, Rebecca, Heddy, Julia, Elizabeth, Hannah, Polly, and Lidda

Nicholas Forney and Elizabeth Sponsailer married 28 Apr. 1807 by John Stough — Lutheran Church Marriage Records, Columbiana County Court House, Lisbon, Ohio. Columbiana County History books state that Nicholas Forney died in that county but Mr. and Mrs. Forney are buried in North Canfield Cemetery, located on Ohio State Route 46 where the Ohio Turnpike crosses; also, his will was probated in Mahoning County.

(Will of Nicholas Forney)

Year 1857 Mahoning County, Austintown Twp., Ohio

Next of Kin — Children

Fredrick Forney — Son		Heddy Kale	— Dau.
Samuel	" "	Julia Meinor	"
George	" "	Elizabeth Meinor	"
Isaac	" "	Hannah Cort	"
Eli	" "	Polly Handwork	"
Susan Shepler	— Dau.	Lidda Cort	"
Rebecca Hawk	"		

Witness - Thomas Hoffert
Joseph Forney

Mahoning County Court House Records - Book #2, Page 4.

Nicholas Forney - First Regiment, Second Brigade, Fourth Division, Ohio Militia organized 8 May 1806 in Columbiana County, Ohio. Capt. John Nichols' Co.

ABRAHAM FORNEY

Son of Abraham and Susanna Forney
b. 1780 m. Mary (Polly) Curtis d. 2 June 1856
CHILDREN
Joseph, Elizabeth, Mary A., Solomon, Frederick, John, Sophia, Eli, and Susan H.

Abraham Forney was born in Frederick County, Maryland. In 1801 Abraham married Mary Curtis and the couple located in Baltimore.

In 1811 Abraham Forney came to Wheeling Township, Guernsey County, Ohio. This was the year after the county was organized. He settled on 400 acres of land. Upon arrival, Abraham and Mary found the county in its primitive state, but they set to work clearing the forest and placing under improvement the large tract they had entered. They kept adding to their original entry and as a result of their prudence and energy, the wide productive acres of the Forneys attracted much attention.

Forney liked to hunt and, as the woods abounded in game, he had ample opportunity to engage in the sport when duties in his clearings did not require all his time. In his later years he used to tell how near his home he killed 400 deer, also many bear and wild turkeys.

The story is told that Mary, when a small girl, was kidnapped, carried away and sold. She was ransomed and returned to her native city of Baltimore. Mary was an intelligent and cultured lady whose influence was an important factor in the intellectual and social development of Wheeling Township in the early day.

Mr. Forney shouldered his musket during the War of 1812, assisting in finally driving the British from American soil.

Mr. and Mrs. Forney are buried in the Guernsey Cemetery. At one time the Birds Run Church stood on the edge of this cemetery; this, no doubt, was part of the homestead. At the mouth of Birds Run, a short distance from their home, was an Indian town whose chief was the notorious Doughty. Although not hostile to the white settlers, the Indians annoyed them at times and there was much relief when they began to leave that section.

MARY (POLLY) FORNEY

Daughter of Abraham and Susanna Forney
b. 1775 m. Charles Timmons d. 5 Aug. 1850

Mary Forney and Charles Timmons married about 1793, probably in West Va. Mr. Timmons came from Martinsburg, West Va.

SUSANNA FORNEY

Daughter of Abraham and Susanna Forney
m. - - - - - Rabe

FREDERICK FORNEY

Son of Abraham and Susanna Forney
b. 28 Aug. 1787 m. Deborah Harris d. 26 Oct. 1854
CHILDREN
Sophia, Susanna, Mary Ann, John H., Eliza M., Catherine, and Alice

Frederick Forney did not receive much education when a boy; notwithstanding this deprivation, he applied himself earnestly to study and became one of the well educated men of his county. He always took a prominant and leading part in public movements of his time. During the War of 1812 he recruited a company of men and was elected captain. He was a Wig in politics and took a deep interest in the welfare of his party. October 29, 1812 he was married to Deborah Harris, whose family were among the early settlers of Harrison County. Mr. Forney died in 1854; his wife survived until 21 June 1873. For several years after their marriage, Mr. and Mrs. Forney lived in Cadiz Township, but in 1827 moved to Nottingham Township, Harrison County, Ohio, where they purchased a farm. They were industrious, economical, persevering, and succeeded in amassing quite an extensive property. Mrs. Forney was 68 yrs., 1 mo., 28 days old at the time of her death. Mr. and Mrs. Forney are buried in the Minksville Cemetery.

SAMUEL S. FORNEY

Son of Adam and Rachel Shriver Forney
b. 6 Mar. 1790 m. Eliza Swope d. 2 Aug. 1879
CHILDREN
Elizabeth, Henry S., Louisa A., Josephine, David S., and John S.

Samuel S. Forney was born in Hanover, Pa. After Mr. and Mrs. Forney were married, they settled in Gettysburg, Pa., where they spent the balance of their lives. He was engaged in the drug business. They were members of the Reformed Church. Eliza Forney died 4 Sept. 1863, aged 64 years.

GEORGE FORNEY

Son of Samuel and Susanna Karle Forney
b. 24 July 1789   m. Elizabeth Young   d. 27 Mar. 1849

CHILDREN

Josiah, Angeline, Ephraim Young, Jesse Young, James Henry, and Adolphus William

George Forney was born in York County, near Hanover, Pennsylvania. Elizabeth Young Forney was the daughter of Henry Young. She died 27 Apr. 1850. Mr. and Mrs. Forney are buried in St. Matthews old Lutheran Cemetery at Hanover, Pa. They raised their family "Pennsylvania Dutch" and all were confirmed in the Lutheran Faith. Soon after Mr. and Mrs. Forneys' deaths, their five sons went west to Illinois.

5th Generation

ANDREW FORNEY

Son of John and Christine Rohrbach Forney
b. 1791 m. Margaret (Peggy) Cort m. Eve - - - - d. 3 Dec. 1844
Peggy Cort Forney died 2 Nov. 1840

CHILDREN

Isaac, Emanuel, Fredrick, John, Elizabeth (Patsy), Margaret (Peggy), Daniel, and Jessie

Andrew Forney was born in York County, Pennsylvania and came to Ohio with his parents when just a child. His Baptismal Record states his Godfather's name was Rohrbach, who, no doubt, was an uncle. Andrew Forney and Peggy Cort, sometimes spelled "Court," were married 24 Jan. 1822. Peggy was a daughter of Fredrick and Barbra Cort of Darlington, Pennsylvania. Mr. and Mrs. Cort are buried in the Old Conkle farm, Beaver County, Pa., on Route 168 about five miles from Darlington, Pa. – (private cemetery known as Cort and Conkle).

> Andrew Forney – First Company, Second Regiment, First Brigade, Sixth Division, Ohio Militia, 2 Sept. 1842. (Taken from original roll which is now in the possession of Capt. Summer's Granddaughter, Mrs. Vernon Crouse, North Lima, Ohio.)

Mr. Forney was a farmer and owned and operated a sawmill.

(Excerpts from the estate of Andrew Forney)

"To all to whom these presents shall come, greetings. Whereas here-to-fore towit on the fifteenth day of February, in the year of our Lord, one thousand eight hundred and forty five, Isaac Forney of Columbiana County in the State of Ohio, filed in his certain petition in the Court of Common Pleas of said County of Columbiana, against Frederick Forney, John Forney, Elizabeth Forney, Margaret Forney, and Daniel Forney, Minor children and heirs at law, and Eve Forney, Widow of Andrew Forney, late of the afore said county, deceased, setting forth among other things that he the said Isaac Forney hath the legal title and right to and was seized in fee simple of one undivided sixth part of the following real estate – Situate lying and being in the south west quarter of Section number nine (9) in Township number thirteen (13) in Range number two (2) in Columbiana County, in the State of Ohio."

William Jellisen (Sheriff)

(Taken from Mahoning County, Court House Deeds, Index Page 146 - Page 422 of Volume U, Item 1126).

HENRY FORNEY

Son of John and Christine Rohrbach Forney
b.   m. Cathorine Musser
CHILDREN
Christeina, John Miller, Elias A., and Mary M.

Henry Forney was killed in a coal mine at Brier Hill, Youngstown, Ohio during a cave-in. He is buried at Brunsteter Cemetery, West Austintown, Ohio.

Cathorine Musser Forney Shrum

Cathorine Musser, no doubt, was a granddaughter of Peter Musser who was the first to establish himself in what is now New Springfield, Ohio. He came from York Co., Pa., and, having considerable means, purchased the four sections in the southeast corner of the township, living a little north of the present village of Petersburgh.

After the death of Mr. Forney, Mrs. Forney married Peter Shrum a native of Germany. To this union there were five children. Mrs. Shrum died 25 July 1878, lifetime 68 yrs., 9 mo., 25 days. She is buried at Brunsteter Cem. Her coffin cost $40.00; she had a linen shroud and robe that cost $7.00. The funeral was conducted by a Methodist Minister with services at the church and house.

ALEXANDER FORNEY

Son of John and Christine Rohrbach Forney
b. 28 Dec. 1807   m. Catherine - - - -   d. 13 July 1880

Alexander Forney was a farmer his entire life. He inherited his father's farm. He is buried at Salem Evangelical and Reformed Church Cemetery Unity, Ohio. Death Records Columbiana County, Court House, Lisbon, Ohio. Page 84 (spelled Alexandora at Court House) July 13, 1880 aged 72 years, 6 months, 17 days.

JOHN PETER FORNEY, JR.

Son of John Peter and Fanny Gundy
b. 1796   m. Mary E. Shultz
CHILDREN
George, Daniel, Susanna, Margret, Harry, Aaron, Elizabeth, Hiram, Rachel Cordelia, and infant daughter

Little is known of John Peter, Jr., as his mother must have died when he was young. His father married Fanny Gundy in 1823. He is listed in the fifth census of the United States (1830), Ohio, Vol. 3 as John Furney, Jr., under Forney Family - Unity Township, Columbiana County, Ohio. He, no doubt, was a farmer his entire life. John Peter Forney, Jr. was lister, or assessor, of Springfield Township, Ohio and paid the levy of $94.69 to Columbiana County.

ANDREW FORNEY

Son of Andrew and Catharine Forney
b. 1817 m. Susanna H. Mowen (or Marvan)

Lutheran Church once called Salem (Old Forney) Marriages Page 134. Marriage Records Mahoning County, Court House Youngstown, Ohio, page 115, Andrew Forney and Susanna H. Marvan, 4 Feb. 1855.

JOSEPH FORNEY

Son of Andrew and Catharine Forney
b. 11 June 1825 m. Martha Smith d. 4 Sept. 1899
CHILDREN
Catherine, Ella, and William H.

Joseph Forney was born in Unity Township, Columbiana County, Ohio. He was confirmed on the 3rd day of Nov. 1841 in the Presbyterian Church at Unity, Ohio. Joseph Forney and Martha Smith were married 1 Nov. 1854. He is buried in the North Canfield Church Cemetery.

(Patent by Joseph Forney)
United States Patent Office. No. 202,806.

Joseph Forney of Canfield, Ohio April 23, 1878 a T-shaped catch on traces of harness to the wiffletrees of wagons or carriages.

(Will of Joseph Forney)

Widow Martha Forney
Ella Strock, Daughter, Canfield, Ohio
Katharine Minard, Daughter, Youngstown, Ohio
Wm. H. Forney, Son, New Castle, Pa.

(The above will was copied from Will Book #15 Mahoning County Court House, Youngstown, Ohio).

ELIZABETH FORNEY

Daughter of Andrew and Catharine Forney
b. 12 Apr. 1817 m. - - - - Rummel m. Benjamin Blott d. Feb. 1904
CHILDREN
With Mr. Rummel: Ann, Mary, Samuel, Sarah, and John
With Mr. Blott: Frank, and Emery

Elizabeth Forney was born in Unity Twp., Columbiana, Ohio. She was a very religious woman and worked hard, often doing a man's work in the field. She and her husband, Benjamin Blott, are buried in a cemetery north of North Jackson, on Ohio Route #45.

BENJAMIN FORNEY

Son of Adam and Sarah May Forney
b. 18 Feb. 1819   m. Mary (Polly) King   d. 11 Dec. 1891

CHILDREN

Maria, Sophia, Martha, Gilbert, Louise, Milton M., Wilson, Harvey F., Sara, Lucy, Mary Ida, Albert, and Morgan Thomas

Birth records taken from books of the United Reformed and Lutheran Church of Springfield Twp., Ohio. Sponsor, William May and Polly.

Benjamin Forney was born and raised in Unity Township, Columbiana County, Ohio. He was a Trustee of the Methodist Episcopal Church of Unity, Ohio which received corporate powers from the state 12 Nov. 1862. He was Unity Township Clerk 1852-53, 1859-78. Mr. Forney served in the army during the Civil War, O.V.I., 19th Regiment, Co. D. He was mustered out 24 July 1863. Marriage Records Columbiana County, Court House, Lisbon, Ohio - Benjamin Forney and Mary (Polly) King, daughter of Thomas King, Leetonia, Ohio 20 Sept. 1842. Mary (Polly) King was born 11 May 1826, died 11 May 1904. Mr. and Mrs. Forney are buried in the Salem Evangelical and Reformed Church once called Salem (Old Forney) Cemetery Unity, Ohio.

SAMUEL FORNEY

Son of Adam and Sarah May Forney
b. 25 Oct. 1811 d. 13 Dec. 1811

SOPHIA FORNEY

Daughter of Adam and Sarah May Forney
b. 22 Oct. 1812 m. Jessie Clark

Birth Records taken from books of the United Reformed and Lutheran Church of Springfield Twp., Ohio. Sponsor, Elizabeth Glas.

MARY FORNEY

Daughter of Adam and Sarah May Forney
b. 20 June 1814 m. Edward Clipper d. 17 Sept. 1834

Birth Records taken from books of the United Reformed and Lutheran Church of Springfield Twp., Ohio. Sponsor, Abraham Nagel and Magalina.

DAVID FORNEY

Son of Adam and Sarah May Forney
b. 6 Feb. 1816 m. Eliza Copeland d. about 1894
CHILDREN
Cornelius, Orange A., David, Wilson, James, Mary, and Elmer

Birth Records taken from books of the United Reformed and Lutheran Church of Springfield Twp., Ohio. Sponsor, William May.

David Forney is buried in the Little Beaver Cemetery, in Pennsylvania. He was married two times but there are no records to prove this statement.

ANNE FORNEY

Daughter of Adam and Sarah May Forney
b. 31 Mar. 1818 m. Edward P. Young d. 27 Jan. 1849
CHILDREN
Thomas P., and Martha A.

Birth Records taken from books of the United Reformed and Lutheran Church of Springfield Twp., Ohio. Sponsor, Yacob May and Sophia.

Anne Forney and E. P. Young were married 17 Dec. 1838.

SARAH FORNEY

Daughter of Adam and Sarah May Forney
b. 16 Dec. 1821

Birth Records taken from books of the United Reformed and Lutheran Church of Springfield Twp., Ohio.

MOSES FORNEY

Son of Adam and Sarah May Forney
b. 3 June 1823

LEVI FORNEY

Son of Adam and Sarah May Forney
b. 6 Sept. 1825 m. Susannah Musser
CHILDREN
Angelina, Lavina, and Maurice Charles

Levi Forney was born in Unity Township, Columbiana County, Ohio. He was a trustee of the Methodist Episcopal Church of Unity, Ohio which received corporate powers from the state, 12 Nov. 1862. Birth Records taken from books of the United Reformed and Lutheran Church of Springfield Twp., Ohio. Levi Forney and Susannah Musser were married in 1843. Marriage Records Columbiana County Court House, Lisbon, Ohio. Mr. Forney was a tailor by trade. Mr. and Mrs. Forney moved to West Branch, Iowa in 1872 where they died and are buried.

HANNAH FORNEY

Daughter of Adam and Sarah May Forney
b. 3 Aug. 1827 m. Daniel J. Forney d. 4 May 1903
CHILDREN
John, Alban W., Sarah, Oliver Daniel, Mary A., Calvin Lancaster,
and Elizabeth Alice (John drowned as a boy)

Birth Records taken from books of the United Reformed and Lutheran Church of Springfield Twp., Ohio and Columbiana County Court House, Lisbon, Ohio, Page 78.

Hannah and Daniel J. Forney were married 2 Nov. 1844. It is not known if they were related in any way; it is believed he came from Pennsylvania, although he would never say anything about his boyhood. He was born 14 Mar. 1824 and died in 1920. Mr. Forney was a farmer and live stock

Hannah and Daniel J. Forney

dealer. He was a Unity Township Trustee 1873-74-75. Hannah and Daniel J. Forney are buried at Salem Evangelical and Reformed Church Cemetery, Unity, Ohio.

SARAH P. FORNEY

Daughter of Adam and Sarah May Forney
b. 18 Nov. 1830   d. 11 Mar. 1853

Birth Records taken from books of the United Reformed and Lutheran Church of Springfield Twp., Ohio.

ADAM FORNEY

Son of Adam and Sarah May Forney
b. 4 June 1836

Birth Records taken from books of the United Reformed and Lutheran Church of Springfield Twp., Ohio.

Adam Forney was taken prisoner during the Civil War and was supposed to have died in either Libby or Andersonville Prison.

ANJALINE FORNEY

Daughter of Adam and Sarah May Forney

b. 24 Sept. 1844

MORRACE LEWIS FORNEY

Son of Adam and Sarah May Forney
b. 24 Sept. 1847

FREDRICK FORNEY

Son of Nicholas and Elizabeth Sponsailer Forney
(no records)

GEORGE FORNEY

Son of Nicholas and Elizabeth Sponsailer Forney
b. 29 Mar. 1819

Birth Records taken from books of the United Reformed and Lutheran Church of Springfield Twp., Ohio. Sponsor, Peter Forney and Elizabeth.

SAM'L FORNEY

Son of Nicholas and Elizabeth Sponsailer Forney

Historical Records of Public Library of Youngstown, and Mahoning County, Ohio.

HANNAH FORNEY

Daughter of Nicholas and Elizabeth Sponsailer Forney
m. Cori - - - -

Historical Records of Public Library of Youngstown, and Mahoning County, Ohio.

ISAAC FORNEY

Son of Nicholas and Elizabeth Sponsailer Forney
(no records)

SUSAN FORNEY

Daughter of Nicholas and Elizabeth Sponsailer Forney
m. - - - -Shepler

Historical Records of Public Library of Youngstown, and Mahoning County, Ohio.

REBECCA FORNEY

Daughter of Nicholas and Elizabeth Sponsailer Forney
m. - - - - Hawk

Historical Records of Public Library of Youngstown, and Mahoning County, Ohio.

MARY (POLLY) FORNEY

Daughter of Nicholas and Elizabeth Sponsailer Forney
m. John Handwork

Historical Records of Public Library of Youngstown, and Mahoning County, Ohio and, Genealogical and Family History of Eastern Ohio.

HEDDY FORNEY

Daughter of Nicholas and Elizabeth Sponsailer Forney
m. - - - - Kale

Historical Records of Public Library of Youngstown, and Mahoning County, Ohio.

JULIA FORNEY

Daughter of Nicholas and Elizabeth Sponsailer Forney
m. - - - - Minor

Historical Records of Public Library of Youngstown, and Mahoning County, Ohio.

ELIZABETH FORNEY

Daughter of Nicholas and Elizabeth Sponsailer Forney
b. 20 Oct. 1814

Birth Records taken from books of the United Reformed and Lutheran Church of Springfield Twp., Ohio. Sponsor, John Forney and Christiana.

LIDDY or LEDDY FORNEY

Daughter of Nicholas and Elizabeth Sponsailer Forney
m. - - - - Cerl

Historical Records of Public Library of Youngstown, and Mahoning County, Ohio.

MARIA FORNEY

Daughter of Nicholas and Elizabeth Sponsailer Forney
b. 12 Apr. 1821

Birth Records taken from books of the United Reformed and Lutheran Church of Springfield Twp., Ohio. Sponsor, Heinrick Forney and Rosina.

LIDIA FORNEY

Daughter of Nicholas and Elizabeth Sponsailer Forney
b. 21 Feb. 1826

Birth Records taken from books of the United Reformed and Lutheran Church of Springfield Twp., Ohio.

ELI FORNEY

Son of Nicholas and Elizabeth Sponsailer Forney
b. 22 May 1830 m. Elizabeth Hunslman

Marriage Records of Trumbull County from 1803-1865. Historical Records of Public Library of Youngstown, and Mahoning County. Ohio. Birth Records taken from books of the United Reformed and Lutheran Church of Springfield Twp., Ohio.

JANA FORNEY

Daughter of Nicholas and Elizabeth Sponsailer Forney
b. 5 Mar. 1823

Birth Records taken from books of the United Reformed and Lutheran Church of Springfield Twp., Ohio. Sponsor, Polly Forney.

JOSEPH FORNEY

Son of Abraham and Mary (Polly) Curtis Forney

b. 28 Feb. 1800 m. Susan Miskimen m. Mary Elizabeth Starker Peterman
d. 31 Jan. 1887

CHILDREN

With Susan Miskimen: Jennie R., and A.Z. (Abe)
With Mary Elizabeth: Soloman, Abel, Barbra, Cathem, Martha, Rose Ellen, Jacob, Simon, David, John M., and Daniel.

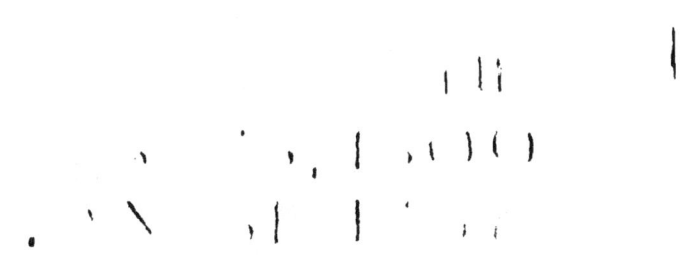

Joseph Forney was born in Pennsylvania or Maryland on the "Disputed Land," and came to Ohio with his parents when he was a boy. His first wife was Susan Miskimen, a native of Ohio. Of Irish descent, she was a daughter of James and Catharine Bartmess Miskimen. His second wife was Elizabeth Starker Peterman, also a native of Ohio. Mr. Forney was a farmer and operated sawmills. He never learned to speak English - always spoke German or Pennsylvania Dutch. Joseph Forney is buried in the (old) Shanesville Cemetery; his grave is on the south side of the cemetery.

SOLOMON FORNEY

Son of Abraham and Mary (Polly) Curtis Forney
b. 1812 m. Mary Ann - - - - d. 31 July 1879

CHILDREN

Abraham, John, Will, Fred, Linder, and Casius Milton
(Casius Milton died 12 Dec. 1862 aged 3 yrs., 10 mo., and 16 days.)

Solomon Forney was the first white child born in Wheeling Township, Guernsey County. He lived his entire life and died in Guernsey County. Mr. Forney was 67 yrs., 3 mo., and 16 days old at the time of his death.

FREDRICK FORNEY

Son of Abraham and Mary (Polly) Curtis Forney
Fredrick Forney went to Iowa (no records).

JOHN FORNEY

Son of Abraham and Mary (Polly) Curtis Forney
b. 1816 m. Eliza J. Wilson m. Ellen Walker d. 1898

CHILDREN

By Eliza J. – Josephus, Isiah, Gilbert, Lafayette, James Hamilton, Eli, Charlotte, Vilet, and another child who died young. *Eliza J. Wilson Forney died 3 July 1867, aged 48 yrs., 2 mo., and 22 days.*

By Ellen – Viola, Chloe, Ollie, Edna, Walter, and Jasper

Ellen Walker Forney was born in 1844, and died in 1907. John Forney and Ellen Walker were married in 1868. John Forney probably did more than any of the other Forneys in Wheeling Township to keep the Forney name alive, he being the father of fifteen children. Mr. Forney lived at home and worked on his father's farm until 1840 when he married Eliza J.

Wilson. The young couple established a home in an old abandoned tobacco house in the woods, which they made habitable by cutting doors and windows and daubing the crevices between the logs with mud. They remained there only long enough to erect a brick residence across the road into which they moved. Mr. Forney opened a store, operated a sawmill, and farmed. He kept adding land to his farm until he was the owner of 1300 acres. John Forney cast his first presidential vote in 1840 for the Wig candidates, and when the Republican party was organized, he became a believer in its principals, as have the Forneys generally since that day. In religion, they were Methodists.

ELI FORNEY

Son of Abraham and Mary (Polly) Curtis Forney
Eli Forney went to Iowa (no records).

SOPHIA FORNEY

Daughter of Frederick and Deborah Harris Forney
b. 6 Sept. 1813

SUSANNA FORNEY

Daughter of Frederick and Deborah Harris Forney
b. 3 Nov. 1814

MARY ANN FORNEY

Daughter of Frederick and Deborah Harris Forney
b. 6 Aug. 1817

JOHN H. FORNEY

Son of Frederick and Deborah Harris Forney
b. 29 Nov. 1817   m. Nancy Johnson
CHILDREN
Ephraim J.

John H. Forney was born in Cadiz Township, Harrison County, Ohio, where he spent his boyhood. He received his education at the subscripttion schools, which were the only ones existing at that time in his neighborhood. He married Nancy Johnson, daughter of Ephraim Johnson, of Morefield, Harrison Co., 26 Sept. 1844 - Rev. Robert Cook being the Minister. After their marriage they settled in Nottingham Twp., where for many years they rented a small farm. They then went to Morefield, where they remained four years, after which they purchased a farm in Tuscarawas Co., Ohio. They remained there ten years and then came back to Nottingham Twp., where they purchased the old home place. Their prosperity was due entirely to their own efforts, as they began life with nothing but their own energy and perseverance. In public matters Mr. Forney was always among the leading and progressive men. He was a Republican in politics. He held the office of Township Trustee. He and his family were members of the Disciples Church.

ELIZA M. FORNEY

Daughter of Frederick and Deborah Harris Forney
b. 6 July 1825

CATHERINE FORNEY

Daughter of Frederick and Deborah Harris Forney
b. 8 July 1827

ALICE FORNEY

Daughter of Frederick and Deborah Harris Forney
b. 4 July 1829

JOHN SWOPE FORNEY

b. 17 Feb. 1830 m. Mary Shriver
CHILDREN
Louisa, Susan E., and David Julian

John S. Forney was born in Gettysburg, Pa. He married Mary Shriver 21 Feb. 1861. He received his education at Oak Ridge Academy and Pennsylvania College. In 1849 he joined a company going to California. They spent the winter of '49 and '50 at Salt Lake with the Mormons. Continuing their journey in the spring, they crossed the Sierra Madre mountains with no guidance but blazed trees at long intervals. He began prospecting in 1851, but not being successful he left California for Oregon, where he remained a year.

He returned to his home in Gettysburg in 1859. The following year he bought a farm, 1¼ miles north of Gettysburg, on Seminary Ridge. This farm is part of the historic battlefield of Gettysburg, where today the Eternal Light Peace Monument stands. About June 28, 1863, Jenkin's Cavalry, an advance scouting party of the Confederate Army, occupied the place; a few days later, during the battle, the house was made headquarters of General Ewell. The largest gun of the Confederate Army was placed just above the house, which discharged its shell over Gettysburg to Round Top, a distance of four miles. Everything about the place was completely destroyed by the battle except the house and barn, and they were well riddled by shot and shell. The buildings were removed in 1937, to make way for the Eternal Light Peace Monument. A section of the joists of the Forney house is now in the Gettysburg National Museum.

JOSIAH FORNEY

Son of George and Elizabeth Young Forney
b. 20 Mar. 1817   m. Sarah Boxwell   d. 24 Dec. 1881
CHILDREN
Henry Clay

Josiah Forney married Sarah Boxwell in the fall of 1857, and they went to housekeeping on his farm, section #35 Clayton Township, Woodford County, Ill. They finally acquired 320 acres, retiring to Minonk, Ill., later in life. Josiah died in 1881 while on a visit to his home town, Hanover, Pa., and is buried in St. Matthews old Lutheran Cemetery, by the side of his parents. He had a lingering illness as the epitaph on his gravestone implies: *"Afflictions sore for years I bore, Physians were in vain, at length God pleased to give ease, and free me from my pain."* Mrs. Forney was born in 1834 and died in 1895. She is buried at Minonk, Illinois.

ANGELINE FORNEY

Daughter of George and Elizabeth Young Forney
m. Abraham Rife
CHILDREN
Ephraim Forney, and Helen Elizabeth

Angeline Forney married Abraham Rife (Rife was probably spelled Reiffe, but the short is being used). We were unable to obtain much information on this family. They resided at Hanover, Pa., where they were both born. Some time after their marriage, they moved to White Hall, Pa., where they had a general store.

EPHRAIM YOUNG FORNEY

Son of George and Elizabeth Young Forney
b. 1820   m. Elizabeth E. Switzer   d. 1897
CHILDREN
William S., died in infancy; Clyde Califax and John Wayne died at age 6.

Ephraim Young Forney was born in York County, near Hanover, Pa., and went to Peoria County, Illinois in 1859. He settled at Oak Hill, northwest of Peoria, Ill., where he had a general store. He married Elizabeth E. Switzer in 1867. She was born in 1842 and died in 1902. Mr. and Mrs. Forney are buried at Oak Hill, Ill. cemetery.

JESSE YOUNG FORNEY

Son of George and Elizabeth Young Forney
b. 24 May 1822 m. Catharine Feeser d. 25 Jan. 1900
CHILDREN
David Zook, Lillie Frances, Luella Young, Karle Herbert, Georgia Etta, and Luta May. (Three died young - Lillie, Luella, and Karle.)

Jesse Young Forney and Catharine Feeser were married 25 Mar. 1852 at York, Pa., and went to Peoria County, Ill., 17 May 1852. They settled in Kickapoo Twp., section #5, where they bought their first farm 29 Sept. 1852. He was a prominent farmer and livestock raiser and finally owned 400 acres of land. Catharine Feeser Forney was born in 1824 and died in 1905. Mr. and Mrs. Forney are buried in a cemetery at Kickapoo, Ill.

JAMES HENRY FORNEY

Son of George and Elizabeth Young Forney
b. 25 July 1825 m. Margaret Ann Allewelt d. 23 May 1892
CHILDREN
Henry, Adolphus Levi, Clara, Belmina, Ephram Young, Leander (Lee) Edmund, James Lawrence, and Cora Irene

James Henry Forney married Margaret Ann Allewelt, in York County, near Hanover, Pa., 28 Mar. 1848. Their first child, Henry, was born there. They went to Peoria County in 1852 and settled in Jubilee Twp., section #7, where their other children were born. Margaret Ann Allewelt Forney was born in 1829 and died in 1905. Mr. and Mrs. Forney are buried at Brimfield, Illinois.

ADOLPHUS WILLIAM FORNEY

Son of George and Elizabeth Young Forney
b. 9 Feb. 1831 m. Mary Ann Diehl d. 16 Aug. 1911
CHILDREN
Harrison William Henry, Alfred Eugene, Bertrum Delmore, Denver Jesse, Charles Whitney, and Elmer Diehl

Adolphus W. Forney married Mary Ann Diehl, a daughter of Daniel Diehl.

She was born at Littletown, Pa., (near Hanover); went to Marshall County with her father and stepmother, when ten years old, and settled west of Henry, Illinois in 1852, where she grew to womanhood. She married Adolphus W. Forney in 1860. They went to housekeeping on his farm in Clayton Township, Woodford County, near Benson, Ill., where he already had been farming for six years. They lived one-quarter mile from old Clayton Baptist Church, where they both became members. She was organist and he was Superintendent of the Sunday School and also was Church Deacon. Their land adjoined his brother Josiah's land on the south. The barn he built there in 1880 or 81 still stands and is an old landmark today. Their family of six boys was born and raised on this farm. They sold out in Illinois, 7 July 1888, moving their family to Daykin, Nebraska the next spring. They arrived there 15 Mar. 1889 and settled on ground they had purchased eighteen years before, 26 Nov. 1870. All the sons stayed with them in Nebraska, except Alfred Eugene, who returned to Illinois because his fiancee, whom he later married, lived there. The land A. W. Forney and family occupied in Nebraska was purchased from a traveling agent. They finally owned 400 acres. Adolphus W. and wife retired to Daykin, Nebraska in the summer of 1899, where he died twelve years later. His wife was born in 1841 and died 11 Jan. 1933. They are buried in Eureka Cemetery, near Daykin, Neb.

6th Generation

GEORGE FORNEY

Son of John and Mary E. Shultz Forney
b. 29 Mar. 1819   m. Lydia Simons   d. 6 Apr. 1883
CHILDREN
Addison, William Henry, John George, Albert (Colonel), Susanna, Ellen, Matilda, Frank B., Mary, Margaret, Sarah, and Julio

George Forney was born in Unity Township, Columbiana County, Ohio. He married Lydia Simons 4 Mar. 1841. She was born in Boardman Township, Mahoning County, Ohio. She was a daughter of Peter and Margaret Simons. The Family Bible states that she was the mother of twelve (12) children and that she died in 1905. George and Lydia Forney are buried at St. John's Reformed Church Cemetery, Southington, Trumbull County, Ohio. Albert Forney's name is on the headstone with his parents (he never married).

DANIEL FORNEY

Son of John and Mary E. Shultz Forney
b. 1821   m. Sarah Rummell

Marriage Records in Columbiana County Court House, Lisbon, Ohio from 1833 to 1848.

GIRL UNKNOWN

Daughter of John and Mary E. Shultz Forney
b. 1822

SUSANNA FORNEY

Daughter of John and Mary E. Shultz Forney
b. 1824

HARRY FORNEY

Son of John and Mary E. Shultz Forney
b. 1826

MARGRET FORNEY

Daughter of John and Mary E. Shultz Forney
b. 1830   m. Lazarus Kunkle

Lutheran Church once called Salem (old Forney) Marriages, page 95. Marriage Records, Mahoning County Court House, Youngstown, Ohio, page 314 - 26 June 1859.

AARON FORNEY

Son of John and Mary E. Shultz Forney
b. 1832 m. Catherine Swank
CHILDREN
James W., Elles Ann, John, and Della

Lutheran Church once called Salem (old Forney) Marriages, page 322, 25 Dec. 1859. Birth Records, Mahoning County Court House, Youngstown, Ohio, page 24.

ELIZABETH FORNEY

Daughter of John and Mary E. Shultz Forney
b. 1834

HIRAM FORNEY

Son of John and Mary E. Shultz Forney
b. 4 May 1837 m. Sarah Kunkle d. 13 Aug. 1916
CHILDREN
Charlotte A., and Clara A.

Hiram Forney and Sarah A. Kunkle were married 26 Mar. 1857. They were living at 311 S. 3rd Street, Cuyahoga Falls, Ohio, at the time of his death. The certificate of death lists apoplexy as the cause of his death. He is buried in the Oakwood Cemetery, Cuyahoga Falls, Ohio, Permit #G. 42 Grave #1, Lot #46, Section L. 1850 Census, Milton Township, Mahoning County, Ohio. Civil War Pension File, Hiram Forney.

RACHEL CORDELIA FORNEY

Daughter of John and Mary E. Shultz Forney
b. 1842

ISAAC FORNEY

Son of Andrew and Peggy Cort Forney
b. 9 Dec. 1823 m. Nancy Diller d. 15 Mar. 1888
CHILDREN
Daniel, Henry, Rohama, Samuel, Mary, Kate, John, Susanah, Elizabeth,

and Debra

The last four children died before reaching sixteen years of age; two more presumed stillborn - no record of burial. Mr. Forney was a farmer. He and his brother, John, went west to Lima, Ohio, some time after 1845. He homesteaded when the County was in its infancy. Mr. and Mrs. Forney are buried in Salem Cemetery, about two miles south of Gomer, Ohio. This cemetery is commonly known as "Dutch Hollow" and it lies across the road from the Mennonite Church.

EMANUEL FORNEY

Son of Andrew and Peggy Cort Forney
b. 25 Dec. 1824   d. Aug. 1842

FREDERICK FORNEY

Son of Andrew and Peggy Cort Forney
b. 20 Apr. 1827   d. 10 Jan. 1849

John Forney and Wife

JOHN FORNEY

Son of Andrew and Peggy Cort Forney
b. 19 Oct. 1829 m. Elizabeth Lehman d. 11 Dec. 1891
CHILDREN
David H., Sarah A., Isach T., Clara E., John W., Lewis, Nandy,
Daniel F., Mary L., and an infant

Mr. Forney went west with his older brother Isaac and homesteaded north of Celina, Ohio, building himself a log cabin and clearing the forest of more than two hundred acres. He was engaged in the raising of sugar beets and farming. Mr. Forney joined the army and served during the Civil War. (G.A.R. Post #429 Ohio). Mr. Forney suffered the rest of his life with dysentery which he said was caused from eating cabbage leaves and roots to keep from starving.

Elizabeth Lehman Forney died 3 Jan. 1893, age 68 years, 2 months, and 14 days. Mr. and Mrs. Forney are buried at Stringtown Cemetery, north of Celina, Ohio.

Elizabeth Forney Calvin and Husband

ELIZABETH (PATSY) FORNEY

Daughter of Andrew and Peggy Cort Forney
b. 9 Dec. 1831 m. John W. Calvin d. 4 Sept. 1888

CHILDREN

Pierce D., Hannah, Minerva, Jacob, Resilva Annetta, Marquis, Clara, and Amy

Mrs. Calvin and her husband were farmers who lived in Green Township. The soil of Green Township is well adapted to the cultivation of fruit trees and is well known for its fine apples. The Calvin Family was one of the early settlers of this section, arriving here about 1815 from New Jersey. These sections are yet chiefly in the possession of the family. John W. Calvin died 11 Dec. 1893 aged 65 years, 10 months, and 1 day. Lutheran Church once called Salem (Old Forney) Marriages, Page 70.

Marriage Records Mahoning County Court House, Youngstown, Ohio. Page 68, 6 Oct. 1853. Mr. and Mrs. John W. Calvin are buried at Locust Grove Baptist Church Cemetery, Salem, Ohio.

Margret Forney Conkle and Husband

MARGARET (PEGGY) FORNEY

Daughter of Andrew and Peggy Cort Forney
b. 14 June 1834 m. Michael Conkle d. 1 Feb. 1909
CHILDREN
J. Edward and Willie

Mr. and Mrs. Conkle were farmers who owned and operated one of the finest farms in Beaver County. Marriage Records in Mahoning County Court House, Youngstown, Ohio. Page 193, 15 Oct. 1856. Lutheran Church once called Salem (Old Forney) Marriages 8 Oct. 1856. Mr. and Mrs. Conkle are buried on old Conkle farm, Beaver County, Darlington, Pennsylvania. (Private Cemetery known as "Cort - Conkle").

Daniel Forney and Wife

DANIEL FORNEY

Son of Andrew and Peggy Cort Forney
b. 3 Jan. 1837 m. Catharine Furhman d. 3 Oct. 1921
CHILDREN
Elizabeth A., Angeline, Mary Ann, Emanuel E., and Harriet (Hattie)

Daniel Forney was a quiet, conservative man, a good father and fine husband. He was a farmer his entire life; for many years he cared for

Mrs. Forney while she was bedfast. Mr. and Mrs. Forney lived about midway between Canfield and Columbiana, Ohio, on what is now Ohio State Route #46. Catharine Furhman Forney was born 1 Aug. 1837 and died 23 Dec. 1914. Mr. and Mrs. Forney are buried in the Midway Mennonite Church Cemetery, Columbiana, Ohio. Lutheran Church once called Salem (Old Forney) Marriages, page 34. Marriage Records Mahoning County Court House, Youngstown, Ohio. Page 254, 20 Feb. 1858.

(Will of Daniel Forney)
(Docket 26 Page 298 Will No. 14367 Vol. 44 P. 192)
"Know all men these presents that I, Daniel Forney, being of sound mind and fully able to transact my business do hereby appoint my Son E.E. Forney and authorize him to be my Executor and Administrator of my Estate after my death and to pay all expenses incurred prior to my decease and distribute the balance of my property among my lawful heirs according to law, also that said E.E. Forney shall not be required to give bond for the trust imposed on him. In testimony hereof I hereunto set my hand this sixteenth (16) day of October 1917."

                                  Daniel Forney   Seal

Witness: Estella Geis
          Wm. Geis
          (New Buffalo, Ohio October 16, 1917)
   Mrs. Angeline Calvin (Dau.)   Mrs. Mary A. Calvin (Dau.)
   Emanuel E, Forney (Son)   Mrs. Hattie Bixler (Dau.)

JESSE FORNEY

Son of Andrew and Peggy Cort Forney
b. 22 Jan. 1840 d. 10 Dec. 1840

CHRISTEINA FORNEY

Daughter of Henry and Cathorine Musser Forney
b. 16 May 1830 m. John Shellhouse m. Charles Reynolds
CHILDREN
Margaret

After the death of Mr. Shellhouse 2 Oct. 1848, Christeina married Mr. Reynolds; they lived at Norfolk, Virginia.

Christeina Forney

JOHN MILLER FORNEY

Son of Henry and Cathorine Musser Forney
b. 6 Dec. 1831 m. Eliza McFarland m. Sarah A. Elliott d. 17 Nov. 1918

John Miller Forney

CHILDREN
Elias A., Henry Zebulion, Mary C., William C., George D., Ida May,
and Cathern

John M. Forney spent practically his entire lifetime in Youngstown, Ohio and was widely known. He was a veteran of the Civil War, having served with Co. F., 114th Regiment of Illinois Inf. He enrolled on the 15th Sept. 1864, and was discharged 14 July 1865 at Springfield, Illinois. Birth Records Mahoning County Court House, Youngstown, Ohio, Page 120 - Calvin Henry Forney, son of J.F. and Sarah A. Elliott Forney. Born in Beaver Township, Mahoning County Ohio 1 May 1873. Sarah A. Elliott Forney died 25 Apr. 1914. John M. and Sarah A. Forney are buried in the Brunsteter Cemetery, West Austintown, Ohio.

ELIAS A. FORNEY

Son of Henry and Cathorine Musser Forney
b. 9 Aug. 1833 m. Jane Cook
CHILDREN
Bernelt, Oliver, and Josiphine

Elias A. Forney went to Kansas and later settled in Sulpher Springs, Arkansas. Elias Forney was a veteran of the Civil War. He was a member of the School Board in Green Township, Mahoning County, Ohio in 1865. Birth Records Mahoning County Court House, Youngstown, Ohio. Lutheran Church once called Salem (Old Forney) Marriages, Page 118, 7 Sept. 1854. Marriage Records Mahoning County Court House, Youngstown, Ohio.

Elias A. Forney and Wife

MARY M. FORNEY

Daughter of Henry and Cathorine Musser Forney
b. 26 Jan. 1835 m. John J. Burns
CHILDREN
Eli, John, Emma, and Ida who married a Mr. Payne

Mary M. Forney married Mr. Burns 2 Apr. 1857 and they later moved to Fort Wayne, Ind. John J. Burns was a veteran of the Civil War. Lutheran Church once called Salem (Old Forney) Marriages, Page 234. Marriage Records Mahoning County Court House, Youngstown, Ohio.

John J. Burns

KATHARINE FORNEY

Daughter of Joseph and Martha Smith Forney
b. 1856 m. James B. Minard Jr. d. 1910

There were no children born to this union. Mr. Minard was a farmer and he managed the Logan Farm in Youngstown, Ohio for years. He was born in 1865 and died in 1908. Mr. and Mrs. Minard are buried in the Canfield Village Cemetery, Canfield, Ohio.

WILLIAM H. FORNEY

Son of Joseph and Martha Smith Forney
b. 2 Nov. 1857 m. Mary Sayers d. 25 Nov. 1938
CHILDREN
Joseph Henry, Frank Sayers, and William Harrison

William H. Forney was an engineer for the Erie Railroad and he had the Niles and Lisbon, Ohio run. Mr. Forney had the misfortune of losing his right leg on the railroad. He was kicking the sand bag to sand wet tracks when he slipped and fell. Mr. Forney lived in New Castle, Pa. for many years but returned to Niles, Ohio where he died. He and his wife are buried in the Union Cemetery in that city. Mary Sayers Forney was the daughter of Mr. and Mrs. Frank Sayers.

MARY ELLA FORNEY

Daughter of Joseph and Martha Smith Forney
b. 22 Oct. 1867   m. Lorenzo Dow Strock   d. 13 June 1937
CHILDREN
Chester Earl, and Olga

Mary Ella Forney was born in Canfield, Ohio, just west of the city limits. She married Lorenzo D. Strock 12 Nov. 1877. Mr. Strock was born 28 Dec. 1855 and died 24 Oct. 1944. He was a carpenter most of his life. Mr. and Mrs. Strock are buried in the Canfield Village Cemetery, Canfield, Ohio. Marriage Records Mahoning County Court House, Youngstown, Ohio.

MARIA FORNEY

Daughter of Benjamin and Polly King Forney
m. Peter Miller

SOPHIA FORNEY

Daughter of Benjamin and Polly King Forney
m. Melchor Mellinger

MARTHA FORNEY

Daughter of Benjamin and Polly King Forney
m. Armenus Ruch

GILBERT FORNEY

Son of Benjamin and Polly King Forney
(no records)

LOUISE FORNEY

Daughter of Benjamin and Polly King Forney
m. Simon Eyster

MILTON M. FORNEY

Son of Benjamin and Polly King Forney
b. 6 Aug. 1857 d. 10 Nov. 1877

Milton M. Forney is buried in the Salem Evangelical and Reformed Church Cemetery, Unity, Ohio. Death Records Columbiana County Court House, Lisbon, Ohio, Page 80 lists Milton M. Forney as having died 10 Feb. 1877, 20 years of age.

WILSON FORNEY

Son of Benjamin and Polly King Forney
m. Elma or Ema Sitler
CHILDREN
Louise, born 22 Jan. 1853

HARVEY F. FORNEY

Son of Benjamin and Polly King Forney
m. Laura V. Rukenbrod
CHILDREN
Albert L.

Marriage Records Columbiana County Court House, Lisbon, Ohio.

SARAH FORNEY

Daughter of Benjamin and Polly King Forney
m. Issac Rantz

LUCY FORNEY

Daughter of Benjamin and Polly King Forney
m. Melvin Day

MARY IDA FORNEY

Daughter of Benjamin and Polly King Forney

b. 6 Aug. 1869   d. 9 Oct. 1900

Mary Ida Forney is buried in the Salem Evangelical and Reformed Church Cemetery, Unity, Ohio.

ALBERT B. FORNEY

Son of Benjamin and Polly King Forney
b. 4 Jan. 1864   m. Albertha Witherspoon   d. 28 Aug. 1890

Marriage Records Columbiana County Court House, Lisbon, Ohio

Albert B. Forney is buried in the Salem Evangelical and Reformed Church Cemetery, Unity, Ohio. Death Records Columbiana County Court House, Lisbon, Ohio, list Albert Forney as having died 28 Aug. 1890, aged 26 years, Unity Township.

MORGAN THOMAS FORNEY

Son of Benjamin and Polly King Forney
b. 1844   m. Elizabeth Mossman   d. 1906
CHILDREN
Charles, and Roscoe Calvert

Morgan Thomas Forney was a merchant in Leetonia, Ohio. Elizabeth Mossman was born in 1842 and died in 1913. Mr. and Mrs. Forney are buried in the Oakdale Cemetery, Leetonia, Ohio.

CORNELIUS A. FORNEY

Son of David and Eliza Jane Copeland Forney
b.   m.   d.
CHILDREN
Frank, Ada, and Odessa

ORANGE A. FORNEY

Son of David and Eliza Jane Copeland Forney
b.   m.   d.

DAVID FORNEY

Son of David and Eliza Jane Copeland Forney
b.   m. Celicia Ritchie d.
CHILDREN
Claude, George, and Myrtle

WILSON FORNEY

Son of David and Eliza Jane Copeland Forney
b.   m.   d.

Wilson Forney and his brother James went west to Kansas and Nebraska.

JAMES FORNEY

Son of David and Eliza Jane Copeland Forney
b.   m.   d.

James Forney and his brother Wilson went west to Kansas and Nebraska.

MARY FORNEY

Daughter of David and Eliza Jane Copeland Forney
b.   m. William Richard Minner

ELMER FORNEY

Son of David and Eliza Jane Copeland Forney
b.   m.   d.

SARAH FORNEY

Daughter of Hannah and Daniel J. Forney
b. 1848 m. Chauncey Zeigler d. 22 Mar. 1916
CHILDREN
Maude, who died when just a child

OLIVER DANIEL FORNEY

Son of Hannah and Daniel J. Forney
b. 26 Jan. 1851 m. Asenith Irene Courtney Wright d. Sept. 1933
CHILDREN
Ruth, and Merle W.

Asenith Irene Courtney Wright was born 7 Jan. 1859 and died 11 Oct. 1943.

MARY A. FORNEY

Daughter of Hannah and Daniel J. Forney
b. 1861   d. 1931

Mary A. Forney is buried in the East Palestine, Ohio Cemetery.

CALVIN LANCASTER FORNEY

Son of Hannah and Daniel J. Forney
b. 3 Aug. 1863   m. Elizabeth Stallsmith   d. 4 May 1938
CHILDREN
Wilbur Dean

Calvin L. Forney was born near Unity, Ohio. He was a painting contractor. Mr. Forney suffered an acute heart attack from which he never rallied. Calvin L. Forney and Elizabeth Stallsmith were married 24 Sept. 1885. She was born in Mercer County, Pa., 3 Oct. 1858, a daughter of George and Esther Stallsmith. Mrs. Forney was a member of the Methodist Episcopal Church and of the Eastern Stars. Elizabeth Stallsmith Forney died 11 Jan. 1938.

Calvin Lancaster Forney and Wife Elizabeth

ELIZABETH ALICE FORNEY

Daughter of Hannah and Daniel J. Forney
b. 2 June 1870   m. Elmer Hisey   d. 27 May 1938
CHILDREN
Irene, Marsella, and Avis

Elmer Hisey was born 25 Dec. 1867 and died 17 Mar. 1933. Birth Records Columbiana County Court House, Lisbon, Ohio. Lizzie Alice Forney born 2 June 1870.

ALBAN WALTER FORNEY

Son of Hannah and Daniel J. Forney
b. 1846   m. Harriet Emeline Sheets   d. 1 Oct. 1909
CHILDREN
Kitty Bell, Minnie Harriet, Charles D., and Walter Alban

Alban W. Forney was born in Unity, Columbiana County, Ohio. Harriet E. Sheets was born in Unity, Columbiana County, Ohio, in 1845 and died 11 Apr. 1873. Alban W. Forney and Harriet E. Sheets were married in Salem, Ohio. Marriage Records Columbiana County Court House, Lisbon, Ohio. Mr. Forney served in the Civil War 1861-1865, Co. B. 19th O.V.I. Mr. and Mrs. Forney are buried in the Salem Evangelical and Reformed Church Cemetery, Unity, Ohio.

ANGELINA FORNEY

Daughter of Levi and Susannah Musser Forney
m. Jacob W. Law

Mr. and Mrs. Law were parents of six children.

LEVINA E. FORNEY

Daughter of Levi and Susannah Musser Forney
b. 7 Apr. 1860   m. E. Morgan Cover   d. 28 Sept. 1936
CHILDREN
Mabel, Pearl, and Earl C.

Vina E. Forney was a small girl when her parents sold their farm at Unity, Ohio and went to West Branch, Iowa. E. Morgan Cover was born 13 Nov. 1851 and died 19 Dec. 1932. He was a brick mason by trade. Mr. and Mrs. Cover are buried at Forest Lawn Cemetery, Youngstown, O.

MAURICE CHARLES FORNEY

Son of Levi and Susannah Musser Forney
CHILDREN
Earl Levi, Lester Burgess, and Harry I.

Maurice Charles Forney lived in Lincoln, Nebraska.

A. Z. (ABE) FORNEY

Son of Joseph and Susan Miskimen Forney
b. 14 Apr. 1828 m. Hulda Doty
CHILDREN
Clark D., Harriet, Joseph W., Franklin, John A., Sarah, Rachel, and James F.

A. Z. Forney was a farmer in Linton Township, Coshocton County, Ohio. He married Hulda Doty, 7 Oct. 1849. She was the daughter of Isaac and Maria Shaw Doty; born in New Jersey and came to Coshocton County when a little girl.

JENNIE R. FORNEY

Daughter of Joseph and Susan Miskimen Forney
m. Perry C. Knisely
CHILDREN
Jesse Clyde, and Ralph

Jennie R. Forney married Perry C. Knisely 20 Jan. 1876. Mr. Knisely was the son of Joseph and Jane Slutts Knisely, natives of Fairfield Township. Mr. Knisely bought the Forney farm; he farmed in the summer and spent the winters teaching school. Mrs. Kinsely was a member of the Plains M.E. Church. Mr. Knisely was a Republican.

JOHN M. FORNEY

Son of Joseph and Mary Elizabeth Peterman Forney
m. Mary Curtis m. Sarah Taylor
CHILDREN
With Mary Curtis: Jess, Frank, Blanche, Laura, Mary, and Lida
With Sarah Taylor: Bertha, Irene, Wilbur, Charles, and Nettie

John M. Forney is buried in Fairfield Cemetery.

SOLOMAN FORNEY

Son of Joseph and Mary Elizabeth Peterman Forney

Soloman Forney was killed at the battle of Kenesaw Mt. in the Civil War. His brother David later received a bronze medal in memory of his work.

ABEL FORNEY

Son of Joseph and Mary Elizabeth Peterman Forney

Abel Forney was killed by a falling tree.

BARBRA FORNEY

Daughter of Joseph and Mary Elizabeth Peterman Forney
m. - - - - Smeltzley

Barbra Forney Smeltzley and her husband lived in the area of Daviess and Washington Counties, Indiana.

CATHERN FORNEY

Daughter of Joseph and Mary Elizabeth Peterman Forney

Cathern Forney lived in the area of Daviess and Washington Counties, Indiana.

MARTHA FORNEY

Daughter of Joseph and Mary Elizabeth Peterman Forney
m. Geo. Lebengood

Mr. and Mrs. Lebengood lived in Sugarcreek, Ohio.

ROSE FORNEY

Daughter of Joseph and Mary Elizabeth Peterman Forney
(died when young)

ELLEN FORNEY

Daughter of Joseph and Mary Elizabeth Peterman Forney
m. - - - Uhl

Mr. and Mrs. Uhl lived in Parral, just north of Dover, Ohio.

JACOB FORNEY

Son of Joseph and Mary Elizabeth Peterman Forney
CHILDREN
Charles D., Albert, Elizabeth, Mary, and Emma

SIMON FORNEY

Son of Joseph and Mary Elizabeth Peterman Forney

Simon Forney went west. As far as is known, he never married.

JOHN FORNEY

Son of Joseph and Mary Elizabeth Peterman Forney

John Forney was married two times. He lived and died in Uhrichsville, O.

DAVID FORNEY

Son of Joseph and Mary Elizabeth Peterman Forney
b. 14 Apr. 1833 m. Abigial Hensel d. 21 Oct. 1921
CHILDREN
Sarah Idella, Alice Elizabeth, John William, Jessie Shirman, Charles Ledley, David Rufus, Kate Ann, Samuel Ellsworth, Jacob Birchard, Grace Edna, and Ralph Barton

Abigial Hensel Forney was born in 1842 and died in 1924.

CASIUS MILTON FORNEY

Son of Solomon and Mary Ann Forney

Casius M. Forney died 14 Dec. 1862, aged 3 years, 10 months, 16 days.

LINDER JAMES FORNEY

Son of Solomon and Mary Ann Forney
b. 1841 d. 1900
CHILDREN
Joe, Frank, Brady Mary, and Vada

Linder James Forney was born in Guernsey County, Ohio. Dr. Forney was married 30 Jan. 1870 and died in Cherokee, Kansas where he was a practicing physician.

ELI FORNEY

Son of John and Eliza J. Wilson Forney

Died 15 Aug. 1850, aged 5 months, and 2 days.

CHARLOTTE FORNEY

Daughter of John and Eliza J. Wilson Forney

She died 7 Jan. 1846.

VILET FORNEY

Daughter of John and Eliza J. Wilson Forney

Vilet Forney died 4 Sept. 1852, aged 1 year and 6 days.

JOSEPHUS W. FORNEY

Son of John and Eliza J. Wilson Forney
b. 26 Sept. 1841 m. Sarah E. Ergenbright d. 21 July 1910,
aged 68 years, 9 months, 25 days
CHILDREN
May, Nora, John W., Lydia, James Garfield, and a daughter Minnie, who died in infancy and was buried in the Belle Plaine Cemetery.

Col. Josephus W. Forney

Josephus W. Forney was born in Guernsey County, Ohio. He lived with his parents on a farm, attended school, and grew to manhood. He attended Madison College, after which he taught nine terms in the public schools. He then studied law with Col. Taylor, of Cambridge, Ohio. He was admitted to the bar in 1867, and practiced law, most of the time, the remainder of his life. At the age of 21, enlisted as a private soldier with the first 75,000 troops called for by President Lincoln. He served 2½ years. During the latter part of the war he was with Gen. Thomas. He was promoted to lieutenant and then to captain but, being on detached service, was never mustered as captain. At the close of the war he was in charge of the government supplies at Louisville, Kentucky.

He moved to Winterset, Iowa, in 1867, and in 1870 was married to Sarah E. Ergenbright. In June 1871 he left Iowa in a "prairie schooner" and went to Kansas arriving 7 July 1871 a few miles southeast of Belle Plaine. He took a "claim" of government land; after "proving up" on his claim he settled in Belle Plaine. He helped in building up the town and community. He served as judge "pro tem" of the District Court in Sumner Co., and as city attorney for Belle Plaine. In 1888 he was elected to the State Senate where he served four years. For distinguished services in the State Senate, his name was placed upon a roll of honor with five others. In 1893 he was appointed a Regent of the State University at Lawrence on which board he served eight years with honors.

He and his brother, A.G. Forney, were in full partnership in business since 1867 and they together owned 800 acres of Ninnescah Valley Land, which they brought to a high state of cultivation from the prairie sward. He was a Republican, a Mason, a charter member of the A.O.U.W. of Belle Plaine, and an honored member of the G.A.R., which fraternity he loved very much. He and his wife were members of the M.E. Church in Belle Plaine. He was church chorister and Sunday School teacher for years. Col. Forney had been ill a long time before his death with that direful malady, creeping paralysis.

This writer wishes to thank Senator Frank Carlson, Senator from Kansas, for valuable information.

ISIAH FORNEY

Son of John and Eliza J. Wilson Forney
b. 1843

Isiah Forney was born in Guernsey County, Ohio. He was the father of five children; he owned a farm in Guernsey County, and another in Sumner County, Kansas. Mr. Forney served in the Civil War, and died in Belle Plaine, Kansas.

Isiah Forney

ANDERSON GILBERT FORNEY

Son of John and Eliza J. Wilson Forney
b. 3 Dec. 1847 m. Samantha Dull
CHILDREN
Amanda B., Frank W., Jennie H., Cora, Rosa Nell, Charles D., Mary D., Josie, Benjamin Harrison, also Emma and Sylvester who died in infancy.

Anderson Gilbert Forney was born in Guernsey County, Ohio. His primary studies were conducted in the common school, and later he entered Cambridge College, Ohio. When leaving school he taught school during the winters of '67, '68, '69, and '70. In 1867 he was married in his native county, to Samantha Dull, daughter of David and Eliza J. Hamilton Dull. Mrs. Forney was also born in that county. Her father was a native of Pennsylvania, and her mother, of Ohio. In 1869 Mr. Forney took a trip to Iowa, having in view a permanent home, but finding nothing desirable, returned to Ohio, where he remained until the spring of 1871. His next venture took him to Sumner County, Kansas. He took a claim on what was known as the Osage Diminished Reserve. He put up a frame shanty which he occupied with his little family for several months, and commenced at the construction of a farm from the primitive soil. During the war, he served in Company G, 47th Regiment Battalion, Ohio National Guard. He was Township Clerk 2 terms and Clerk of the School Board for 21 years. He also was once elected Justice of the peace but did not qualify. He was delegate to 3 national presidential conventions, 2 congressional, 3 state, and one silver convention. Being a pharmacist, he spent 3 years in the drug business. The 28th Senatorial District, consisting of the County of Sumner, the Peoples Party elected Senator A.G. Forney of Belle Plaine, for two successive terms. Mr. Forney gave his political support to the Republican Party. He was a member of the A.O.U.W. Lodge No. 83, of Belle Plaine.

After years of wise investement Mr. Forney and his brother, J.W. Forney, not only had their original entry but they had about one thousand acres of land dealing largely in good grades of cattle, of which they usually fed about five hundred head annually, besides draft and road horses. They also had two other good farms and property in Wichita, Wellington, and Belle Plaine. Anderson G. Forney could usually be found at his headquarters on Section 7, Palestine Township, where he had a comfortable home, and apparently everything around him to make life desirable.

This writer wishes to thank Senator Frank Carlson, Senator from Kansas, for valuable information.

Anderson Gilbert Forney

LAFAYETTE D. FORNEY

Son of John and Eliza J. Wilson Forney
b. 1849 m. Arminda Lanning d. 1934
CHILDREN
Howard W., Blanche, John Wilbur, James Clark, Essie, and an infant daughter that died 10 June 1882, aged 2 days

Lafayette D. Forney

Lafayette D. Forney was born in Guernsey County, Ohio. Mr. Forney was a well-known farmer and stock breeder in Guernsey County. He was preceded in death by Arminda Lanning Forney in 1930, who was born in 1875.

JAMES HAMILTON FORNEY

Son of John and Eliza J. Wilson Forney
b. 1854 m. Mattie Anderson
CHILDREN
Bertha, Faye, Clarence, and Donovan

James Hamilton Forney

Hamilton Forney was born in Guernsey County, Ohio, and as a young man taught school in Kansas; also he operated a hardware store in Belle Plaine. Mattie Anderson Forney was from Joplin, Missouri. Mr. Forney moved to Colorado in 1927. He died at Fort Collins, Colorado. Aged 90 years.

VIOLA FORNEY

Daughter of John and Ellen Walker Forney
m. Harry Hammersley
CHILDREN
Mary, Cleo, and Stella

CHLOE FORNEY

Daughter of John and Ellen Walker Forney
m. William Tipton
CHILDREN
Jean, and Mildred

Chloe Forney Tipton lived in Newcomerstown, Ohio.

OLIVE FORNEY

Daughter of John and Ellen Walker Forney
m. - - - - Shaffer and William Duesenbury
CHILDREN
Clarence, and Lawrence

Olive Forney Duesenbury lives in Newcomerstown, Ohio.

EDNA FORNEY

Daughter of John and Ellen Walker Forney
m. Dan Beiter

Edna Forney Beiter lives in Temple, Texas.

WALTER FORNEY

Son of John and Ellen Walker Forney

CHILDREN
Ruth, and Doris

JASPER FORNEY

Son of John and Ellen Walker Forney
m. Mary Mathews
CHILDREN
Ruth, and Doris

DAVID JULIAN FORNEY

Son of John S. and Mary Shriver Forney
m. Mary Crawford

CHILDREN
David Crawford, George Douglas

HENRY CLAY FORNEY

Son of Josiah and Sarah Boxwell Forney
b. 3 Jan. 1859 m. Carrie Edmona Wilcox d. 13 Nov. 1938
CHILDREN
Samuel Wilcox, Helen Darlene

Henry Clay Forney went by his second name. He was born in Clayton Township. Mrs. Forney was a Minonk doctor's daughter. Mr. and Mrs. Forney had a furniture store and undertaking establishment in Minonk, Illinois.

WILLIAM S. FORNEY

Son of Ephraim Young and Elizabeth E. Switzer Forney
b. 1868   d. 1868

William S. Forney died in infancy.

CLYDE CALIFAX FORNEY

Son of Ephraim Young and Elizabeth E. Switzer Forney
b. 1869 m. Laura Sentz d. 1941
CHILDREN
Allene

Clyde C. Forney was a mail carrier in the city of Peoria, Ill. for years, retiring a few years before he died. Clyde C. and daughter Allene are buried in Park View Cemetery on University Ave., Peoria, Ill.

DAVID ZOOK FORNEY

Son of Jesse Young and Catherine Feeser Forney
b. 12 Feb. 1854 m. Annie Karnaghan d. 9 Nov. 1921
CHILDREN
Everitt

David Z. Forney and Annie Karnaghan were married 14 Dec. 1882. She was born 22 Aug. 1856 and died 15 Mar. 1943.

LILLIE FRANCES FORNEY

Daughter of Jesse Young and Catherine Feeser Forney
b. 2 July 1856 d. 26 Nov. 1866

LUELLA YOUNG FORNEY

Daughter of Jesse Young and Catherine Feeser Forney
b. 31 Dec. 1859 d. 26 Sept. 1864

KARLE HERBERT FORNEY

Son of Jesse Young and Catherine Feeser Forney
b. 2 Jan. 1862 d. 5 Mar. 1866

GEORGIA ETTA FORNEY

Daughter of Jesse Young and Catherine Feeser Forney
b. 1864 m. James Henry Ford d. 1947

CHILDREN
Edna Beulah, Jesse James, Roy Forney, Mabel Marguerite, and Willis Jay

Georgia E. Forney and James H. Ford were married 16 Jan. 1884.

LUTA MAY FORNEY

Daughter of Jesse Young and Catherine Feeser Forney
b. 1867 m. Charles Ford d. 1954
CHILDREN
Walter Kneer, Fern Luella, and Merle Howard

Luta May Forney and Charles Ford were married 11 Jan. 1888.

HENRY FORNEY

Son of James Henry and Margaret Ann Allewelt Forney
b. 29 June 1849 m. Fanny Shambrook d. 21 Apr. 1920
CHILDREN
Josephine Louise (died in infancy)

Henry Forney was born in York County, Pennsylvania, and is buried at Roberts, Illinois.

ADOLPHUS LEVI FORNEY

Son of James Henry and Margaret Ann Allewelt Forney
b. 19 Oct. 1853 m. Eliza Corney d. 22 Nov. 1903

Adolphus L. Forney lived at Kickapoo, Ill., and he dealt in horses.

BELMINA FORNEY

Daughter of James Henry and Margaret Ann Allewelt Forney
b. 2 Aug. 1857 m. Joseph Hart
CHILDREN
Leroy, Cora, John, Mayme, Mabel, Henry, Mina, Ruby, and Clay Dunham

Belmina Forney and Joseph Hart were married 12 Feb. 1878 in Peoria County, Illinois. Joseph Hart was born 2 Mar. 1852 and died 11 Mar. 1922.

EPHRAIM YOUNG FORNEY

Son of James Henry and Margaret Ann Allewelt Forney
b. 7 Apr. 1858 m. Ella E. Shane d. 10 Feb. 1911
CHILDREN
Pearle Reiffe, Ora Clifford, Clifton Elroy, Chalmers, and Faye

Ella E. Shane was born 28 June and died 23 April 1912.

LEANDER (LEE) EDMUND FORNEY

Son of James Henry and Margaret Ann Allewelt Forney
b. 31 July 1859 m. Nancy Caldwell, Elizabeth Rodison, and Jennie Dickson d. 2 April 1931
CHILDREN
Ethel, Daisy, Gilbert Allewelt, and George Franklin

Lee Forney was born at Brimfield, Ill.; he was married three times:- First marriage to Nancy Caldwell; they had one child, Ethel. Second marriage to Elizabeth Robinson at Wichita, Kansas in Feb. of 1889.

They went to Oklahoma and were in the "Land Rush" at Oklahoma City, Oklahoma, Sept. 16, 1893 when one million acres were given away in 160 acre-farms to settlers. They had three children, all born at Cherokee, Oklahoma; Daisy, Gilbert Allewelt, and George Franklin. Third marriage to Jennie Dickson - no children.

JAMES LAWRENCE FORNEY

Son of James Henry and Margaret Ann Allewelt Forney
b. 1863 m. Tressa McDonald d. 1936
CHILDREN
John Earl, Maude Mary, Frances, and Margureta Ann

Tressa McDonald was born 1862 and died in 1926. Mr. and Mrs. Forney are buried in a cemetery at Brimfield, Illinois.

CORA IRENE FORNEY

Daughter of James Henry and Margaret Ann Allewelt Forney
b. 5 Dec. 1866 m. William Lincoln Hayward d. 1 May 1945
CHILDREN
Edna, Burt Forney H., and Hazel

HARRISON WILLIAM HENRY FORNEY

Son of Adolphus William and Mary Ann Diehl Forney
b. 14 Jan. 1861 d. 21 Jan. 1821

Harrison W. H. Forney, who never married, was a painter and decorator. His remains lie in Eureka Cemetery near Daykin, Nebraska.

ALFRED EUGENE FORNEY

Son of Adolphus William and Mary Ann Diehl Forney
b. 24 Mar. 1863 m. Carrie Susanna Tallyn d. 11 Oct. 1944
CHILDREN
Emory Owen, and Roy Cranston

Alfred E. Forney and Carrie S. Tallyn were married 17 Feb. 1892 at Benson, Ill. They started farming on eighty acres, which was located about the center of Clayton Twp., on ground then owned by his uncle, Jesse Y. Forney of Peoria County, Illinois. The latter bought this ground from his brother, Adolphus W. Forney. Nine rods square was given off the southeast corner of this property for school purposes, and the Clayton Center school building was erected thereon. Their two sons were born while living there. They lived there nine years and bought a quarter-section near the northwest corner of Clayton Twp., (Section #7) known as part of Houck Estate, in Feb. of 1900, moving there that same spring. They retired from farming, moving to Benson, Ill., in Dec. 1916. Carrie Susanna Tallyn was born 28 Aug. 1858 and died 16 Nov. 1941. Mr. and Mrs. Forney are buried in Clayton Township cemetery at Benson, Illinois.

BERTRAM DELMORE FORNEY

Son of Adolphus William and Mary Ann Diehl Forney
b. 2 Sept. 1865 m. Jessie Gertrude Champlin d. 20 Oct. 1927
CHILDREN
Harry Theodore, Alvina Mildred, Dorothy Gertrude, Robert Henry, and Mary Louise

Bertram D. Forney and Jessie G. Champlin were married in Nebraska Sept. 1896. They farmed on his mother's farm in Saline County, northeast of Daykin, Nebraska, which she purchased 3 Sept. 1892 for $17.00 per acre. This farm was just across the county line from his parent's other two farms in Jefferson County, where his other two brothers, Charles W. and Elmer D. Forney, farmed. Bertram D. and his wife had three children born while living there: Harry T., Alvina M., and Dorothy G. They sold out in Nebraska, going to Meridian, Idaho in the spring of 1904, where their other two children were born: Robert H., and Mary Louise. Jessie Gertrude Champlin was born in Bloomington, Ill., 11 Aug. 1873 and died 7 Dec. 1949.

DENVER JESSE FORNEY

Son of Adolphus William and Mary Ann Diehl Forney
b. 2 July 1868 m. Carrie Deems m. Mae M. Borland d. 2 Mar. 1944
CHILDREN
Helen, Claire, Richard H., and Louise

Denver J. Forney, a painter and decorator, lived at Kansas City, Missouri, where their four children were born. Mr. Forney's second marriage was to Mae M. Borland. She was killed in a car accident when their car skidded on a gravelled road, throwing her out; he wasn't seriously hurt. Both are deceased at this writing and are buried at a cemetery near Tobias, Nebraska.

CHARLES WHITNEY FORNEY

Son of Adolphus William and Mary Ann Diehl Forney
b. 13 Oct. 1871   m. Lelia Floyd Wolf   m. Henrietta Hewitt   m. Hattie Schappaugh   d. 30 Oct. 1931

CHILDREN

Lulu May, Floyd Whitney, Alfred Eugene, Lois Maude, Wayne Irving, Ethel Lucille, Grace Arline, and Violet Louise (Vicky)

Charles W. Forney, born at Benson, Ill., went to Nebraska with his parents when 17 years old. He married Lelia F. Wolf in Nebraska 5 Dec. 1894. She was born at Hendersonville, North Carolina, coming to Syracuse, Nebr., with her parents. After her marriage to Charles W. Forney, they went to housekeeping on his mother's farm, northeast of Daykin, where six of their seven children were born. They left Daykin and moved out to Ledge Pole, in the western part of Nebraska in the spring of 1918, where they had purchased 320 acres of land. Another daughter Grace A., was born there. Lelia F. Wolf was born 8 Dec. 1879 and died 3 Dec. 1920. Charles W. Forney and Henrietta Hewitt were married 22 Mar. 1923. To this union one daughter was born, Violet Louise (Vicky). Henrietta H. Forney died 23 June 1924 and is buried at Lodge Pole, Nebr. His third marriage was to Hattie Schappaugh 9 Dec. 1925; no children to this union. Charles and his first wife are buried in Eureka Cemetery near Daykin, Nebraska.

ELMER DIEHL FORNEY

Son of Adolphus William and Mary Ann Diehl Forney
b. 25 Aug. 1874   m. Viola Graves   d. 27 Jan. 1960

CHILDREN

Rollin Albion, Lester Wayne, Helen Myrtle, and Florence Viola

Elmer D. Forney, born at Benson, Ill., moved to Daykin, Nebraska with his parents when fourteen years of age, where he grew to manhood. He married Viola Graves 27 Dec. 1898; they went to housekeeping on his father's quarter section northeast of Daykin, where his parents had been farming. His parents retired to Daykin, Nebr., the following summer. Mr. and Mrs. Forney's four children were born while living on this farm. Elmer D. and wife, Viola, moved to a farm north of Daykin, in March of 1916, which was given them by her father, Mr. Graves. Later, they retired to Western, Nebraska, and their son, Rollin, and wife took the farm. Mr. and Mrs. Forney celebrated their sixtieth wedding anniversary with open house at Western Methodist Church, 28 Dec. 1958. They lived to see their sixty-first anniversary, and he passed away just one month later. He is buried in Eureka Cemetery near Daykin.

7th Generation

ADDISON D. FORNEY

Son of George and Lydia Simons Forney
m. Mary M. Taylor
CHILDREN
Roy and Grace

Marriage Records Portage County Court House, Ravenna, Ohio. A.D. Forney to Mary M. Taylor 25 Sept. 1873.

WILLIAM HENRY FORNEY

Son of George and Lydia Simons Forney
b. 8 Mar. 1865 m. Minnie Nicely d. 9 Mar. 1929
CHILDREN
William Ed., Clarence O., Bert, Gertrude, Forest, and Clyde, who died when an infant

Mr. and Mrs. Forney are buried in the East Palestine, Ohio, Cemetery.

JOHN GEORGE FORNEY

Son of George and Lydia Simons Forney
b. 1850 m. Mary Ellen Helsel d. 1905
CHILDREN
Alfred, and Elmer C., (Twins) Frank, Orrie S., Dessie, Ida, and Nora

Marriage Records Portage County Court House, Ravenna, Ohio. John Forney to Mary Helsel 4 July 1872. Mr. and Mrs. Forney are buried at the Hartzell Cemetery, North Benton, Ohio.

ALBERT B. (COLONEL) FORNEY

Son of George and Lydia Simons Forney
b. 1861 m. no d. 1921

Albert B. Forney is buried next to his parents; his name is on the headstone with his parents.

SUSANNA FORNEY

Daughter of George and Lydia Simons Forney
m. Sam Miller d. about 1929
CHILDREN

Louise, Pearl, Raymond, and Jessie

ELLEN FORNEY

Daughter of George and Lydia Simons Forney
m. no

MATILDA FORNEY

Daughter of George and Lydia Simons Forney
m. no

FRANK B. FORNEY

Son of George and Lydia Simons Forney
b. 1859   m. Celina Allie Robison   d. 1940
CHILDREN
John Henry, William Earl, George, May Edith, and Minnie Pearl

Frank B. Forney was a dairy farmer. Mr. and Mrs. Forney are buried at Pine Crest Cemetery, Southington, Ohio.

Frank B. Forney and Wife

SARAH FORNEY

Daughter of George and Lydia Simons Forney
b. 15 Nov. 1843 m. John Henry d. 12 Jan. 1889

CHILDREN

Jennie --------- m. Benjamin Franklin Blott
Ametta) Twins m. Aubrey Mansell
Mary   )   m. Jacob Reebel
Charles -------- m. Minnie Fear
Grace ---------- m. Will Lewis and Thomas Crawford

John Henry, Husband of Sarah Forney

Sarah Forney and John Henry were married 27 Nov. 1862 in Lutheran Church, once called Salem (Old Forney). Church Marriage Records Page 82. Marriage Records Mahoning County Court House, Youngstown, Ohio.

JULIO FORNEY

Daughter of George and Lydia Simons Forney
m. Judson Buell

MARY FORNEY

Daughter of George and Lydia Simons Forney
m. Tom Kincaid

Mr. and Mrs. Kincaid went to Nebraska.

MARGARET FORNEY

Daughter of George and Lydia Simons Forney
b. 2 Feb. 1857 m. Andrew Miner d. 4 Nov. 1911
CHILDREN

Mr. and Mrs. Miner are buried at the St. John's Reformed Church Cemetery, Southington, Ohio.

Margaret Forney

JAMES W. FORNEY

Son of Aaron and Catherine Swank Forney
b. 22 Sept. 1869

Birth Records Mahoning County Court House, Youngstown, Ohio.

ELLES ANN FORNEY

Daughter of Aaron and Catherine Swank Forney
m. Frank C. - - - -

Marriage Records Mahoning County Court House, Youngstown, Ohio. Page 433 Ok'd, by Aaron Forney 20 Sept. 1882.

JOHN FORNEY

Son of Aaron and Catherine Swank Forney

DELLA FORNEY

Daughter of Aaron and Catherine Swank Forney

CHARLOTTE A. FORNEY

Daughter of Hiram and Sarah A. Kunkle Forney

CLARA A. FORNEY

Daughter of Hiram and Sarah A. Kunkle Forney
b. 5 Jan. 1862 m. H.M. Lambright d. 27 Mar. 1949
CHILDREN

Sarah A. Forney and H.M. Lambright were married in 1879. This writer wishes to thank Mrs. Robert H. *(Rosemary Lambright)* Taylor of Plainfield, New Jersey for assistance in her line. Mrs. Taylor is a granddaughter of Clara A. Forney Lambright.

DANIEL FORNEY

Son of Issac and Nancy Diller Forney
b. 1860 m. Janette Hunt d. 1930

Janette Hunt Forney was born 1868 and died in 1915. Mr. and Mrs. Forney are buried in the Salem Cemetery, about two miles south of Gomer, Ohio. This Cemetery is commonly known as "Dutch Hollow" and it lies across the road from the Mennonite Church. There were no children born to this union.

Henry Forney

HENRY FORNEY

Son of Issac and Nancy Diller Forney
b. 29 Sept. 1870 m. Cora Westenbarger d. 20 Aug. 1926
CHILDREN
Glen, Mable, Rudolph, Kenneth, and Eva who died as an infant

Cora Westenbarger Forney was born 28 June 1880 and died 26 Feb. 1952.

SAMUEL FORNEY

Son of Issac and Nancy Diller Forney
b. 1872 m. Ella Haffer d. 5 Oct. 1895, aged 23 yrs., 4 mo., and 14 days
CHILDREN
Emerson

Mr. Forney is buried in the Salem Cemetery, about two miles south of Gomer, Ohio.

ROHAMA FORNEY

Daughter of Issac and Nancy Diller Forney
m. John Bare

There were no children born to this union. Mr. Bare had two girls by a former marriage; they are supposed to have lived in or around Columbus Grove, Ohio.

Rohama Forney Bare and Husband John

MARY FORNEY

Daughter of Issac and Nancy Diller Forney
m. Noah Harris

Mary Forney Harris and her husband had ten or twelve children. This writer has been told they moved to Paulding County, Ohio, but after making a search of that county no one seems to know anything about them. It is possible that they may have moved farther west, as people often did then.

KATE FORNEY

Daughter of Issac and Nancy Diller Forney
m. Jake Derickson m. - - - - Snarey

There were two daughters by Mr. Derickson. After his death, Kate married a Mr. Snarey.

JOHN FORNEY

Son of Issac and Nancy Diller Forney

John Forney died 28 July 1861, aged 5 years, 6 months, and 9 days. Little John is buried in the Salem Cemetery, about two miles south of Gomer, Ohio.

SUSANNAH FORNEY

Daughter of Issac and Nancy Diller Forney

Susannah Forney died 27 Jan. 1872, aged 4 years, 5 months, and 24 days. She is also buried in the Salem Cemetery, about two miles south of Gomer, Ohio.

DAVID H. FORNEY

Son of John and Elizabeth Lehman Forney
b. - - m. Lois Nolan d. 16 Mar. 1944, aged 91 yrs.
CHILDREN
Louis

Mr. David H. Forney visited my mother's home in 1933. At that time he was 81 years of age but he looked much younger. It was he who was responsible for starting this writer on Forney genealogy, as he gave me a small list of four generations and aroused interest in my ancestors.

ELIZABETH FORNEY

Daughter of Issac and Nancy Diller Forney

Elizabeth Forney died 22 May 18--, aged 20 years, 11 months, and 2 days.

Elizabeth Forney

DEBRARY FORNEY

Daughter of Issac and Nancy Diller Forney

The birth date of Debrary is unknown but she died 30 July 1861.

SARAH A. FORNEY

Daughter of John and Elizabeth Lehman Forney
m. Cashmere Wright
CHILDREN
Will, Mandy, Fanny, Dora, George, and Perry

ISACH T. FORNEY

Son of John and Elizabeth Lehman Forney
(died young)

CLARA E. FORNEY

Daughter of John and Elizabeth Lehman Forney
m. Issac Hooper

JOHN WESLEY FORNEY

Son of John and Elizabeth Lehman Forney
m. Henretta Muttersbaugh d. 21 Sept. 1939, aged 76 yrs.
CHILDREN
Nelly, Volma, John Fred, Minnie, and Cora

LEWIS FORNEY

Son of John and Elizabeth Lehman Forney
(died young)

NANDY FORNEY

Daughter of John and Elizabeth Lehman Forney
(died young)

DANIEL FREEMAN FORNEY

(no records)

MARY L. FORNEY

Daughter of John and Elizabeth Lehman Forney
b. 10 Oct. 1875 m. Sherman Fast
CHILDREN
Lee, Ocie, and Q. V. Dove

Mrs. Mary L. Fast lives at Celina, Ohio with her daughter, Mrs. H.G. Meyer. We are sorry our visit with her was so short, as I am sure she would be able to tell a lot of Forney History.

Mary L. Forney Fast

Five Generations

Pictured above holding her great-great grandson, David William Althouse, is Mrs. Emanuel E. Forney, the writer's mother. Standing (l to r) are: the child's great-grandmother, Mrs. Homer Stackhouse; the father, The Reverend Glenn Althouse; and the grandmother, Mrs. Elmer Althouse.

ELISABETH A. FORNEY

Daughter of Daniel and Catharine Furhman Forney
b. 11 Aug. 1858

Elisabeth A. Forney played with the fire in the heating stove when she was a small girl, and her clothes caught on fire; she died a terrible death.

ANGELINE FORNEY

Daughter of Daniel and Catharine Furhman Forney
b. 10 May 1860 m. Aaron Calvin d. 21 Sept. 1937
CHILDREN
Alice

Angeline Forney married Aaron Calvin 23 June 1878. Mr. Calvin was a hard-working and very fine farmer. He was born 1849; died 1914. Mrs. Calvin was a very beautiful woman, but for many years before her death she suffered ill health. Mr. and Mrs. Calvin are buried in the Locust Grove Baptist Church Cemetery, Salem, Ohio. Marriage Records Mahoning County Court House, Youngstown, Ohio. Page 45, 23 June 1878.

Angeline F. Calvin; Husband Aaron; and Daughter Alice

MARY ANN FORNEY

Daughter of Daniel and Catharine Furhman Forney
b. 21 May 1864   m. Urban D. Calvin   d. 1947
CHILDREN
Infant Gii. Gladys, born 12 Sept. 1900

Mary Ann Forney Calvin was a very fine lady, always willing to give a helping hand to anyone in need. She was known to many as *"Aunt Mary Ann"*. Mr. Calvin was a farmer; he was born 1860 and died 1932. Mr. and Mrs. Calvin are buried in the Locust Grove Baptist Church Cemetery, Salem, Ohio. Marriage Records Mahoning County Court House, Youngstown, Ohio. Page 377 - 23 Sept. 1886.

Mary Ann Forney Calvin

EMANUEL E. FORNEY

Son of Daniel and Catharine Furhman Forney
b. 5 Mar. 1868 m. Viola L. Lesher d. 16 Sept. 1932

CHILDREN

Myrtle Mae, Monroe McKinley, Elwood Roosevelt, Howard Glen, and Leroy Leonard

Emanuel E. Forney and Wife

Emanuel E. Forney was born in Beaver Township, Mahoning County, Ohio, where he lived his entire life. Mr. Forney was very active in politics and civic affairs, serving on the Election Board for 31 years as a Republican. He served on the board of managers of the Mahoning

County Agricultural Society for 13 years, was Clerk and Treas. of Beaver Township School Board for many years. Mr. Forney was a rural mail carrier for 26 years; he was a member of I.O.O.F., Panora Lodge No. 410, Columbiana, Ohio.

Mr. Forney married Viola L. Lesher, who is a direct descendant of Sebastian Lesher, a native of Shauffhasen, Switzerland, who emigrated from Rotterdam, Holland, landed at Philadelphia, Pa., 23 Sept. 1734, on the Ship Hope of London, when he was fifteen years old.

Marriage Records Mahoning County Court House, Youngstown, Ohio. Page 461, 22 Dec. 1892. Mr. Forney is buried in the Midway Mennonite Church Cemetery, Columbiana, Ohio.

(Emanuel E. Forney - Will 1932)

"I, Emanuel E. Forney of the Township of Beaver, County of Mahoning and State of Ohio, being of full age and sound mind and memory, do make, and publish and declare this to be my last will and testament hereby revoking and annulling any and all wills by me heretofore made.

Item 1. I direct that all my just debts and funeral expenses be paid out of my estate as soon as practicable after my decease.
Item 2. I direct that the balance of my property both realestate, chattels and moneys to be given to my wife Viola L. Forney to be hers.
Item 3. I nominate and appoint Monroe M. Forney and Elwood R. Forney executors of this, my last will and testament, without bond.
In witness whereof, I have hereunto set my hand to this, my last will and testament, at Canfield this twenty-first day of March in the year of our Lord, 1931."

    I. W. Coy   Emanuel E. Forney
    E. W. Coy

Application states decendant died testate on or about Sept. 16, 1932 leaving Viola L. Forney his Widow and the following persons his only next of kin: Myrtle Stackhouse (Dau); Monroe M. Forney (Son); Elwood R. Forney (Son); Howard G. Forney (Son); and Leroy L. Forney (Son).

(The above will was copied from Probate Court Record of Wills, Volume 69, Page 362).

HARRIET (HATTIE) E. FORNEY

Daughter of Daniel and Catharine Furhman Forney
b. 14 Aug. 1870 m. Noah Bixler d. 1953

Harriet Forney Bixler

CHILDREN
Emanuel and Homer

Harriet E. Forney was born in Beaver Twp., Mahoning Co., Ohio, remaining in the Township all her life. She married Noah Bixler in 1890. Mr. Bixler was a son of Rev. Joseph Bixler, a Mennonite minister. Mr. Bixler was a man of many occupations, some of which were farmer, carpenter, mason and butcher. Birth Records, Page 38, 19 Oct. 1870, and Marriage Records Page 40, 27 Dec. 1890 Mahoning County Court House, Youngstown, Ohio. Mr. and Mrs. Bixler are buried in the Midway Mennonite Church Cemetery, Columbiana, Ohio.

ELIAS A. FORNEY

Son of John Miller and Sarah A. Elliott Forney
b. 1867   m. Anna Lewis   d. 1926 or 27
CHILDREN
Clifford, Mildred (Toots), Ellen and Howard

Mr. Forney was born and raised in Youngstown, Ohio. He worked on the railroad for many years. Anna Lewis was born in Youngstown, Ohio, in 1877 and died 7 Jan. 1950. Mr. and Mrs. Forney are buried in the Brunsteter Cemetery, West Austintown, Ohio.

Elias A. Forney

HENRY ZEBULION FORNEY

Son of John Miller and Sarah A. Elliott Forney
b. 6 May 1873 m. Margaret R. Johnson d. 2 Mar. 1956
CHILDREN
John William, Margaret Ruth, Henry Zebulion, Jr. and Theresa May, who died 22 Feb. 1912 at 6 months of age

Henry Z. Forney was born and raised at Youngstown, Ohio. He worked at the Youngstown Sheet and Tube Co., as a sheet heater in No. 7 Mill. Margaret R. Johnson was born 30 Nov. 1874. Mr. and Mrs. Forney are buried at The Belmont Park Cemetery, Youngstown, Ohio.

JESSIE WILLIAM FORNEY

Son of John Miller and Sarah A. Elliott Forney
b. 9 Sept. 1876 m. Zuma Ella Fuller d. 4 Sept. 1920

Jessie William Forney lived at 557 South Main Street, Akron, Ohio, at the time of his death. Mr. Forney was electrocuted by touching a fallen trolley wire at the corner of Howard and Market Streets. He was buried at Mt. Peace Cemetery, Akron, 8 Sept. 1920. Bureau of Vital Statistics, certificate of death registration No. 2248. State of Ohio.

GEORGE D. FORNEY

Son of John Miller and Sarah A. Elliott Forney
b. 21 May 1877 m. Mary Elizabeth Fullerman, Alice Stamp, Mary Gluckner, and Mary Jane - - - - d. 1 May 1945
CHILDREN

With Mary Elizabeth Fullerman: Lawrence, Elizabeth, and Catherene
With Mary Gluckner: George, Mary Catherine who died when 3 months old; also 2 still-born

George D. Forney was born and raised in Youngstown, Ohio. He was a carpenter by trade.

IDA MAY FORNEY

Daughter of John Miller and Sarah A. Elliott Forney
b. 29 Sept. 1881 m. David Long and Jacob W. Shiley d. Feb. 1960
CHILDREN
Margaret May, and George

Ida May Forney was born at Youngstown, Ohio. She died at Poplar Bluff, Missouri after an illness of a month. Mrs. Shiley moved to Butler County, Missouri in 1953, where she lived with her daughter, Mrs. Margaret May Ricks. She is buried at the Brunsteter Cemetery, West Austintown, Ohio.

MARY CATHERN FORNEY

Daughter of John Miller and Sarah A. Elliott Forney
d. Dec. 1888, aged 20 years, 3 months, 21 days

Cathern Forney is buried in the Brunsteter Cemetery, West Austintown, O.

BERNELT FORNEY

Son of Elias A. and Jane Cook Forney
b. 15 June 1875

Birth Records Mahoning County Court House, Youngstown, Ohio. It is supposed Bernelt went west with his folks, as no further record can be found of him.

JOSEPH HENRY FORNEY

Son of William H. and Mary Sayers Forney
b. 20 Aug. 1888 m. Marie Johnson m. Jean Glenn
CHILDREN
Russel H.

Joseph H. Forney was born in Niles, Ohio. When he was two years old his parents moved to New Castle, Pa. Mr. Forney learned the machinist trade at the Carnegie Steel Co., and then he worked for the American Can Co. for eight years. After leaving there he started a shop in his garage, which grew to become Forney's Inc., of which he is president and his son is secretary-treasurer. Forney's Inc. is a factory which manufactures special purpose machine tools. Marie Johnson Forney died in 1932.

FRANK SAYERS FORNEY

Son of William H. and Mary Sayers Forney
b. 16 Aug. 1892 m. Nell Wilkinson
CHILDREN
Elnor June, and Frank Gordon

Frank S. Forney was born in New Castle, Pennsylvania. He attended Westminister College and followed the accounting profession for years. He was manager of the Warren and Niles, Ohio Ice Company; later he started the Ohio Cement Products Company of Niles, Ohio, of which he is now president. Mr. and Mrs. Forney live in Niles, Ohio. Mrs. Forney also is a native of New Castle, Pennsylvania.

WILLIAM HARRISON FORNEY

Son of William H. and Mary Sayers Forney
b. 11 Mar. 1902 m. Bernadine Albiez
CHILDREN
Janice, and William Harrison Jr.

William H. Forney was born in New Castle, Pennsylvania. He attended school in that city until his junior year when his parents moved to Niles, Ohio, where he finished high school. He then attended Westminister College. Mr. Forney is Vice President and General Manager of The Eckman Coal and Supply Co. in Girard, Ohio, where he now lives. Bernadine Albiez Forney is the daughter of Richard and Julia Stemnerich Albiez. She was born in Pittsburgh, Pa., 3 Mar. 1906.

CHARLES FORNEY

Son of Morgan Thomas and Elizabeth Mossman Forney
m. Celia Bradley
CHILDREN
Morgan Thomas, and Paul Mossman

Mr. and Mrs. Forney went to California.

ROSCOE CALVERT FORNEY

Son of Morgan Thomas and Elizabeth Mossman Forney
b. 11 Jan. 1878   m. Julia Gillespie   d. 20 June 1955
CHILDREN
Kenneth G., Francis, Roscoe Calvert Jr., Albert J., Wilfred Guy, Charles William and Elizabeth

Roscoe C. Forney was born and raised in Leetonia, Ohio. He later went to Pittsburgh, and then settled in Aliquippa, Pennsylvania. Mr. Forney was a member of the St. James Elks Lodge in Beaver, Pa. Julia C. Gillespie was born 27 July 1880 in Leetonia, Ohio, a daughter of Mr. and Mrs. W. R. Gillespie. She was a graduate of Leetonia High School and Ursuline Academy Residence. She was a member of The Woodlawn Presbyterian Church, Coraopolis, Pa. Mrs. Forney died 11 Mar. 1958. Mr. and Mrs. Forney are buried in the Oakdale Cemetery in Leetonia, O.

HARRY I. FORNEY

Son of Maurice Charles and ---- ---- Forney
b.   m.
CHILDREN
Charles Diecks, Clair Elaine, Illa May, Harry I. Jr., Laura Dee, and G. Cress

FRANK R. FORNEY

Son of Cornelius and ---- ---- Forney
m. Mabel
CHILDREN
Leroy M., Marvin D., and Lavonne

The above information was sent to me by Frank R. Forney, who was living in Baudette, Minn. at the time.

ADA FORNEY

Daughter of Cornelius and ---- ---- Forney
m. ---- Alshouse

ODESSA FORNEY

Daughter of Cornelius and ---- ---- Forney
m. ---- Sams

KITTY BELL FORNEY

Daughter of Alban W. and Harriet E. Sheets Forney
b. 27 July 1867   d. 23 Nov. 1873

Kitty Bell Forney was born in Unity, Ohio, Columbiana County, Ohio. Birth Records Columbiana County Court House, Lisbon, Ohio, page 72. Death Records Columbiana County Court House, Lisbon, Ohio, page 76 - 6 years, 2 months, Unity, Ohio.

MINNIE HARRIET FORNEY

Daughter of Alban W. and Harriet E. Sheets Forney
b. 19 Mar. 1869   d. 14 June 1880

Minnie Harriet Forney died in Massillon, Ohio.

CHARLES D. FORNEY

Son of Alban W. and Harriet E. Sheets Forney
b. 28 July 1870   m. Charlotte Crocker
CHILDREN
Richard Alban, Virginia Lois, Elizabeth Harriet, and Kathryn Margaret, who was born 27 June 1910 and died 25 May 1911

Charlie D. Forney and Charlotte Crocker were united in marriage in Cleveland, Ohio, 26 July 1899 by Rev. Mr. Tagg.

WALTER ALBAN FORNEY

Son of Alban W. and Harriet E. Sheets Forney
b. 3 Mar. 1873   m. (Annie) Christiana L. Schaeffer
CHILDREN
Harry Alban, Frederick Cattell, Walter Alban Jr., and Isaac William

Walter A. Forney was born in Beloit, Ohio. Walter A. and Christiana L. Schaeffer were married 22 May 1895 in New Waterford, Ohio. Marriage Records Columbiana County Court House, Lisbon, Ohio. Mr. Forney worked for the B. & O. and Wheeling and Lake Erie Rail Roads his entire life. He is buried in the Sunset Hills Burial Park at Canton, Ohio.

RUTH FORNEY

Daughter of Oliver Daniel and Asenith Irene Courtney Wright Forney
b. 3 Mar. 1886   m. John L. Gross

Ruth Forney and John L. Gross were married in 1920. John L. Gross was born 15 Mar. 1892.

MERLE W. FORNEY SR.

Son of Oliver Daniel and Asenith Irene Courtney Wright Forney
b. 5 Mar. 1884 m. Hannah Hough
CHILDREN
Merle W. Jr.

Merle W. Forney and Hannah Hough were married in 1923. Hannah Hough Forney was born 8 May 1900.

WILBUR DEAN FORNEY

Son of Calvin Lancaster and Elizabeth Stallsmith Forney
b. 29 Mar. 1888 m. Jennie Luella Morris
CHILDREN
Dorothy Jean

Wilbur Forney and Luella Morris were married 29 June 1914. Marriage Records Columbiana County Court House, Lisbon, Ohio. Jennie Luella Morris Forney was born 31 May 1892 and died 28 Aug. 1942.

Wilbur Dean Forney and wife Luella

Wilbur Dean Forney was born in Unity, Ohio. He attended public school in Unity and in East Palestine, Ohio, graduating from the East Palestine High School. While in high school he was very active in athletics. He later moved to East Palestine, Ohio, working as bookkeeper, office and traffic manager at the W.S. George Pottery Co. for nearly fifty years.

JAMES F. FORNEY

Son of A. Z. and Hulda Doty Forney
b. 4 Sept. 1859 m. Charlotte Hamersley

James F. Forney, who resided in Linton Township, Coshocton County, Ohio, was born in Linton Township. On the day that James F. attained his majority, he formed a partnership with his brother, John A., and they were the largest importers of French Percheron horses in that part of Ohio. In 1882, James F. Forney was married to Miss Charlotte Hamersley.

CHARLES D. FORNEY

Son of Jacob and ---- ---- Forney
CHILDREN
Floyd F., and Howard

Charles D. Forney was a farmer and lived at Dover, Ohio.

ALBERT FORNEY

Son of Jacob and ---- ---- Forney
m. Bertha Sheline
CHILDREN
Camilla

ELIZABETH FORNEY

Daughter of Jacob and ---- ---- Forney
m. James Coventry

MARY FORNEY

Daughter of Jacob and ---- ---- Forney
m. ---- Avore

Mary Forney Avore went west to Idaho. She was the mother of twin boys.

EMMA FORNEY

Daughter of Jacob and ---- ---- Forney

Emma Forney had two husbands, a Mr. Wegle, and Ramseyer.

SARAH IDELLA FORNEY

Daughter of David and Abigial Hensel Forney
b. 18 May 1861 m. J. Calvin Milar d. 8 June 1911
CHILDREN
J. Thurman

ALICE ELIZABETH FORNEY

Daughter of David and Abigial Hensel Forney
m. Ed. Eckert d. 1915

Mr. Eckert ran a grocery store and livery stable in New Philadelphia, O.

JOHN WILLIAM FORNEY

Son of David and Abigial Hensel Forney
m. Louisa Ankney, Hattie Rorer, and Amelia Jacobs d. 9 May 1947

Mr. John W. Forney lived in Canton, Ohio at the time of his death and is buried there.

JESSIE SHERMAN FORNEY

Son of David and Abigial Hensel Forney
m. Adeline Foss d. 1951
CHILDREN
Birchard, Beulah, Margaret, and Genevive

Jessie S. Forney went to Silver Springs, Colorado.

CHARLES LEDLEY FORNEY

Son of David and Abigial Hensel Forney
m. Emma Blauser
CHILDREN
Carl, Paul Barton, and Lelia

DAVID RUFUS FORNEY

Son of David and Abigial Hensel Forney
b. 7 May 1879 m. Mrs. Anna Winsper, Nora Carpenter, and Effie Foutz

KATE ANN FORNEY

Daughter of David and Abigial Hensel. Forney
b. 20 Mar. 1871 m. Sheldon Helmick d. 1955

CHILDREN
Clyde David, Ralph, Harlan, Roland, Jessie Howard, Birchard, and Joe

SAMUEL ELLSWORTH FORNEY

Son of David and Abigial Hensel Forney
b. 12 Sept. 1874 m. Cora Winsper
CHILDREN
Russell

Samuel E. Forney was a school teacher when he was a young man. Mr. Forney is a York Rite Mason, Columbus Commandery No. 39, a past Master of York Lodge # 562 Columbus, Ohio.

JACOB BIRCHARD FORNEY

Son of David and Abigial Hensel Forney
b. 9 May 1875 m. Maria Addleman d. Mar. 1903

Jacob B. Forney was killed on the Cleveland Lorain and Wheeling Railroad, which is now the B. & O.

GRACE EDNA FORNEY

Daughter of David and Abigial Hensel Forney
b. 26 Feb. 1878 m. Henry S. Ballard d. 15 Jan. 1959
CHILDREN
Henry S., Jr.

Mrs. Ballard lived in New Philadelphia, Ohio.

RALPH BARTON FORNEY

Son of David and Abigial Hensel Forney
b. 12 Aug. 1880 m. Nora L. Schwab d. 20 Sept. 1958
CHILDREN
Helen Kathryn, and Alice Elizabeth

Ralph B. Forney was born at Stone Creek Valley, Ohio. Mrs. Nora L. Forney died 1 Sept. 1959. Mr. and Mrs. Forney lived in New Philadelphia, Ohio.

JOE W. FORNEY

Son of Linder James and - - - - Forney

b. 1871
CHILDREN
Lysle M. (Joe)

Joe W. Forney was born in St. Charles, Iowa.

MAY FORNEY

Daughter of Josephus and Sarah Ergenbright Forney
m. - - - Wilson

NORA FORNEY

Daughter of Josephus and Sarah Ergenbright Forney
m. - - - - Dawson

LYDIA FORNEY

Daughter of Josephus and Sarah Ergenbright Forney
m. - - - - Guinn

CORA FORNEY

Daughter of Anderson Gilbert and Samantha Dull Forney
m. - - - - Price

Cora Forney Price lives in Wichita, Kansas.

ROSA NELL FORNEY

Daughter of Anderson Gilbert and Samantha Dull Forney
m. - - - - Hatfield

HOWARD W. FORNEY

Son of Lafayette D. and Arminda Lanning Forney
m. Josie Roe   d. 6 Nov. 1957
CHILDREN
Arminda, Elberta, and Aaron
Elberta and Aaron are twins.

Howard W. Forney was a farmer who lived on his grandfather's (John Forney) farm.

BLANCHE FORNEY

Daughter of Lafayette D. and Arminda Lanning Forney
m. Walter Trott

Blanche Forney Trott lives in Columbus, Ohio.

JOHN WILBUR FORNEY

Son of Lafayette D. and Arminda Lanning Forney
b. 15 May 1883 m. Sarah Eliza Caldwell d.
CHILDREN
Robert Lafayette, Fred Freeman, and John W. Jr.

Mr. and Mrs. Forney were born in Wheeling Township, Guernsey County, Ohio. Mr. Forney worked for the Pennsylvania Railroad for 50 years. He was a Scottish Rite Mason, and has a 50-year pin in the Blue Lodge. Mr. and Mrs. Forney lived in Columbus, Ohio at the time of his death.

JAMES CLARK FORNEY

Son of Lafayette D. and Arminda Lanning Forney
b. 13 Aug. 1885 m. Amanda Forest Asher
CHILDREN
John V., Irene, and Doris

James C. Forney was born in Guernsey County, Ohio. Mr. Forney was a farmer and a railroader before his retirement. Mr. and Mrs. Forney now live in Newcomerstown, Ohio.

ESSIE FORNEY

Daughter of Lafayette D. and Arminda Lanning Forney
b. 4 May 1892 m. Ira Murphy
CHILDREN
Robert Hayes

Essie Forney was born in Wheeling Township, Guernsey County, Ohio. Mr. and Mrs. Murphy live in Orrville, Ohio.

BERTHA FORNEY

Daughter of James Hamilton and Mattie Anderson Forney
m. - - - - Boardman

FAYE FORNEY

Daughter of James Hamilton and Mattie Anderson Forney
m.

CLARENCE L. FORNEY

Son of James Hamilton and Mattie Anderson Forney
b.   m. Alice - -

Clarence L. Forney was born near Enid, Oklahoma. Mrs. Forney was killed in an automobile accident in Colorado. Mr. Forney now lives in Toledo, Ohio.

J. DONOVAN FORNEY

Son of James Hamilton and Mattie Anderson Forney
b.   m.

J. Donovan Forney was born near Enid, Oklahoma. He left there in 1925 to attend college at Fort Collins, Colorado. Mr. Forney is president of The Forney Mfg. Company which celebrated its silver anniversary with 25 years of manufacturing and business experience. Covering one wall of the office of J. D. Forney is a huge map pinpointing 75 distribution centers in the United States and Canada for Forney Arc Welders. The company is the world's oldest and largest builder of farm welders. The plant has one of the largest heat-treating furnaces between Los Angeles and Wichita. Forney Films, Inc., produces industrial motion pictures. The Don-Art Publishing Co. is also a Forney enterprise, as are the radio and generator divisions of the parent company.

DAVID CRAWFORD FORNEY

Son of David J. and Mary Crawford Forney
b.   m. Bette Mason   d. 3 Mar. 1961
CHILDREN
Marilyn D., David Crawford Jr., George M., Stephen M., and John R.

David C. Forney was born in Adams County, Pa., and he was a life-long resident of that county. He attended the public schools of Gettysburg, the Gettysburg Academy, the George School, Doylestown, and Mt. St. Mary's College, Emmitsburg. He was associated with the National Garage on Chambersburg St., established by his father, and was the Packard dealer for many years. At the time of his death he was conducting an automobile business in Gettysburg and was associated with the Wayne Motor Co. of Waynesboro. Mr. Forney was a member of the Gettysburg Presbyterian Church and of the Elks Lodge. He was also well known for his swimming and diving ability. He is survived by his widow and five children. Mrs. Forney is a teacher at Gettysburg High School and a former laboratory technician at the Warner Hospital.

We spent a very enjoyable visit with Mr. and Mrs. Forney in their beautiful home on Herr's Ridge, Gettysburg, Pa., and this writer is indebted to Mrs. Forney for some of the Forney History in this book.

SAMUEL WILCOX FORNEY (DR)

Son of Henry Clay and Carrie Edmona Wilcox Forney
b. 29 Dec. 1883 m. Vera Aldrich
CHILDREN
Richard Aldrich, and William Dwight

Samuel W. Forney became a doctor and went to Boise, Idaho to start his practice, where he married Vera Aldrich, 15 Mar. 1911. Vera Aldrich Forney was born 24 July 1887 and died 1 July 1945.

HELEN DARLENE FORNEY

Daughter of Henry Clay and Carrie Edmona Wilcox Forney
b. 5 Oct. 1889 m. Ernest James Henderson
CHILDREN
Helen Edmona, and James Forney H.

Helen D. Forney married Ernest J. Henderson of Elpaso, Illinois, 1 Oct. 1913. They resided at Minonk, Ill., where he was a prominent attorney. Ernest James Henderson was born 13 Oct. 1884 and died 3 Nov. 1940.

ALLENE FORNEY

Daughter of Clyde Califax and Laura Sentz Forney
m. Howard Felton
CHILDREN
Patricia

Allene Forney Felton died of tuberculosis when her daughter Patricia was just six years old.

EVERETT FORNEY

Son of David Zook and Annie Karnaghan Forney
b. 14 Mar. 1887 m. Emilie Ulrich m. Anna Duffy

Everett Forney and Emilie Ulrich were married 5 Sept. 1927. She died 9 Sept. 1929. His second wife, Anna Duffy, whom he married 4 Mar. 1942, was born 21 Sept. 1887. There were no children born to these two unions.

CLIFTON ELROY FORNEY

Son of Ephraim Young and Ella E. Shane Forney
m. Pearl Irene Murnan d. 1927
CHILDREN
Leigh (Lee) Clifton, Millard Chester, Maynard Amiel, Marie Pearl,
and Verna

CHALMERS DEAN FORNEY

Son of Ephraim Young and Ella E. Shane Forney
m. Neva Irene Catton m. Susan Camp
CHILDREN
Ira Dale, and Miriam Irene

Chalmers D. Forney married Neva Catton, who died in 1947. They had two children, Ira Dale, who died when seven years of age from infant diabetis in two days' time; and Miriam Irene, who died when eight years old of blood poison from a cat scratch. Chalmers' first job was mail carrier for one year. He kept three horses to travel a twenty-five mile route per day at a salary of $75.00 per month. He became a farmer and owned several farms in the vicinity of Brimfield, Illinois. Later, he retired to Brimfield and worked at the carpenter trade.

FAY FORNEY

Daughter of Ephraim Young and Ella E. Shane Forney
m. Walter Miller
CHILDREN
Murry, Bernice, and Joanne

ETHEL FORNEY

Daughter of Leander Edmund and Nancy Caldwell Forney
m. Wilbur Simmons
CHILDREN
Irene (She lives at Saunimen, Ill.)

DAISY FORNEY

Daughter of Leander Edmund and Elizabeth Robinson Forney

b. 7 May 1890 m. Floyd A. Hague
CHILDREN
Loraine, and Jack

Daisy Forney and Floyd A. Hague were married 25 May 1910. Floyd A. Hague was born 26 April 1886 and died 12 July 1953.

GILBERT ALLEWELT FORNEY

Son of Leander Edmund and Elizabeth Robinson Forney
b. 1 Aug. 1896 m. Mary Overstreet d. 24 Jan. 1925
CHILDREN
Jackie, and Lee Junior

Gilbert A. Forney lives at Brewster, N. Y.

GEORGE FRANKLIN FORNEY (DR.)

Son of Leander Edmund and Elizabeth Robinson Forney
b. 28 Nov. 1900 m. Ruth Green
CHILDREN
Franklin, and Thomas

Dr. George F. Forney, a dentist at Cherokee, Oklahoma, married Ruth Green in 1931.

JOHN EARL FORNEY

Son of James Lawrence and Tressa McDonald Forney
b. 5 Jan. 1888 m. Maude Mulvaney m. Evelyn McGuire
CHILDREN
Gerald Lorin, Robert Elmore, Donald Rowland, and Mabel Elizabeth (by second marriage)

John E. Forney and Maude Mulvaney were married 27 Dec. 1911. They ran a farm and dairy near Brimfield, Ill. His second marriage was to Evelyn McGuire 29 April 1929. She was born 23 Feb. 1909. They have a shoe store in Princeville, Ill.

MAUDE MARY FORNEY

Daughter of James Lawrence and Tressa McDonald Forney
b. 10 Mar. 1890 m. Lloyd Hasselbacker d. 1 July 1955
CHILDREN
Margaret

Maude M. Forney and Lloyd Hasselbacker were married 26 Jan. 1917. He was born 11 Jan. 1892.

FRANCES FORNEY

Daughter of James Lawrence and Tressa McDonald Forney
b. 4 Aug. 1892 m. Raymond Kingdom
CHILDREN
Bernice Eileen, and John Francis

Frances Forney married Raymond Kingdom at Brimfield, Illinois. Later they moved to California.

MARGURETA ANN FORNEY

Daughter of James Lawrence and Tressa McDonald Forney
b. 11 Feb. 1900

Margureta Ann, who never married, went to California later in life.

EMORY OWEN FORNEY

Son of Alfred Eugene and Carrie Susanna Tallyn Forney
b. 11 July 1893 m. Ethel Myra Ehringer
CHILDREN
Marjorie Elaine, Lowell Eugene, Melvin Lee, and Eldon DeLong

Emory O. Forney was born and raised in Clayton Twp., near Benson and west of Minonk, Illinois. When thirteen years of age, he united with the Benson Baptist Church at meetings then held every Sunday afternoon at the Jefferson County School house, which was located about a quarter mile from his home. The pulpit was filled by the Pastor from the Benson Church and Emory was the organist for several years. These meetings were discontinued with the coming of the automobile, in the "teens", probably about 1915. This community was formerly called Yankeetown. For two winters, when he was not needed to help his father on the farm, Emory attended business college at Dixon, Ill. Later he went to Valparaiso University at Valparaiso, Indiana, but quit school to enlist in the Navy, after World War 1 started. He enlisted as an apprentice seaman, but after three months got transferred to the Great Lakes Naval Band, where he played (trombone) many times under the late Lieutenant John Philip Sousa, the March King. He participated in band duties at training station and with the band away from station — on Liberty Loan Drives, etc. After serving about eighteen months, he was honorably discharged.

He was married to Ethel M. Ehringer at Washburn, Ill., Feb. 12, 1920. They started farming on his parents' farm, where they have resided ever since, although he is now retired from active farming. They attended the Christian Church at Pattonsburg, a small village three miles northwest of their home. Both were active in the musical department of the church, he singing bass in choir and with a male and mixed quartet. His wife was the soprano with the latter. When their children started to high school in Minonk, they went to Minonk Baptist Church where he started a quartet from the Fellowship Class of that church. They called themselves the Fellowship Male Quartet after their class name. Besides singing at local church services, they had numerous out-of-town engagements, singing at Evangelistic Meetings and special church services.

Mr. and Mrs. Emory O. Forney

This quartet sang two summers over Bloomington, Ill. radio station; they sang nothing but sacred songs.

This writer is indebted to Mr. Forney for the fine job of collecting the history of his branch of the family; it is proof he did a lot of research. We had the pleasure of having Mr. and Mrs. Forney visit us in our home.

ROY CRANSTON FORNEY

Son of Alfred Eugene and Carrie Susanna Tallyn Forney
b. 18 July 1898 m. Harriet Robbins

CHILDREN
Ellen Elizabeth, John Richard, Ruth Aileen, Roy Cranston, Harriet Jeanne, and Roger Franklin

Roy C. Forney and Harriet Robbins were married in Linn Township, near Washburn, Ill., 17 Feb. 1921. They farmed in Linn and Clayton Townships. Six years later they moved to a farm in Roberts Township, Marshal County, southwest of Varna, Ill., where they resided for nineteen years. They purchased a farm in Bureau County, Wheatland Township, northwest of Henry, near Whitefield, Ill., moving there in 1947. They sold that farm in 1956 and moved to a farm they purchased southeast of Varna, or northeast of Toluca, Ill., moving there the next spring.

HARRY THEODORE FORNEY

Son of Bertram Delmore and Jessie G. Champlin Forney
b. 20 July 1898 m. Lena May Scheer
CHILDREN
Marlane Duane

Harry T. Forney and Lena May Scheer were married 15 Jan. 1928. Mr. Forney works for the Hines Lumber Co. in Oregon.

MILDRED ALVINA FORNEY

Daughter of Bertram Delmore and Jessie G. Champlin Forney
b. 14 Aug. 1900 m. Theodore Herbert Fisher
CHILDREN
Wayland Irving, and Weldon Theodore

Mildred A. Forney and Theodore H. Fisher were married 26 Nov. 1922. Mr. Fisher was born 26 Aug. 1885 at Audubon, Iowa. He had a son, Edgar, by a former marriage.

DOROTHY GERTRUDE FORNEY

Daughter of Bertram Delmore and Jessie G. Champlin Forney
b. 8 Mar. 1903 m. Lory Earl Rice
CHILDREN
Twins, Robert Allen and Richard Bertram; also William Forney R, who died at three years of age

Dorothy G. Forney and Lory E. Rice were married 6 June 1926 at Meridian, Idaho. Mr. Rice died in 1948.

ROBERT HENRY FORNEY

Son of Bertram Delmore and Jessie G. Champlin Forney
b. 9 Oct. 1904   m. Geneva Valentine Gritton
CHILDREN
Robert Lester, and Keith George

Robert H. Forney, who resides at Melba, Idaho, is employed with Forest Service. It is not uncommon for this company to replant 350,000 trees as replacement in a spring. In the summer he has a fire lookout headquarters. Robert H. Forney and Geneva V. Gritton were married 17 July 1922. She was born 14 Feb. 1905 and died 26 June 1929.

MARY LOUISE FORNEY

Daughter of Bertram Delmore and Jessie G. Champlin Forney
b. 17 Sept. 1911   m. Leonard Jensen
CHILDREN
Marvin Leonard, and Shirley Ilene

Mary Louise Forney and Leonard Jensen were married 4 Nov. 1928. He was born in 1904.

LULU MAY FORNEY

Daughter of Charles W. and Lelia F. Wolfe Forney
b. 5 Sept. 1895   m. Marion A. Wolfe   d. 15 Sept. 1957
CHILDREN
Arline (stillborn), and Elaine

Lulu M. Forney was born near Daykin, Jefferson County, Nebraska. Lulu M. Forney and Marion A. Wolfe were married 9 Sept. 1914. They farmed on his parents' farm near Western, Nebraska. Lulu and husband separated in 1925. She and daughter, Elaine, went to California in December of 1925. For years she ran a lunch route in Los Angeles, California, where she was married three more times.

FLOYD WHITNEY FORNEY

Son of Charles W. and Lelia F. Wolfe Forney
b. 28 Dec. 1896   m. Helena Beatrice Modisette   d. 29 Apr. 1961
CHILDREN
Virginia May, Doris Helen, Marguerite Louise, Agnes Florene, Beverly

Joyce, and Richard Floyd

Floyd W. Forney and Helena B. Modisette were married 19 July 1920 at Lodge Pole, Nebraska.

ALFRED EUGENE FORNEY

Son of Charles W. and Lelia F. Wolfe Forney
b. 15 Jan. 1898 d. 13 Mar. 1907

Alfred E. Forney died of pneumonia at nine years of age.

MAUDE LOIS FORNEY

Daughter of Charles W. and Lelia F. Wolfe Forney
b. 12 July 1899 m. Frank Vorce m. Al Hasler
CHILDREN
Kenneth Emory, and Keith Arnold

Maude L. Forney was born near Daykin, in Jefferson County, Nebraska. She and Frank Vorce were married at Lodge Pole, Nebraska, 18 June 1919.

WAYNE IRVING FORNEY

Son of Charles W. and Lelia F. Wolfe Forney
b. 30 Oct. 1902 m. Goldie May Vorce
CHILDREN
Robert Wayne, Mary Louise, and Marguerite Lucille

Wayne I. Forney and Goldie M. Vorce were married at Western, Nebraska, 29 Oct. 1924. They reside at Brule, Nebr., where they own a farm.

ETHEL LUCILLE FORNEY

Daughter of Charles W. and Lelia F. Wolfe Forney
b. 30 Sept. 1907 m. Paul Dyck
CHILDREN
Roberta Ethelyn, Gloria Jean, and Bonnie Gail

Ethel L. Forney and Paul Dyck were married at Los Angeles, California 30 June 1928. They formerly had a lunch route; now, have apartments and a Trailer Park in Inglewood.

GRACE ARLINE FORNEY

Daughter of Charles W. and Lelia F. Wolfe Forney
b. 20 Nov. 1918 m. Martin Luther Melton m. Earl Winston Ward
CHILDREN
With Martin L. Melton: Martin Luther, and Donald George
With Earl W. Ward: Linda Kay

Grace A. Forney was born at Lodge Pole, Nebraska. Her mother died when she was two years old. She grew to womanhood in Nebraska, going to California later to be with her brother and sisters.

VIOLET LOUISE FORNEY

Daughter of Charles W. and Henrietta Hewitt Forney
m. George L. Watters

Violet L. and her husband reside at Lincoln, Nebraska. There are no children to this union.

ROLLIN ALBION FORNEY

Son of Elmer Diehl and Viola Graves Forney
b. 11 Mar. 1900 m. Katharine Broeder
CHILDREN
Raymond, Mary Lucille, Betty Jean, and Carol

Rollin A. Forney operates a dairy farm near Daykin, Nebraska. He and Katharine Broeder were married 7 Feb. 1923. Katharine Broeder Forney was born 5 Jan. 1905.

LESTER WAYNE FORNEY, M.D.

Son of Elmer Diehl and Viola Graves Forney
b. 6 Jan. 1902 m. Della Schultz
CHILDREN
Larry Wayne, and Lewis Elmer

Dr. and Mrs. Forney live at Crete, Nebraska where he is a medical doctor. They were married 1 July 1926.

HELEN MYRTLE FORNEY

Daughter of Elmer Diehl and Viola Graves Forney
b. 13 Apr. 1906 m. Clyde Damke
CHILDREN
Betty Lee, and Bonnie

Helen and her husband reside at Western, Nebraska. They were married 18 June 1933.

FLORENCE VIOLA FORNEY

Daughter of Elmer Diehl and Viola Graves Forney
b. 12 Feb. 1911 m. Kermit Roland Erickson
CHILDREN
Patricia Jean, and Kermit Roland, 2nd.

Mr. and Mrs. Erickson reside at Arcadia, Nebraska, where she teaches music and he has an insurance agency. They were married 11 July 1937. Kermit R. Erickson was born 4 Dec. 1906.

8th Generation

ROY FORNEY

Son of Addison and Mary M. Taylor Forney
m. no

GRACE FORNEY

Daughter of Addison and Mary M. Taylor Forney
m. - - - - Mackintosh

WILLIAM ED. FORNEY

Son of William and Minnie Nicely Forney

CLARENCE O. FORNEY

Son of William and Minnie Nicely Forney
m. Margret Diehl

BERT FORNEY

Son of William and Minnie Nicely Forney

FOREST FORNEY

Son of William and Minnie Nicely Forney
CHILDREN
Clyde, Donna, Robert, Delmar, and Mildred

Forest lives in McKeesport, Pennsylvania.

GERTRUDE FORNEY

Daughter of William and Minnie Nicely Forney
m. Chas. Sansenbacher

CLYDE D. FORNEY

Son of William and Minnie Nicely Forney
Clyde died as an infant.

ALFRED FORNEY
(a twin)
Son of John George and Mary Ellen Helsel Forney
b. 1 Sept. 1873 m. Dora Bonner

Birth Records Portage County Court House, Ravenna, Ohio. Born in Deerfield, Ohio. Marriage Records Portage County Court House, Ravenna, Ohio. Alfred Forney to Dora Bonner 2 July 1902.

ELMER C. FORNEY
(a twin)
Son of John George and Mary Ellen Helsel Forney
b. 1 Sept. 1873 m. Maud L. Hoyle d. 1937

Birth Records Portage County Court House, Ravenna, Ohio. Born at Deerfield, Ohio. Mr. Forney is buried at West Berlin Center, Cemetery. Maud L. Hoyle Forney was born in 1879.

FRANK C. FORNEY

Son of John George and Mary Ellen Helsel Forney
b. 1880 m. Elie Adrin m. Adda Kale d. 1932

Frank C. Forney is buried in the Hartzell Cemetery, North Benton, Ohio. Adda Kale Forney was born in 1888.

ORRIE S. FORNEY

Son of John George and Mary Ellen Helsel Forney
b. 1891 d. 1899

Orrie S. Forney is buried in the Hartzell Cemetery, North Benton, Ohio.

DESSIE P. FORNEY

Daughter of John George and Mary Ellen Helsel Forney
b. 3 Feb. 1885 m. Ford Hoyle

Mrs. Hoyle lives in Youngstown, Ohio.

IDA M. FORNEY

Daughter of John George and Mary Ellen Helsel Forney
b. 1875 m. Arthur W. Lewis d. 1944

Marriage Records Portage County Court House, Ravenna, Ohio. Ida Forney to Arthur W. Lewis 27 May 1902. Mr. and Mrs. Lewis are buried in the Hartzell Cemetery, North Benton, Ohio.

NORA FORNEY

Daughter of John George and Mary Ellen Helsel Forney
b. 1873 m. Oscar Rakestraw d. 1919
CHILDREN
Pearl

Marriage Records Portage County Court House, Ravenna, Ohio. Nora Forney to Oscar Rakestraw 5 Feb. 1901. Mr. and Mrs. Rakestraw are buried in the Hartzell Cemetery, North Benton, Ohio.

JOHN HENRY FORNEY

Son of Frank B. and Celina Allie Robison Forney
b. 20 July 1885 m. Inez Shaw m. Mildred Amelia Prime
CHILDREN
With Inez Shaw: Florence
With Mildred A. Prime: Eva Mae, Maree, and Virginia Mae

Birth Records Portage County Court House, Ravenna, Ohio. Born at Hiram, Ohio. John Henry Forney worked 48 years for the Nickle Plate Railroad. Started in 1906 and retired in 1954 in Vermilion, Ohio. Since Mr. Forney retired they have moved to Florida. They now live in Sylvan Shores, Mt. Dora, Fla.

GEORGE FORNEY

Son of Frank B. and Celina Allie Robison Forney
b. 1884 d. 1892 aged 8 yrs.

MINNIE PEARL FORNEY

Daughter of Frank B. and Celina Allie Robison Forney
b. 29 Sept. 1891 m. Isaac Reed Hays d. 1952
CHILDREN
Isaac Reed Hays, Jr.

Birth Records Portage County Court House, Ravenna, Ohio. Born at Mantua Township. Marriage Records Portage County Court House, Ravenna, Ohio. Minnie Forney to Reed Hays 8 June 1910. Isaac Reed Hays was born in 1885 and died in 1953. Mr. and Mrs. Hays are buried in Hiram, Ohio.

MAY EDITH FORNEY

Daughter of Frank B. and Celina Allie Robison Forney
b. 20 Apr. 1880 or 87 m. O. J. Clark

CHILDREN
Helen, who married Clark Hutcheson of Frankfort, Indiana.

Birth Records Portage County Court House, Ravenna, Ohio. Born at Hiram, Ohio. On the 6th of May 1959, the Clarks observed their 50th wedding anniversary with an open reception in Florida, where they live.

WILLIAM EARL FORNEY

Son of Frank B. and Celina Allie Robison Forney
b. 20 July 1890 m. Marie Otrick

Birth Records Portage County Court House, Ravenna, Ohio. Born at Hiram, Ohio. William Earl Forney and Marie Otrick were married in Darlington, Pennsylvania.

LOUIS FORNEY, SR.

Son of David and Louise Townsend Forney
m. Etta Mae Andrews
CHILDREN
Louis, Jr., Madge Marie, and Donald

Louis Forney is a retired employee of the Standard Oil Company. He lives on Breese Road, Lima, Ohio.

JOHN FRED FORNEY

Son of John Wesley and Henretta Muttersbaugh Forney
b. 1 Oct. 1895 m. Lottie German

John F. Forney owns and operates the farm where his grandfather, John Forney, settled and built a log cabin. This farm is located on Ohio Route 707 just west of Rockford, Ohio. There were no children born to this union.

MABLE FORNEY

Daughter of Henry and Cora Westenbarger Forney
m. Earl Keyser
CHILDREN
Earl, Robert, and Doris

Mabel Forney was born at Fort Jennings, Ohio and now lives in Columbiana, Ohio.

GLEN FORNEY

Son of Henry and Cora Westenbarger Forney
b. 1904 m. Irene Braddick
CHILDREN
Glen A.

Glen Forney and his brother Kenneth have Radio Station WHLL, 1600 on the dial. This station is located off Route 40 in West Virginia.

RUDOLPH FORNEY

Son of Henry and Cora Westenbarger Forney
b. 1908 m. Ruth Ellen Dilling
CHILDREN
James, and Ruth Ellen

KENNETH FORNEY

Son of Henry and Cora Westenbarger Forney
b. 1919

EMERSON FORNEY

Son of Samuel and Ella Haffer Forney
b. 1872
CHILDREN
Lois, and Robert

MYRTLE MAE FORNEY

Daughter of Emanuel E. and Viola L. Lesher Forney
b. 15 Oct. 1893 m. Homer Stackhouse
CHILDREN
Gertrude, Helen, and Alta Mae

Myrtle M. Forney was born in Beaver Twp., Mahoning County, Ohio. Mr. Stackhouse was a native of Columbiana County, Ohio. Mr. and Mrs. Stackhouse lived for many years in Winona, Ohio. He operated a store a few years and for many years was employed in a nursery. Mr. Stackhouse is buried in the Midway Mennonite Church Cemetery, Columbiana, Ohio.

Myrtle M. Forney Stackhouse and Husband

MONROE McKINLEY FORNEY

Son of Emanuel E. and Viola L. Lesher Forney
b. 14 Aug. 1896 m. Elta Miller
CHILDREN
Donald Floyd

Monroe M. Forney

Monroe M. Forney was born in Beaver Twp., Mahoning County, Ohio. Mr. Forney served in World War #I Quartermaster Corps., Serial No. 38 57534. He lives in Canfield, Ohio and is well known as an exhibitor of fine ponies ("Forney's Midget Ponies"). They have hundreds of ribbons, trophies, and cups that they have won at fairs and horse shows. They have shown as far west as Oklahoma and throughout the east. The Forneys know pony breeders all over the United States.

ELWOOD ROOSEVELT FORNEY

Son of Emanuel E. and Viola L. Lesher Forney
b. 22 Oct. 1904 m. Ruby Blosser
CHILDREN
Robert L., Virgiana, Richard, and Fredric

Elwood R. Forney and Wife

Elwood R. Forney was born in Beaver Twp., Mahoning County, Ohio. Mr. Forney has been an active member of Locust Grove Baptist Church, Salem, Ohio. He has served as Deacon, Sunday School Supt., and various other posts. He lives in Columbiana, Ohio, and is a man with much energy; he loves to garden and grow shrubbery as a hobby.

Seated Monroe, holding Leroy; standing, rear, Elwood, and, in front, Howard.

Left to right; Joyce and Joann Forney,
age 2 years.

L-R; Joyce and Joann Forney,
age 16 years.

HOWARD GLEN FORNEY

Son of Emanuel E. and Viola L. Lesher Forney
b. 26 Feb. 1911 m. LaVerne Huxley m. Mary Louise Barhoover
CHILDREN
Joyce Delaine, and Joann Elaine *(twins)*

Howard G. Forney and Wife Mary Louise

There may be some who might be interested in the most important events in my life.

I, Howard Glen Forney, was born on Feb. 26, 1911 on a small farm just outside of Calla, Ohio, a village in Mahoning County that once teemed with business activity and enterprise. Calla derived its name from the Calla lily. Calla today is scarcely more than a shadow of its former self. Calla was the seat or location of the old Templin Seed Company whose history dates back to the early eighties, and it had almost a national reputation. It was a pretty little village, with a store, post office, railway depot, a little Evangelical Church and a contented and happy populace.

After the first World War, my parents purchased a farm in Beaver Township, Mahoning County, Ohio, where I went to school and grew to manhood. When I was a boy I was baptized in the Locust Grove Baptist Church, the result of having a fine Christian mother.

I am the father of twin daughters, Joyce and Joann, by my first marriage; both are married and Joyce has two daughters, Karen and Nancy.

In 1940 I moved to Warren, Ohio, and from there I entered the army in World War #2; my serial number was 35608140. I served in the Mediterranean Theater of operations, and received the Bronze Star, Purple Heart, Presidential Citation and others.

After the war, I returned to Warren, Ohio, met and married Mary Louise Barhoover.

I am employed at Packard Electric, a Division of General Motors Corporation. I am a member of Carroll F. Clapp Lodge No. 655, F. & A.M.; Warren Council No. 58, Mahoning Chapter No. 10 Royal Arch Masons; Warren Commandery No. 39 Knights Templar; Ali Baba Grotto; Society of the Third Infantry Division; The Huguenot Society of Ohio, and the Ethan Allen Chapter of the Ohio Society Sons of the American Revolution.

My grandfather was responsible for my interest in genealogy. He was a fine old gentleman, very proud and mysterious as far as his family was concerned. Perhaps he was mysterious because he became an orphan when just a small boy, and had no knowledge of his ancestors; however, I know a man of his character had to be a man of fine breeding and have good ancestry. So when I was old enough and time would permit, I would wonder and work on the family history. My first start was given to me by a cousin, David Forney, from Lima, Ohio, in 1933. Since then I have traveled and visited Forney families, cemeteries, courthouses and archives in many states in America, and concluded my search in 1963 with a trip to Europe to verify records by visiting Forneys and searching records in archives there.

I am sorry I have not been able to connect all the Forneys with whom I have corresponded and met. I feel sure they are related and are fine people, but time does not permit any further research.

LEROY LEONARD FORNEY

Son of Emanuel E. and Viola L. Lesher Forney
b. 12 Oct. 1914 m. Anna Keck Kasza
CHILDREN
Harold, Mrs. Forney's child by a former marriage

Leroy L. Forney and Wife

Leroy L. Forney was born in Beaver Twp., Mahoning County, Ohio. He served in World War #2, Serial No. 35024363, with the 25th Division Co. M. 161st. Inf. Mr. Forney served with the 25th Division during the Guadalcanal Campaign and many other major battles in the Pacific.

He and his wife live at "Ten-N-Half Acres," on South Range Road, Columbiana, Ohio, where he enjoys his hobby of raising flowers and shrubbery.

MILDRED "TOOTS" FORNEY

Daughter of Elias A. and Anna Lewis Forney
b. 14 July m. David Bailey
CHILDREN
Eleanor Mae (married Dean Cranmer who is now Mayor of Salem, Ohio)

Mrs. Bailey has lived in Youngstown, Ohio most of her life.

ELLEN FORNEY

Daughter of Elias A. and Anna Lewis Forney
b. 12 July 1900 m. Lloyd T. Shell

Ellen Forney was born and raised in Youngstown, Ohio. Mr. Shell died in March 1950. Mrs. Shell now resides in St. Petersburg, Florida.

HOWARD FORNEY

Son of Elias A. and Anna Lewis Forney
b. 25 Nov. 1905 m. Helen Hofmeister
CHILDREN
Evelyn, Marjorie, and Marilyn Jean

Howard Forney was born and raised in Youngstown, Ohio. He was appointed Captain of the Salem, Ohio Police Force 16 Feb. 1943. He is a member of the Independent Hose Club of Salem, Ohio, The Loyal Order of Moose, and the Fraternal Order of Police (Quaker Lodge #88). Helen Hofmeister Forney is the daughter of Harry and Maud Seiter Hofmeister.

CLIFFORD FORNEY

Son of Elias A. and Anna Lewis Forney
d. 7 years of age

Clifford Forney was killed while playing with some boys at the Heller Bro's Lumber Company in Youngstown, Ohio. He fell and ran a piece of wood through his head.

JOHN WILLIAM FORNEY

Son of Henry Zebulon and Margeret R. Johnson Forney
b. 17 Oct. 1901 m. Luella Dunkle

John W. Forney was born in Youngstown, Ohio, and lives in Struthers, O.

MARGARET RUTH FORNEY

Daughter of Henry Zebulon and Margeret R. Johnson Forney
b. 22 Aug. 1906 m. John Hiet and Luthe Burbaker
CHILDREN
Isabel May, daughter of John Hiet

Margaret R. Burbaker resides in Struthers, Ohio.

HENRY ZEBULON FORNEY, JR.

Son of Henry Zebulon and Margeret R. Johnson Forney
b. 10 Sept. 1909 m. Willie Holbrook
CHILDREN
John William

Henry Z. Forney, Jr. was born in Youngstown, Ohio, where he now resides. Mr. Forney served in World War #2, Serial No. 35303317. Willie Holbrook Forney is a native of Texas.

LAWRENCE FORNEY

Son of George D. and Mary Elizabeth Fullerman Forney
b. 29 Jan. 1908 m. Rena Lawson

Mr. and Mrs. Forney live in Rural Hall, North Carolina. Mrs. Forney is a native of that state.

ELIZABETH FORNEY

Daughter of George D. and Mary Elizabeth Fullerman Forney
b. 4 Sept. 1910 m. William H. Reed
CHILDREN
William Hamilton, Jr., Carolyn Irene, Robert Eugene, Catherine Eileen, and Nancy Lee

Mr. Reed was born in New Philadelphia, Ohio. Mr. Reed died in 1962. Mrs. Reed lives in Warren, Ohio.

CATHERENE FORNEY

Daughter of George D. and Mary Elizabeth Fullerman Forney
b. 17 Mar. 1913 m. Peter Marino

Mr. and Mrs. Marino live in Brooklyn, New York.

GEORGE FORNEY

Son of George D. and Mary Gluckner Forney
b. 3 Nov. 1918 m. Olga Lawson

At this writing George Forney could not be located. Olga Lawson Forney is a native of North Carolina. She is a sister of Rena Lawson Forney, wife of Lawrence Forney.

MORGAN THOMAS FORNEY

Son of Charles and Celia Bradley Forney

Mr. Forney lives in California.

PAUL MOSSMAN FORNEY

Son of Charles and Celia Bradley Forney

Mr. Forney lives in California.

KENNETH GILLESPIE FORNEY

Son of Roscoe Calvert and Julia Gillespie Forney
b. 18 Jan. 1907 m. Agnes Slater d. 1937
CHILDREN
Mary Ann

Cadet Kenneth G. Forney

Kenneth G. Forney was born in Beaver, Pa. He was admitted to the United States Military Academy as a Cadet 2 July 1928, and was discharged 7 Jan. 1929.

FRANCIS FORNEY

Daughter of Roscoe Calvert and Julia Gillespie Forney
b. 13 Aug. 1910 m. R. Kenneth Baerwald
CHILDREN
Velma, Kenneth Jr., and Ross

Francis was born in Hayesville, Pa., and now lives in Anniston, Alabama.

ROSCOE CALVERT FORNEY, JR.

Son of Roscoe Calvert and Julia Gillespie Forney
b. 27 Jan. 1913 m. Betty Evans
CHILDREN
Robert Evans

Roscoe C. Forney was born in Rochester, Pa., and now lives in Aliquippa. He is interested in scouting and served in World War #2, Serial No. 13057967. Mr. Forney is a member of the Masonic Lodge of Pennsylvania.

ALBERT JEFFERSON FORNEY

Son of Roscoe Calvert and Julia Gillespie Forney
b. 8 July 1915 m. Charlotte Plunkett
CHILDREN
Martha Grace, Richard, and Shane

Albert J. Forney was born in Aliquippa, Pa., and now lives in Coraopolis Heights, Pa.

WILFRED GUY FORNEY

Son of Roscoe Calvert and Julia Gillespie Forney
b. 13 Jan. m. Anna Jean Bowen
CHILDREN
Julianna, Thomas, and Joanne

Wilfred G. Forney was born in Aliquippa, Pa., and still resides there.

CHARLES WM. FORNEY

Son of Roscoe Calvert and Julia Gillespie Forney
b. 30 June m. Tamanie Sallie
CHILDREN
Cheryl Ann

Charles W. Forney was born in Aliquippa, Pa., and now lives in Santa Barbara, California.

ELIZABETH FORNEY

Daughter of Roscoe Calvert and Julia Gillespie Forney
b. 28 June m. Richard Boyd

Elizabeth Forney was born in Aliquippa, Pa., and now lives in California.

RUSSEL H. FORNEY

Son of Joseph H. and Marie Johnson Forney
b. 23 June 1912 m. Helen Woods
CHILDREN
Karen Woods, Russel Henry, and Lisa

Russel H. Forney was born in New Castle, Pennsylvania. Mr. Forney is secretary-treasurer of Forney's Inc., New Castle, Pa. Helen Woods is a native of New Castle.

ELNOR JUNE FORNEY

Daughter of Frank S. and Nell Wilkinson Forney
b. 15 May 1922 m. Howard T. Eaton, Jr.
CHILDREN
Rebecca, Holly, and Melissa

Elnor J. Forney was born in Trumbull County, Ohio. She and her husband live in Pittsburgh, Pennsylvania.

FRANK GORDON FORNEY

Son of Frank S. and Nell Wilkinson Forney
b. 7 May 1927 m. Mary Reeves
CHILDREN
Frank Gordon Jr., Patrica, and Cynthia

Frank G. Forney was born in Trumbull County, Ohio. He is associated with his father in the Ohio Cement Products Company, Niles, Ohio.

JANICE FORNEY

Daughter of William H. and Bernadine Albiez Forney
b. 13 Feb. 1937 m. Paul L. Miller Jr.

Janice Forney attended Grove City College and Frances Payne Bolton School of Nursing of Western Reserve University. She graduated from Flora Stone Mather College of Western Reserve University, where her sorority was Phi Kappa Zeta. Miss Forney and Paul L. Miller were married 19 Aug. 1960 in Girard, Ohio. They now live in Cleveland, Ohio. Mrs. Miller teaches English at Garfield Heights High School, Cleve., O.

WILLIAM HARRISON FORNEY, JR.

Son of William H. and Bernadine Albiez Forney
b. 23 Mar. 1940

William H. Forney was born in Mahoning County, Ohio. He is a senior student at DePauw University, Greencastle, Indiana where he is majoring in mathematics.

DOROTHY JEAN FORNEY

Daughter of Wilbur and Jennie Luella Morris Forney
b. 12 May 1929

Dorothy Jean Forney was born in Salem, Ohio; attended and graduated from East Palestine Public Schools; graduated from Youngstown University; and received her Master's Degree from Western Reserve University. She has been employed as a librarian at Youngstown University since 1954.

Dorothy Jean Forney

RICHARD ALBAN FORNEY

Son of Charles D. and Charlotte Crocker Forney
b. 29 Apr. 1901 m. Hilda - - - -

VIRGINIA LOIS FORNEY

Daughter of Charles D. and Charlotte Crocker Forney
b. 2 Apr. 1904   m. Wm. G. Chalkley

ELIZABETH HARRIET FORNEY

Daughter of Charles D. and Charlotte Crocker Forney
b. 31 Dec. 1906   m. - - - - Hallett

HARRY ALBAN FORNEY

Son of Walter A. and Christiana L. Schaeffer Forney
b. 29 Feb. 1896   m. Bernice Bowman
CHILDREN
Glen Frederick, Robert (who died in infancy), and Doris Eileen

Harry A. Forney was born in Beloit, Ohio. He moved to Orrville, Ohio in 1911 and in 1920 went to Oakland, Calif., where he now resides. Mr. Forney is employed by the Southern Pacific Railroad.

FREDERICK CATELL FORNEY

Son of Walter A. and Christiana L. Schaeffer Forney
b. 23 Mar. 1900   m. Hazel V. Wakefield
CHILDREN
Raymond Frederick, Infant, and Helen Virginia

Frederick C. Forney was born in Beloit, Ohio. He moved to Orrville, Ohio in 1911 where he now resides, and is a city mail carrier. He served in World War #1 with H. Co. 146th Reg. 37th Division and E. Co. 50th Reg. Provisional Brigade, from June 1917 to May 1920, Serial No. 1521-939. Mr. Forney has been active in the Masonic Lodge; he is a York Rite Mason, Wooster Commandery No. 48 K.T.

WALTER ALBAN FORNEY, JR.

Son of Walter A. and Christiana L. Schaeffer Forney
b. 8 May 1902   m. Juanita Shields
CHILDREN
Phyllis Eileen, Infant, Robert Kaye

Walter A. Forney was born in Ohio Pile, Pennsylvania. He is a district inspector for the Dayton Power and Light Co. and lives in Greenville, O.

ISAAC WILLIAM FORNEY

Son of Walter A. and Christiana L. Schaeffer Forney
b. 27 Sept. 1904 m. Martha Long
CHILDREN
Richard Larry, and Gary Kent

Isaac W. Forney was born in Confluence, Pennsylvania. Mr. Forney is a baker for the Ohio State Reformatory and lives in Mansfield, Ohio.

ROBERT HAYES FORNEY

Son of Essie Forney
b. 17 May 1909 m. Rhea Dietrich
CHILDREN
Alice Jeanette, Donna Mae, and Walter Lee

Robert H. Forney was born in Wheeling Township, Guernsey County, O. Mr. Forney has worked for the Nickle Plate Railroad for many years. Mr. and Mrs. Forney live in Beach City, Ohio.

RICHARD ALDRICH FORNEY, M.D.

Son of Samuel Wilcox and Vera Aldrich Forney
b. 8 Apr. 1914 m. Margaret Magel
CHILDREN
Janet, Richard, Susan, and Frank

Richard A. Forney was born in Boise, Idaho where he is now a doctor. He and Margaret Magel were married 28 Aug. 1941. Margaret was born 12 July 1918.

WILLIAM DWIGHT FORNEY, M.D.

Son of Samuel Wilcox and Vera Aldrich Forney
b. 12 July 1918 m. Mae Shelton
CHILDREN
Drew, and Liza (adopted)

William D. Forney was born in Boise, Idaho where he is now a doctor. He and Mae Shelton were married 24 Dec. 1942. Mae Shelton was born 14 Oct. 1917.

LEIGH (LEE) CLIFTON FORNEY

Son of Clifton Elroy and Pearl Irene Murnan Forney
b. 4 Apr. 1907 m. Nellie Heines
CHILDREN
Carol Lee, Donna Faye, and Kay Cile

Leigh C. Forney resides in Chatsworth, Ill., where he operates a garage. Leigh C. Forney and Nellie Heines, of Brimfield, Ill., were married 19 Feb. 1930. Nellie Heines was born 30 Nov. 1909.

MILLARD CHESTER FORNEY

Son of Clifton Elroy and Pearl Irene Murnan Forney
b. 14 June 1910 m. Alice Blank
CHILDREN
Mary Alice, Margaret Ann, Thomas Millard, and Gerald Arthur

Millard C. Forney is a blacksmith in Princeville, Ill. Millard and Alice Blank were married 23 Nov. 1939. Alice Blank was born 30 May 1916.

MAYNARD AMIEL FORNEY

Son of Clifton Elroy and Pearl Irene Murnan Forney
b. 7 Mar. 1918 m. Gail McKown
CHILDREN
James Lee, Kenneth Eugene, Clifton Maynard, and Jack Lynn

Mr. and Mrs. Forney have a restaurant and ice cream parlor in Elmwood, Ill. Gail McKown was born 25 Mar. 1920.

MARIE PEARL FORNEY

Daughter of Clifton Elroy and Pearl Irene Murnan Forney
b. 9 Oct. m. Robert H. Norton
CHILDREN
Rose Marie

VERNA FORNEY

Daughter of Clifton Elroy and Pearl Irene Murnan Forney
b. 17 July 1921 m. Merlin James Gutshall
CHILDREN
Michael Glenn, James Merlin, and Christine Ann

Verna Forney was married 29 Feb. 1940. Merlin J. Gutshall was born 16 Aug. 1920.

IRA DALE FORNEY

Son of Chalmers and Neva Irene Catton Forney
b. 29 June 1912 d. 27 Sept. 1919

Ira D. Forney died of infant diabetis.

MIRIAM IRENE FORNEY

Daughter of Chalmers and Neva Irene Catton Forney
b. 22 Aug. 1916 d. 22 Jan. 1925

Miriam I. Forney died of blood poison from a cat scratch when she was eight years old.

LEE JUNIOR FORNEY

Son of Gilbert Allewelt and Mary Overstreet Forney
b. 22 Apr. 1923 d. Sept. 1944

JACKIE FORNEY

Daughter of Gilbert Allewelt and Mary Overstreet Forney
b. July 1921 m. Henry Noll
CHILDREN
Jack Lee, James C., and Judy

FRANKLIN FORNEY

Son of George Franklin and Ruth Green Forney
b. 19 Dec. 1933 m. Judy Patton
CHILDREN
Le Anne

Franklin Forney and Judy Patton were married in 1957.

THOMAS FORNEY

Son of George Franklin and Ruth Green Forney
b. 6 Feb. 1940

GERALD LORIN FORNEY

Son of John Earl and Maude Mulvaney Forney
b. 26 Dec. 1913 m. Ruth Manypenny
CHILDREN

Gerald Lorin Jr., Cheryl Ruth, David Bruce, and Bruce Wayne

Gerald L. Forney married Ruth Manypenny in East Liverpool, Ohio, 8 Sept. 1943, where they resided and raised their four children. They now live in Pittsburgh, Pennsylvania.

ROBERT ELMORE FORNEY

Son of John Earl and Maude Mulvaney Forney
b. 13 July 1919 m. Helen Rakai
CHILDREN
Robert Philip, Dennis, and Cecile

Mr. and Mrs. Forney live in Wakefield, Michigan, where their three children were born.

DONALD ROWLAND FORNEY

Son of John Earl and Maude Mulvaney Forney
b. 24 Jan. 1923 m. Rita Neises
CHILDREN
Carolyn Ann, Donald Rowland, Jr., John Joseph, and David Patrick

Mr. and Mrs. Forney live in Temple, Texas, where their four children were born. Rita Neises was born 18 May 1924.

MABEL ELIZABETH FORNEY

Daughter of John Earl and Evelyn McGuire Forney
b. 4 Sept. 1942 m. Ronald Spear
CHILDREN
Renee Elizabeth

Mabel E. Forney and Ronald Spear were married 4 Sept. 1960.

MARJORIE ELAINE FORNEY

Daughter of Emory Owen and Ethel Myra Ehringer Forney
b. 13 Nov. 1923 m. Vernon Dale Pelz
CHILDREN
Vernon Dale, David Randall, Leigh Annette, and Lori Susan

Marjorie E. Forney and Vernon D. Pelz were married in Washburn, Ill., 5 Mar. 1950. They reside on a farm in Clayton Township, Illinois, where their four children were born. Vernon Dale Pelz was born 2 Feb. 1918.

LOWELL EUGENE FORNEY

Son of Emory Owen and Ethel Myra Ehringer Forney
b. 6 Jan. 1926   m. Lisa Ritschel
CHILDREN
Claudia Jean, Evan Dale (stillborn), Sandra Lee, Lyle Eugene,
and Kyle David

Lowell E. Forney and Lisa Ritschel were married in Los Angeles, Calif., 10 Aug. 1946. She was born in Brunswick, Germany, 21 Dec. 1925, a daughter of Henry Ritschel, coming to Los Angeles with her parents when two years old. They reside in Clayton Township, Illinois.

MELVIN LEE FORNEY

Son of Emory Owen and Ethel Myra Ehringer Forney
b. 18 Jan. 1931   m. Doris Elbert
CHILDREN
Steven Lee, infant daughter, stillborn; Therese Rose, Kevin Joseph,
and Annette Marie

Melvin L. Forney and Doris Elbert were married in Metamora, Ill., 30 Apr. 1953. Mr. Forney is a welder at the Caterpillar Tractor Co., Peoria, Ill. They reside in Metamora, Ill., where their children were born. Doris Elbert was born 10 Mar. 1932.

ELDON DELONG FORNEY

Son of Emory Owen and Ethel Myra Ehringer Forney
b. 23 Nov. 1934   m. Joyce Koch
CHILDREN
Pamela Sue, and Paul Owen

Eldon D. Forney and Joyce Koch were married 16 Jan. 1954. Mr. Forney is a mechanic at the Olds-Cadillac Garage in Pontiac, Illinois. Joyce Koch was born 16 Jan. 1934.

ELLEN ELIZABETH FORNEY

Daughter of Roy Cranston and Harriet Robbins Forney
b. 2 Oct. 1923   m. Charles Sager Finley
CHILDREN
Carolyn Ruth, Stephen Roy, Jeannette Marlene, Diane Elizabeth,
and David Reece

Ellen E. Forney and Charles S. Finley were married 16 June 1946. They lived on his parents' farm near Hoopeston, Ill., where two of their five children were born:- Carolyn Ruth and Stephen Roy. They moved to Tuscon, Arizona and then to Pheonix, Ariz., for his health, where he taught agriculture in a high school. Their other three children were born in Arizona.

JOHN RICHARD FORNEY

Son of Roy Cranston and Harriet Robbins Forney
b. 13 Aug. 1925 m. Bernice Edna Gibbs
CHILDREN
Nancy Jean, Larry Richard, and Carol Bernice

John R. Forney and Bernice E. Gibbs were married in Henry, Ill., 22 Feb. 1948. Mr. and Mrs. Forney farmed in Marshall, County; in 1961 they purchased a farm west of McNabb, Illinois, and moved there.

RUTH AILEEN FORNEY

Daughter of Roy Cranston and Harriet Robbins Forney
b. 11 Dec. 1927 m. John Wallace Rodgers
CHILDREN
John Wallace, Ann Marie, Elizabeth Jeanne, and James Cranston

Ruth A. Forney and John W. Rodgers were married in her parents' home in Bureau County, near Whitefield, Ill., 5 Dec. 1948. They resided in Pekin, Ill., where their four children were born; later they moved to Loveland, Colorado. John W. Rodgers was born 20 July 1925.

ROBERT CRANSTON FORNEY

Son of Roy Cranston and Harriet Robbins Forney
b. 10 Apr. 1932 m. Dorothy Ann Drozd
CHILDREN
Lynette Joy

Robert C. Forney and Dorothy A. Drozd were married in Chicago, Ill., 27 Dec. 1953. Robert graduated from the University of Illinois School of Dentistry, in Chicago, Ill., in July 1961. He went to Dallas, Texas that year to start his practice. Dorothy Ann Drozd was born 26 July 1934.

HARRIET JEANNE FORNEY

Daughter of Roy Cranston and Harriet Robbins Forney

b. 22 Apr. 1935 m. John Paul Mudry
CHILDREN
Carolyn Jeanne

Harriet J. Forney married John P. Mudry, a young navy doctor serving at Great Lakes, Ill., 8 Aug. 1959. After his enlistment period expired in 1961, they went to Washington D. C. to serve in a hospital.

ROGER FRANKLIN FORNEY

Son of Roy Cranston and Harriet Robbins Forney
b. 7 Dec. 1939 m. Donna Grasser
CHILDREN
Deborah Susan, Wendy Lee, and Todd Alan

Roger F. Forney and Donna Grasser were married in McNabb, Ill., 30 May 1956. They started farming on Grasser land, west of McNabb, where their three children were born.

MARLANE DUANE FORNEY

Daughter of Harry Theodore and Lena May Scheer Forney
b. 28 Mar. 1933

ROBERT LESTER FORNEY

Son of Robert Henry and Geneva V. Critton Forney
b. 16 June 1923 m. LaVern McClintook
CHILDREN
Douglas Robert, and Deanna Ray

KEITH GEORGE FORNEY

Son of Robert Henry and Geneva V. Critton Forney
b. 26 June 1929 m. Ada Lorene Jones
CHILDREN
Kathy Genel, Loren Keith, and Della Jean

Keith G. Forney and Ada L. Jones were married 5 June 1954. They reside in Walla Walla, Washington.

VIRGINIA MAY FORNEY

Daughter of Floyd Whitney and Helena B. Modisette Forney
b. 6 May 1921 m. Kurt Beldt m. Herbert C. Bailey

CHILDREN
With Kurt Beldt: Roger Kurt
With H. C. Bailey: Elizabeth Virginia, and Robert Herbert

DORIS HELEN FORNEY

Daughter of Floyd Whitney and Helena B. Modisette Forney
b. 28 Dec. 1922 m. Ford W. Thomson, Richard Monteverce, and
Walter Wm. Henshe
CHILDREN
Ford Wesley, and Craig Westley, sons of F. W. Thomson

MARGUERITE LOUISE FORNEY

Daughter of Floyd Whitney and Helena B. Modisette Forney
b. 25 Mar. 1924 m. Joe M. Palkovich
CHILDREN
Jo Linda, and Joe Martin

AGNES FLORENE FORNEY

Daughter of Floyd Whitney and Helena B. Modisette Forney
b. 4 Jan. 1926 m. Alfred N. Sproules
CHILDREN
Alan Carl, and Diane Kristine

BEVERLY JOYCE FORNEY

Daughter of Floyd Whitney and Helena B. Modisette Forney
b. 2 Sept. 1927 m. Adolphus D. Dye
CHILDREN
Michael O'Dean, Stanley Howard, Joyce Christine, and Mary Jane

RICHARD FLOYD FORNEY

Son of Floyd Whitney and Helena B. Modisette Forney
b. 19 Mar. 1935 m. Peggy Jean McLeod
CHILDREN
Richard Wayne, and Darla Sue

ROBERT WAYNE FORNEY

Son of Wayne Irving and Goldie May Vorce Forney
b. 6 Feb. 1926 m. Nelda Kahl
CHILDREN

Lanella Kay

Robert W. Forney and Nelda Kahl were married 24 Nov. 1951. She was born 28 June 1930. They farmed a few years in the western part of Nebraska where their daughter was born. Later, they sold out and moved to Miami, Florida, where he attended Miami University, graduating in business administration. They still reside in Miami.

MARY LOUISE FORNEY

Daughter of Wayne Irving and Goldie May Vorce Forney
b. 8 May 1929 m. Donald Peterson

Mary Louise Forney and Donald Peterson were married in Brule, Nebraska 28 Dec. 1958. They reside in Columbus, Nebr., where he is a chemical engineer for Dale Electronics. Donald Peterson was born 29 Nov. 1929.

MARGUERITE LUCILLE FORNEY

Daughter of Wayne Irving and Goldie May Vorce Forney
b. 8 Sept. 1935 m. Hilmar Fred Krueger
CHILDREN
Shiela Marie, and Cheryl Ann

Marguerite L. Forney and Hilmar F. Krueger were married in Brule, Nebraska, 14 June 1959. They reside in Gilead, Nebraska. Hilmar F. Krueger was born 19 Sept. 1928.

RAYMOND FORNEY

Son of Rollin Albion and Katherine Broeder Forney
b. 30 July 1924 m. Shirley Ann Hewitt
CHILDREN
Raeshelle Jean

Raymond Forney and Shirley Ann Hewitt were married in Fairbury, Nebr., 5 June 1960. Shirley A. Hewitt was born 24 April 1936.

MARY LUCILLE FORNEY

Daughter of Rollin Albion and Katherine Broeder Forney
b. 16 Dec. 1926 m. Leland Root

Mary Lucille Forney and Leland Root were married 22 June 1947. They reside in California.

BETTY JEAN FORNEY

Daughter of Rollin Albion and Katherine Broeder Forney
b. 5 Mar. 1931   m. Marvin J. Gutzmer
CHILDREN
Katherine Louise, and Jayne Lynette

Betty Jean Forney and Marvin J. Gutzmer were married 1 Aug. 1949. They reside in Wichita, Kansas.

CAROL FORNEY

Daughter of Rollin Albion and Katherine Broeder Forney
b. 31 Dec. 1932   m. Joel Jordening   d. 17 July 1953

Carol Forney and Joel Jordening were married 15 Feb. 1953; she died five months later.

LARRY WAYNE FORNEY

Son of Lester Wayne and Della Shultz Forney
b. 30 June 1928   m. Nan Daniels
CHILDREN
David, Luanne, and Daniel Wayne

Mr. and Mrs. Forney reside in Liberty, Texas. Nan Daniels was born 29 Aug. 1932.

LEWIS ELMER FORNEY

Son of Lester Wayne and Della Shultz Forney
b. 8 Dec. 1929

Lewis E. Forney lives in California, where he teaches music.

9th Generation

FLORENCE A. FORNEY

Daughter of John Henry and Inez Shaw Forney
b. 2 Apr. 1910 m. Glen M. Robison
CHILDREN
Gerald Glen, Donald Keith, James Lee, and John William,
who died when 2 months old

Marriage Records Portage County Court House, Ravenna, Ohio. Florence A. Forney to Glenn M. Robison 9 Nov. 1931. Birthplace of Florence A. Forney, Warren, O. Mr. and Mrs. Robison live in Newton Falls, Ohio.

EVA MAE FORNEY

Daughter of John Henry and Mildred Amelia Prime Forney
b. 8 Apr. 1916

Eva Mae only lived five weeks and is buried in Hiram, Ohio.

MAREE FORNEY

Daughter of John Henry and Mildred Amelia Prime Forney
b. 31 Mar. 1917 m. Max G. Hurd
CHILDREN
David Allen, and John Keith

VIRGINIA MAE FORNEY

Daughter of John Henry and Mildred Amelia Prime Forney
b. 26 May 1922 m. George Reese m. Charles Ross Winter
CHILDREN
Michael Allen

Mr. and Mrs. Winter live in Akron, Ohio.

LOUIS FORNEY, JR.

Son of Louis and Etta Mae Andrews Forney
b. 21 Sept. 1924 m. Virgiana Layman
CHILDREN
Rosanne, Stephen, Dana Jo., Kay Ellen, and Kimberly

Louis Forney Jr. had a twin who died at birth. Mr. and Mrs. Forney live in Cridersville, Ohio.

MADGE MARIE FORNEY

Daughter of Louis and Etta Mae Andrews Forney
b. 12 June 1916 m. Donald A. Binkley
CHILDREN
Donald John

Mr. and Mrs. Binkley live on Breese Road, Lima, Ohio.

DONALD FORNEY

Son of Louis and Etta Mae Andrews Forney
b. 4 Oct. 1908 m. Opal Best m. Estelline - - - -
CHILDREN
Ronald, and Cardinal

DONALD FLOYD FORNEY

Son of Monroe M. and Elta Miller Forney
b. 11 Oct. 1919 m. Isabelle Haefke
CHILDREN
Donna Lee

Donald F. Forney was born in Mahoning County, Ohio. Mr. Forney served in World War #2 Serial No. 35526340, 37th. Division 129th. Inf., Co. E. Mr. and Mrs. Forney reside in Canfield, Ohio.

ROBERT L. FORNEY

Son of Elwood R. and Ruby Blosser Forney
b. 9 Jan. 1927 m. Margaret Marie Wellendorf
CHILDREN
Linda Lee, Mary Anne, and Glenn E.

Robert L. Forney and Wife

Robert L. Forney was born in Mahoning County, Ohio. Mr. Forney served in World War #2 Serial No. 35999564. Mr. and Mrs. Forney reside in Columbiana, Ohio.

VIRGIANA LOUISE FORNEY

Daughter of Elwood R. and Ruby Blosser Forney
b. 29 Feb. 1928 m. Carl Farmer
CHILDREN
Richard Leroy, Dale Alen, Kathy Louise, and Larry Carl

Virgiana L. Forney was born in Columbiana County, Ohio. Mr. Farmer also is a native of that county; he is a World War #2 Veteran. Mr. and Mrs. Farmer live in Hanoverton, Ohio.

Virgiana Louise Forney

RICHARD LEE FORNEY

Son of Elwood R. and Ruby Blosser Forney
b.   d.

Richard L. Forney is buried in the Mennonite Church Cemetery, Columbiana, Ohio.

FREDRIC DANIEL FORNEY

Son of Elwood R. and Ruby Blosser Forney
b. 5 Oct. 1935 m. Rachel Alice Esterly

CHILDREN
Fredric Daniel Jr., and Susan Lynne

Fred D. Forney was born in Columbiana, Ohio where he attended school and was graduated from high school in 1953, serving as, among other offices, senior class president and captain of the varsity football team. He won varsity letters in football and track.

Fred was enrolled at Kent State University, Kent, Ohio, in 1953 and was graduated with honors from this University in 1957, obtaining a Bachelor of Science degree in Business Administration. While at Kent State, he was a member of the Reserve Officers' Training Corps and upon graduation was designated a Distinguished Military Graduate by the University president, and was commissioned a Second Lieutenant in the United States Army Reserve. As part of his military activities at Kent State, he was a local member and officer of the National Society of Scabbard and Blade, a scolastic military society. Fred joined the Kent State Chapter of Theta Chi National Fraternity.

On June 20, 1957 Fred was married to the former Rachel Alice Esterly, daughter of A. Russell and Eleanor Esterly of Columbiana, Ohio.

Mr. Forney entered active duty with the Army of the United States in 1958; was promoted to First Lieutenant and completed his active duty in 1960. At present, he is employed in a civilian capacity by the Department of Defense near Washington D. C., and resides with his wife and two children in Hyattsville, Maryland.

Fredric D. Forney and Wife

JOANN E. FORNEY

Daughter of Howard G. and LaVerne Huxley Forney
b. 9 June 1932 m. William E. Cook

Joann E. Forney was born in Beaver Township, Mahoning County, Ohio. Certificate of birth State of Ohio, Registration District No. 5204. Joann is a twin sister of Joyce D. Forney Haydu.

Joann Forney Cook and Husband

She is a member of the Daughters of the American Revolution, National No. 461864. (Henry Forney 1747-1831). She also is a direct descendent of Dan Huxley, 15 May 1748 - 22 July 1822 farmer and Revolutionary Soldier Ref. (The Huxley Family by Jared Huxley), Youngstown, Ohio 18 January 1900.

Joann E. Forney and William E. Cook were married 7 June 1958. They now reside in Youngstown, Ohio.

JOYCE D. FORNEY

Daughter of Howard G. and LaVerne Huxley Forney
b. 9 June 1932 m. John J, Haydu, Jr.
CHILDREN
Karen Jean, and Nancy Ann

Joyce D. Forney was born in Beaver Township, Mahoning County, Ohio. Certificate of birth State of Ohio, Registration District No. 5204. Joyce is a twin sister of Joann E. Forney Cook.

Joyce Forney Haydu and Husband

She is a member of the Daughters of the American Revolution, National No. 461865. (Henry Forney 1747-1831). She also is a direct descendent of Dan Huxley, 15 May 1748 - 22 July 1822 farmer and Revolutionary Soldier Ref. (The Huxley Family by Jared Huxley), Youngstown, Ohio 18 January 1900.

Joyce D. Forney and John J. Haydu, Jr. were married 7 May 1955. They now reside in Youngstown, Ohio.

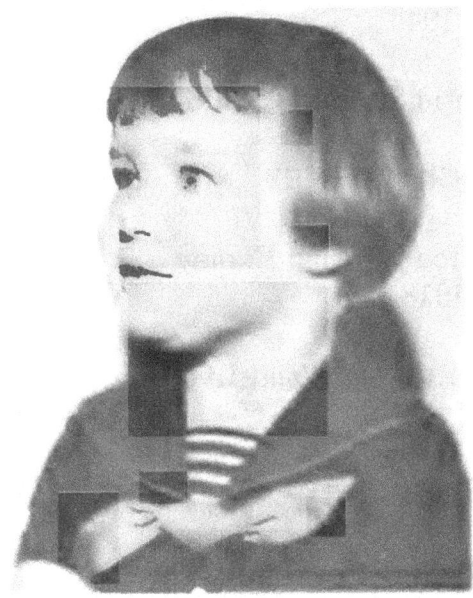
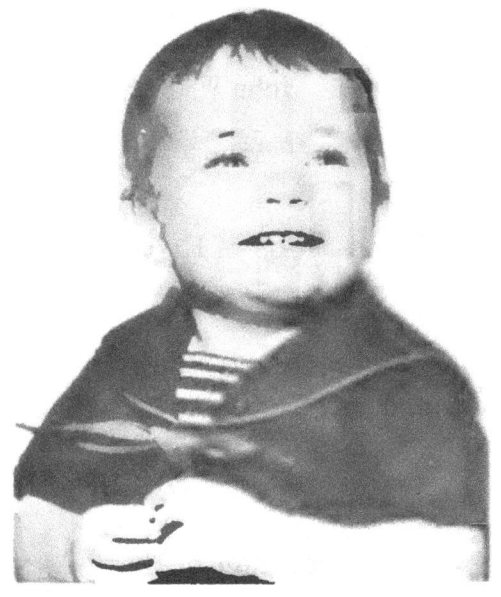

Karen Jean Haydu   **Nancy Ann Haydu**

EVELYN FORNEY

Daughter of Howard and Helen M. Hofmeister Forney
b. 23 Nov. 1926 m. Delmer Will m. Norman Firestone

Evelyn Forney was born in Salem, Ohio.

MARJORIE FORNEY

Daughter of Howard and Helen M. Hofmeister Forney
b. 7 Mar. 1928 m. Otto Crider
CHILDREN
Judy Ann, Richard, Suzanne, and Johnny Ray

Marjorie Forney was born in Salem, Ohio.

MARILYN JEAN FORNEY

Daughter of Howard and Helen M. Hofmeister Forney
b. 6 May 1936 m. Robert Spandauer
CHILDREN
Susan Lee, Robert Lee, and Terri Lee

Marilyn Jean Forney was born in Salem, Ohio.

JOHN WILLIAM FORNEY

Son of Henry Z. Jr. and Willie Holbrook Forney
b. 28 Jan. 1944

John W. Forney was born in Struthers, Ohio.

GLENN FREDERICK FORNEY

Son of Harry A. and Bernice Bowman Forney
b. 21 May 1918

Glenn F. Forney was born in Marshalville, Ohio and lives in Baltimore, Maryland.

DORIS EILEEN FORNEY

Daughter of Harry A. and Bernice Bowman Forney
b. 10 Apr. 1920

Doris E. Forney was born in Wooster, Ohio.

RAYMOND FREDERICK FORNEY

Son of Frederick C. and Hazel V. Wakefield Forney
b. 23 June 1927

Raymond F. Forney was born in Wooster, Ohio.

HELEN VIRGINIA FORNEY

Daughter of Frederick C. and Hazel V. Wakefield Forney
b. 8 Sept. 1933

PHYLLIS EILEEN FORNEY

Daughter of Walter A., Jr. and Juanita Shields Forney
b. 26 July 1926

Phyllis E. Forney was born in Orrville, Ohio.

ROBERT KAYE FORNEY

Son of Walter A., Jr. and Juanita Shields Forney
b. 18 Aug. 1930

Robert K. Forney was born in Greenville, Ohio.

RICHARD LARRY FORNEY

Son of Isaac W. and Martha Long Forney
b. 19 May 1928

Richard L. Forney was born in Orrville, Ohio.

GARY KENT FORNEY

Son of Isaac W. and Martha Long Forney
b. 27 Feb. 1935

Gary K. Forney was born in Orrville, Ohio.

JANET FORNEY

Daughter of Richard Aldrich and Margaret Magel Forney

b. 20 July 1943

RICHARD WILCOX FORNEY

Son of Richard Aldrich and Margaret Magel Forney
b. 18 Jan. 1946

SUSAN FORNEY

Daughter of Richard Aldrich and Margaret Magel Forney
b. 18 Feb. 1947

FRANK FORNEY

Son of Richard Aldrich and Margaret Magel Forney
b. 9 Nov. 1948

DREW FORNEY

Son of William Dwight and Mae Shelton Forney
b. 13 Jan. 1950

LIZA FORNEY

Adopted Daughter of William Dwight and Mae Shelton Forney
b. 16 Sept. 1954

CAROL LEE FORNEY

Daughter of Leigh Clifton and Nellie Heines Forney
b. 28 Sept. 1934 m. Richard John Rosenbloom

Richard J. Rosenbloom was born 15 Apr. 1935.

DONNA FAY FORNEY

Daughter of Leigh Clifton and Nellie Heines Forney
b. 21 Oct. 1936 m. Donald Leroy Snow

Donna F. Forney and Donald L. Snow were married 6 May 1956. Donald L. Snow was born 17 Aug. 1934.

KAY CILE FORNEY

Daughter of Leigh Clifton and Nellie Heines Forney

b. 5 Feb. 1944

MARY ALICE FORNEY

Daughter of Millard Chester and Alice Blank Forney
b. 4 Oct. 1940   m. Lewis M. Haney

MARGARET ANN FORNEY

Daughter of Millard Chester and Alice Blank Forney
b. 25 Nov. 1943

THOMAS MILLARD FORNEY

Son of Millard Chester and Alice Blank Forney
b. 10 Nov. 1945

GERALD ARTHUR FORNEY

Son of Millard Chester and Alice Blank Forney
b. 22 Sept. 1949

JAMES LEE FORNEY

Son of Maynard Amiel and Gail McKown Forney
b. 17 July 1937   m. Evelyn Broadfield

James L. Forney and Evelyn Broadfield were married 22 Oct. 1959. Evelyn Broadfield was born 17 July 1940.

KENNETH EUGENE FORNEY

Son of Maynard Amiel and Gail McKown Forney
b. 26 Nov. 1942   m. Mary Ann Broadfield

CLIFTON MAYNARD FORNEY

Son of Maynard Amiel and Gail McKown Forney
b. 16 Aug. 1945

JACK LYNN FORNEY

Son of Maynard Amiel and Gail McKown Forney
b. 3 Sept. 1951

GERALD LORIN FORNEY, JR.

Son of Gerald Lorin and Ruth Manypenny Forney
b. 27 July 1944

CHERYL RUTH FORNEY

Daughter of Gerald Lorin and Ruth Manypenny Forney
b. 30 Aug. 1947

DAVID BRUCE FORNEY

Son of Gerald Lorin and Ruth Manypenny Forney
b. 19 May 1952

BRUCE WAYNE FORNEY

Son of Gerald Lorin and Ruth Manypenny Forney
b. 15 Dec. 1954

ROBERT PHILIP FORNEY

Son of Robert Elmore and Helen Rakai Forney
b. 11 July 1942

DENNIS FORNEY

Son of Robert Elmore and Helen Rakai Forney
b. 10 Aug. 1947

CECILE FORNEY

Daughter of Robert Elmore and Helen Rakai Forney
b. 19 Dec. 1952

CAROLYN ANN FORNEY

Daughter of Donald Rowland and Rita Neises Forney
b. 12 Dec. 1944

DONALD ROWLAND FORNEY, JR.

Son of Donald Rowland and Rita Neises Forney
b. 4 Dec. 1950

JOHN JOSEPH FORNEY

Son of Donald Rowland and Rita Neises Forney
b. 12 Oct. 1954

DAVID PATRICK FORNEY

Son of Donald Rowland and Rita Neises Forney
b. 7 Sept. 1956

CLAUDIA JEAN FORNEY

Daughter of Lowell Eugene and Lisa Ritschel Forney
b. 29 June 1947

EVAN DALE FORNEY

Son of Lowell Eugene and Lisa Ritschel Forney
b. 17 Oct. 1949 (stillborn)

SANDREA LEE FORNEY

Daughter of Lowell Eugene and Lisa Ritschel Forney
b. 31 Sept. 1951

LYLE EUGENE FORNEY

Son of Lowell Eugene and Lisa Ritschel Forney
b. 13 Dec. 1954

STEVEN LEE FORNEY

Son of Melvin Lee and Doris Elbert Forney
b. 18 Nov. 1955

THERESE ROSE FORNEY

Daughter of Melvin Lee and Doris Elbert Forney
b. 13 Nov. 1958

KEVIN JOSEPH FORNEY

Son of Melvin Lee and Doris Elbert Forney
b. 23 Mar. 1961

PAMELA SUE FORNEY

Daughter of Eldon Delong and Joyce Koch Forney
b. 8 Jan. 1955

PAUL OWEN FORNEY

Son of Eldon Delong and Joyce Koch Forney
b. 20 Jan. 1959

NANCY JEAN FORNEY

Daughter of John Richard and Bernice Edna Gibbs Forney
b. 3 Jan. 1951

LARRY RICHARD FORNEY

Son of John Richard and Bernice Edna Gibbs Forney
b. 29 June 1952

CAROL BERNICE FORNEY

Daughter of John Richard and Bernice Edna Gibbs Forney
b. 14 Apr. 1959

LYNETTE JOY FORNEY

Daughter of Robert Cranston and Dorothy Ann Drozd Forney
b. 3 Sept. 1956

DEBORAH SUSAN FORNEY

Daughter of Roger Franklin and Donna Grasser Forney
b. 17 Aug. 1957

WENDY LEE FORNEY

Daughter of Roger Franklin and Donna Grasser Forney
b. 30 June 1959

TODD ALAN FORNEY

Son of Roger Franklin and Donna Grasser Forney
b. 3 Aug. 1961

DOUGLAS ROBERT FORNEY

Son of Robert Lester and LaVern McClintook Forney
b. 26 Feb. 1944

DEANNA RAY FORNEY

Daughter of Robert Lester and LaVern McClintook Forney
b. 4 Mar. 1947

KATHY GENEL FORNEY

Daughter of Keith George and Ada Lorene Jones Forney
b. 16 July 1955

LOREN KEITH FORNEY

Son of Keith George and Ada Lorene Jones Forney
b. 25 Mar. 1957

DELLA JEAN FORNEY

Daughter of Keith George and Ada Lorene Jones Forney
b. 17 Aug. 1959

RICHARD WAYNE FORNEY

Son of Richard Floyd and Peggy Jean McLoed Forney
b. 17 Nov. 1957

DARLA SUE FORNEY

Daughter of Richard Floyd and Peggy Jean McLeod Forney
b. 1 Jan. 1960

LANELLA KAY FORNEY

Daughter of Robert Wayne and Nelda Kahl Forney
b. 6 Nov. 1952

RAESHELLE JEAN FORNEY

Daughter of Raymond and Shirley Ann Hewitt Forney
b. 15 Aug. 1961

DAVID FORNEY

Son of Larry Wayne and Nan Daniels Forney
b. 16 Aug. 1954

LUANNE FORNEY

Daughter of Larry Wayne and Nan Daniels Forney
b. 16 Sept. 1958

DANIEL WAYNE FORNEY

Son of Larry Wayne and Nan Daniels Forney
b. 27 June 1960

10th Generation

THE PRESENT

DONNA LEE FORNEY

Daughter of Donald F. and Isabelle Haefke Forney
b. 1 May 1948

LINDA LEE FORNEY

Daughter of Robert L. and Margaret M. Wellendorf Forney
b. 22 June 1950

MARY ANNE FORNEY

Daughter of Robert L. and Margaret M. Wellendorf Forney
b. 19 June 1952

GLENN E. FORNEY

Son of Robert L. and Margaret M. Wellendorf Forney
b. 6 Dec. 1956

FREDRIC DANIEL FORNEY, JR.

Son of Fredric D. and Rachel A. Esterly Forney
b. 20 Jan. 1961

SUSAN LYNNE FORNEY

Daughter of Fredric D. and Rachel A. Esterly Forney
b. 21 Jan. 1963

I WISH TO THANK

I wish to thank my wife, Mary Louise Forney, for skillful help in the preparation of this book.

The text of this edition has been prepared in the hope of bringing up to date as much of the Forney History as possible.

If this book achieves its purpose, the promotion of a feeling of unity and pride among members of the Forney Family, then perhaps there will be someone in future generations who will pick up where we stopped and follow it to completion.

H. G. F.

"A GOOD name is rather to be chosen than great riches, and loving favour rather than silver and gold."

– Proverb 22

INDEX

Adams, Walter D.	33
Addleman, Maria	156
Adrin, Elie	173
Albiez, Bernadine	150, 188, 189
Albiez, Julia	150
Albiez, Richard	150
Alden, John	5
Aldrich, Vera	160
Allewelt, Margaret Ann	96, 127, 128
Althouse, David William	143
Althouse, Mrs. Elmer	143
Althouse, Rev. Glenn	143
Anderson, Mattie	123, 158, 159
Andrew, John	60
Andrews, Etta Mae	175, 202, 203
Andrews, James	62
Ankney, Louisa	155
Asher, Amanda Forest	158
Avore, Mr.	154
Bachelder, John B.	30
Baerwald, Kenneth, Jr.	186
Baerwald, R. Kenneth	186
Baerwald, Ross	186
Baerwald, Velma	186
Bailey, David	183
Bailey, Eleanor Mae	183
Bailey, Elizabeth Virginia	198
Bailey, Herbert C.	197
Bailey, Robert Herbert	198
Ballard, Henry S.	156
Ballard, Henry S., Jr.	156
Bankmann, Anna	15
Bapben, Jacob	16
Bare, John	139
Barhoover, Mary Louise	181
Bartmess, Catharine	91
Bayer, Heinrich	63
Beard, Mr.	59
Beck, Susanna	65
Beebe, Walter B.	63
Beiter, Dan	124
Beldt, Kurt	197
Beldt, Roger Kurt	198
Bergner, Maria	1
Best, Opal	203
Binkley, Donald A.	203
Binkley, Donald John	203
Bishop, Jim	32
Bittinger, Lucy Forney	3
Bixler, Emanuel	147
Bixler, Harriet Forney	147
Bixler, Mrs. Hattie	106
Bixler, Homer	147
Bixler, Rev. Joseph	147
Bixler, Noah	146, 147
Blackburn, Moses	62
Blank, Adam	15
Blank, Alice	192, 211
Blank, Wolfgang	15
Blauser, Emma	155
Bloon, Lady	37
Blosser, Ruby	178, 203, 204
Blott, Benjamin	83, 84
Blott, Benjamin Franklin	136
Blott, Emery	83
Blott, Frank	83
Boardman, Mr.	158
Bockmeyer, Barbara Elisabetha	24
Bonner, Dora	172, 173
Borland, Mae M.	129
Bowen, Anna Jean	187
Bowman, Bernice	190, 208
Bowman, Elizabeth	66
Boxwell, Sarah	95, 125
Boyd, Richard	187
Braddick, Irene	176
Bradley, Celia	150, 185, 186
Brendli, Anna	14
Broadfield, Evelyn	211
Broadfield, Mary Ann	211
Broeder, Katherine	168, 199, 200
Buchsel, Peter	15
Buell, Judson	136
Buhl, Dorothea	20
Buhl, Engelhardt	20
Buhler, Hans	10
Buler, Anna	13, 15
Buler, Michel	12
Burbaker, Luthe	184
Burgdorfer	9
Burki, Peter	15
Burns, Eli	109
Burns, Emma	109
Burns, Ida	109
Burns, John	109
Burns, John J.	109
Bush, Mrs. Annie Forney	3
Byland, Barbara	15
Caldwell, Nancy	127, 161
Caldwell, Sarah Eliza	158
Calvin, Aaron	143
Calvin, Alice	143
Calvin, Amy	104
Calvin, Mrs. Angeline	106
Calvin, Clara	104
Calvin, Elizabeth Forney	103
Calvin, Gladys	144
Calvin, Hannah	104
Calvin, Jacob	104
Calvin, John W.	104
Calvin, Marquis	104
Calvin, Mrs. Mary A.	106
Calvin, Mary Ann Forney	145
Calvin, Minerva	104
Calvin, Mr.	103
Calvin, Pierce D.	104

Name	Pages
Calvin, Resilva Annetta	104
Calvin, Urban D.	144
Camp, Susan	161
Carli., Anna	13
Carlson, Senator Frank	120, 122
Carpenter, Nora	155
Catton, Neva Irene	161, 193
Cerl, Mr.	90
Chalkley, Wm. G.	190
Champlin, Jessie Gertrude	129, 165, 166
Clapper, John	59
Clark, Helen	175
Clark, Jessie	85
Clark, O. J.	174
Clipper, Edward	85
Conaugby, David M.	29
Conkle, J. Edward	105
Conkle, Margret Forney	104
Conkle, Michael	105
Conkle, Willie	105
Cook, Jane	108, 149
Cook, Rev. Robert	93
Cook, William E.	206
Cookson, Thomas	37
Cope, Colonel E. B.	30
Copeland, Eliza	85
Copeland, Eliza Jane	112, 113
Corney, Eliza	127
Cort, Andrew	101, 102, 103, 104, 105, 106
Cort, Barbra	80
Cort, Fredrick	80
Cort, Hannah	73
Cort, Lidda	73
Cort, Margaret (Peggy)	80
Cort, Peggy	101, 102, 103, 104, 105, 106
Coventry, James	154
Cover, Earl C.	115
Cover, E. Morgan	115
Cover, Mabel	115
Cover, Pearl	115
Coy, E. W.	146
Coy, I. W.	146
Cranmer, Dean	183
Crawford, Mary	125, 159
Crawford, Thomas	136
Crawford, Jr., Mrs. Webb	3
Crider, Johnny Ray	208
Crider, Judy Ann	208
Crider, Otto	208
Crider, Richard Suzanne	208
Critton, Geneva V.	197
Critton, Geneva Valentine	166
Crocker, Charlotte	152, 189, 190
Cross, John L.	152, 153
Crouse, Mrs. Vernon	80
Curtis, Mary	116
Curtis, Mary (Polly)	74, 90, 91, 92, 93
Dachseggerin, Maria	10
Damke, Betty Lee	168
Damke, Bonnie	168
Damke, Clyde	168
Daniels, Nan	200, 216
Dawson, Mr.	157
Day, Melvin	111
Decker, George	66, 67
Decker, Jacob Forney	67
Decker, Lydia	67
Decker, Salome	67
Deems, Carrie	129
Derickson, Jake	140
Dickson, Jennie	127
Diehl, Daniel	96
Diehl, Margret	172
Diehl, Mary Ann	96, 128, 129, 130
Dietrich, Rhea	191
Digges, John	37, 40, 46, 52
Diller, Nancy	101, 138, 139, 140, 141
Dilling, Ruth Ellen	176
Dixon, Jeremiah	38
Dixon, Joshua	62
Doty, Hulda	116, 154
Doty, Issac	116
Douglass, George	40
Drozd, Dorothy Ann	196, 214
Duesenbury, Clarence	124
Duesenbury, Lawrence	124
Duesenbury, William	124
Duffy, Anna	160, 161
Dull, David	121
Dull, Samantha	121, 157
Dummermuth, Peter	10
Dunkle, Luella	184
du Pont, Alfred Victor	65
du Pont, Eleuthere Irenee	65
du Pont, Pierre S., 3rd.	65
Dyck, Bonnie Gail	167
Dyck, Gloria Jean	167
Dyck, Paul	167
Dyck, Roberta Ethelyn	167
Dye, Adolphus D.	198
Dye, Joyce Christine	198
Dye, Mary Jane	198
Dye, Michael O'Dean	198
Dye, Stanley Howard	198
Early, James	71
Eaton, Holly	188
Eaton, Howard T., Jr.	188
Eaton, Melissa	188
Eaton, Rebecca	188
Eckert, Ed.	155
Egli, Elsbeth	12, 13, 14
Ehrehart, Mrs. C. F. (Amelia)	39
Ehringer, Ethel Myra	163, 194, 195
Elbert, Doris	195, 213
Elliott, Sarah A.	107, 108, 147, 148, 149

Name	Pages
Engel, Elsbeth	13
Ergenbright, Sarah E.	119, 120, 157
Erickson, Kermit Roland	169
Erickson, Kermit Roland, 2nd	169
Erickson, Patricia Jean	169
Erwin, Samuel	60
Esterly, A. Russell	205
Esterly, Eleanor	205
Esterly, Rachel Alice	205, 218
Ettleman, Jacob	59
Evans, Betty	187
Eyster, Simon	111
Farmer, Carl	204
Farmer, Dale Alen	204
Farmer, Kathy Louise	204
Farmer, Larry Carl	204
Farmer, Richard Leroy	204
Farne, Christanus	10
Farne, Christian	26
Farne, Elsbeth	9
Farne, Hans	14
Farne, Hansen	9
Farne, Mattaus	25
Farne, Mattuas	26
Farne, Nicolausen	9
Farne, Steffan	10
Farne, Susanna Catharina	25
Farni, Abraham	12, 13, 11
Farni, Adam	10, 11, 12, 23
Farni, Agathe	15, 10
Farni, Agnesen	10
Farni, Ana	15
Farni, Anna	10, 12, 13, 15, 16
Farni, Anna Elisabetha	24
Farni, Anna Sophia	24
Farni, Anni	15
Farni, Babi	11
Farni, Baby	15
Farni, Barb.	12, 13, 16
Farni, Barbara	12, 13, 15, 16
Farni, Barbli	15
Farni, Benedicta	11
Farni, Benedikta	15
Farni, Cathr.	13
Farni, Cathrin.	11, 12, 13, 15
Farni, Catharina	14
Farni, Cathri	10
Farni, Cathrie	11
Farni, Christen	9, 10, 11, 12, 13, 14, 15
Farni, Christian	9, 23
Farni, Christina	15, 16
Farni, Clauri	10
Farni, Elisabeth	11
Farni, Elsbeth	12, 13, 15, 16
Farni, Hans	10, 11, 12, 13, 14, 15
Farni, Hans Georg	24
Farni, Hansen	11
Farni, Jakob	12
Farni, Johann Georg	26
Farni, Johann Jakob	26
Farni, Johannes	12
Farni, Lucia	10
Farni, Madle	15
Farni, Magdalena	13, 16
Farni, Mari	15, 10
Farni, Maria	10
Farni, Maria Elisabetha	24
Farni, Maria Katharina	24
Farni, Maria Salome	24
Farni, Matthys	12
Farni, Mattys	11
Farni, Michel	10, 11, 12, 13, 15
Farni, Nickel	26, 12
Farni, Niclas	23
Farni, Nicol	11
Farni, Nicolaus	11, 12, 14
Farni, Nikolaus	24
Farni, Peter	10, 11, 12, 13, 14, 15
Farni, Stefan	11, 13
Farni, Steffan	10, 11, 12, 13, 14
Farni, Steffanus	10
Farni, Sybilla Philippina	24
Farni, Uli	10, 11, 12, 14
Farni, Ulrich	12, 14, 13, 15
Farni, Verena	13, 15, 16
Farnie, Cathrie	15
Farnier, Johann Adam	20
Farnier, Maria Eva	20
Farnin, Christine	10
Farnin, Verena	10
Farnir, Christan	10
Farnir, Christina	10
Farnir, Clauri	10
Farnir, Dichtla	10
Farnir, Peter	10
Farnir, Uli	10
Farnoy, Christian	1
Farny, Catharina Margaretha	25
Farny, Hans	23, 24
Farny, Joh. Georg	25
Farny, Johann Jakob	25
Farny, Maria Anna	25
Farree, Rebecca	64
Fast, Lee	142
Fast, Mary L.	142
Fast, Ocie	142
Fast, Q. V. Dove	142
Fast, Sherman	142
Faurney, Adam	40
Fear, Minnie	136
Feeser, Catherine	126, 96
Felton, Howard	160
Felton, Patricia	160
Fili, Hans Georg	19
Finger, Hans	15
Finley, Carolyn Ruth	195
Finley, Charles Sager	195, 196

Finley, David Reece	195
Finley, Diane Elizabeth	195
Finley, Jeannette Marlene	195
Finley, Stephen Roy	195
Firestone, Norman	208
Fisher, Edgar	165
Fisher, Theodore Herbert	165
Fisher, Wayland Irving	165
Fisher, Weldon Theodore	165
Flekingar, Andrew	52
Ford, Charles	126
Ford, Edna Beulah	126
Ford, Fern Luella	126
Ford, James Henry	126
Ford, Jesse James	126
Ford, Mabel Marguerite	126
Ford, Merle Howard	126
Ford, Roy Forney	126
Ford, Walter Kneer	126
Ford, Willis Jay	126
Forne, Adam	37, 38
Forne, Nicholas	38
Forneick, Christian	19
Forneick, Christina	19
Forneick, Rosina Margaretha	19
Forney, Aaron	82, 101, 137, 138, 157
Forney, Abel	91, 117
Forney, Abraham	1, 45, 59, 63, 74, 76, 90, 91, 92, 93
Forney, Ada	112, 151
Forney, Adam	40, 47, 59, 64, 73, 76, 84, 85, 86, 87, 88
Forney, Abraham, Sr.	63
Forney, Addison	100, 172
Forney, Addison D.	134
Forney, Adolphus Levi	96, 127
Forney, Adolphus William	77, 96, 128, 129, 130
Forney, Adolphus W.	97, 128
Forney, A. G.	120
Forney, Agnes Florene	166, 198
Forney, Alban W.	86, 152
Forney, Alban Walter	115
Forney, Albert	84, 118, 154
Forney Albert B. (Colonel)	100, 112, 134
Forney, Albert J.	151
Forney, Albert Jefferson	187
Forney, Albert L.	111
Forney, Alexander	70, 71, 82
Forney, Alfred	134, 172, 173
Forney, Alfred Eugene	96, 97, 128, 130, 163, 164, 167
Forney, Alice	76, 94
Forney, Alice Elizabeth	118, 155, 156
Forney, Alice Jeanette	191
Forney, Allene	125, 160
Forney, Alvina Mildred	129
Forney, Amanda B.	121
Forney, Anderson Gilbert	121, 157
Forney, Andrew	59, 70, 72, 80, 83
Forney, Angelina	86, 115
Forney, Angeline	77, 95, 105, 143
Forney, Anjaline	73, 87
Forney, Anna Catrina	59
Forney, Anna Margaret	45, 57
Forney, Anna Margaretha	56
Forney, Anna Maria	59, 66
Forney, Anna Maria (Polly)	64
Forney, Anna Mary	57
Forney, Anne	73, 85
Forney, Annette Marie	195
Forney, Arminda	157
Forney, Senator A. G.	122
Forney, A. Z.	154
Forney, A. Z. (Abe)	91, 116
Forney, Barbra	91, 117
Forney, Belmina	96, 127
Forney, Benjamin	60, 73, 84, 110, 111, 112
Forney, Benjamin Harrison	121
Forney, Bernelt	108, 149
Forney, Bert	134, 172
Forney, Bertha	116, 123, 158
Forney, Bertram Delmore	129
Forney, Bertrum Delmore	96, 165, 166
Forney, Betty Jean	168, 200
Forney, Beulah	155
Forney, Beverly Joyce	166, 198
Forney, Birchard	155
Forney, Blanche	116, 122, 157
Forney, Brady Mary	118
Forney, Bruce Wayne	194, 212
Forney, Calvin Henry	108
Forney, Calvin Lancaster	86, 114, 153
Forney, Camilla	154
Forney, Cardinal	203
Forney, Carl	155
Forney, Carol	168, 200
Forney, Carol Bernice	196, 214
Forney, Carol Lee	192, 210
Forney, Carolyn Ann	194, 212
Forney, Carolyn Irene	185
Forney, Casius Milton	91, 118
Forney, Catherene	149, 185
Forney, Catherine	45, 57, 59, 76, 82, 83, 94
Forney, Catherine Eileen	185
Forney, Cathern	91, 108, 117
Forney, Cecile	194, 212
Forney, Chalmers	127, 193
Forney, Chalmers Dean	161
Forney, Charles	112, 116, 150, 185, 186
Forney, Charles D.	115, 118, 121, 152, 154, 189, 190
Forney, Charles Diecks	151
Forney, Charles Ledley	118, 155
Forney, Charles W.	129, 166, 167, 168

Forney, Charles Whitney 96, 130
Forney, Charles William 3, 59, 151, 187
Forney, Charlotte 92, 119
Forney, Charlotte A. 101, 138
Forney, Cheryl Ann 187
Forney, Cheryl Ruth 194, 212
Forney, Chloe 124, 92, 92, 124
Forney, Christeina 81, 89, 106, 107
Forney, Christian 1, 36
Forney, Christian Georg 45, 56
Forney, Christina 70, 71
Forney, Claire 129
Forney, Clair Elaine 151
Forney, Clara 37, 96
Forney, Clara A. 101, 138
Forney, Clara E. 103, 141
Forney, Clarence 123
Forney, Clarence L. 159
Forney, Clarence O. 134, 172
Forney, Clark D. 116
Forney, Claude 113
Forney, Claudia Jean 195, 213
Forney, Clifford 147, 184
Forney, Clifton Elroy 127, 161, 192
Forney, Clifton Maynard 192, 211
Forney, Clora 47
Forney, Clyde Califax 95, 125, 160
Forney, Clyde D. 134, 172
Forney, Cora 121, 142, 157
Forney, Cora Irene 96, 128
Forney, Cornelius 85, 151
Forney, Cornelius A. 112
Forney, G. Cress 151
Forney, Cynthia 188
Forney, Daisy 127, 161
Forney, Dana Jo. 202
Forney, Daniel 45, 57, 71, 80, 82,
.... 91, 100, 101, 105, 106,
.... 138, 143, 144, 145, 146
Forney, Daniel F. 103
Forney, Daniel Freeman 142
Forney, Daniel J. 86, 87, 113, 114, 115
Forney, Daniel Smyser 57
Forney, Daniel Wayne 200, 216
Forney, Darla Sue 198, 215
Forney, David 47, 66, 67, 73, 85
.... 91, 112, 113, 117, 118,
.... 155, 156, 175, 200, 216
Forney, David Bruce 194, 212
Forney, David Crawford 125, 159
Forney, David Crawford, Jr. 159
Forney, David H. 103, 140
Forney, David J. 159
Forney, David Julian 94, 125
Forney, David Patrick 194, 213
Forney, David S. 76
Forney, David Shriver 64
Forney, David Rufus 118, 155
Forney, David Zook 96, 126, 160

Forney, Deanna Ray 197, 215
Forney, Deborah Susan 197, 214
Forney, Debra 102
Forney, Debrary 141
Forney, Della 101, 138
Forney, Della Jean 197, 215
Forney, Delmar 172
Forney, Dennis 194, 212
Forney, Denver Jesse 96, 129
Forney, Dessie 134
Forney, Dessie P. 173
Forney, Donald F. 218
Forney, Donald 175, 203
Forney, Donald Floyd 177, 203
Forney, Donald Rowland ... 162, 194, 212, 213
Forney, Donald Rowland, Jr. 194, 212
Forney, Donna 172
Forney, Donna Faye 192, 210
Forney, Donna Lee 203, 218
Forney, Donna Mae 191
Forney, Donovan 123
Forney, Doris 125, 158
Forney, Doris Eileen 190, 208
Forney, Doris Helen 166, 198
Forney, Dorothy Gertrude 165
Forney, Dorothy Jean 153, 189
Forney, Douglas Robert 197, 215
Forney, Drew 191, 210
Forney, Earl Levi 116
Forney, Edmund 96
Forney, Edna 92, 124
Forney, Elberta 157
Forney, Eldon Delong 163, 195, 214
Forney, Eli 73, 74, 90, 92, 93
.... 119
Forney, Elias 71
Forney, Elias A. 81, 108, 147, 148, 149
.... 183, 184
Forney, Elisabeth A. 143
Forney, Eliza 77
Forney, Eliza M. 94, 76, 76, 94
Forney, Elizabeth 47, 56, 57, 65, 66
.... 67, 72, 73, 74, 76
.... 82, 83, 84, 89, 101
.... 103, 118, 141, 149, 151
.... 154, 185, 187, 188
Forney, Elizabeth (Patsy) 80, 104
Forney, Elizabeth A. 105
Forney, Elizabeth Alice 86, 115
Forney, Elizabeth Harriet 152, 190
Forney, Elizabeth Lowisa 2, 36
Forney, Elizabeth M. 32
Forney, Elizabetha Lowisa 45, 46, 47
Forney, Ella 83
Forney, Ellen 91, 100, 117, 135, 147, 183
Forney, Ellen E. 196
Forney, Ellen Elizabeth 165, 195
Forney, Elles Ann 101, 137
Forney, Elmer C. 134, 173

Forney, Elmer 85, 113
Forney, Elmer D. 129
Forney, Elmer Diehl 96, 130, 168, 169
Forney, Elnor June 150, 188
Forney, Elwood Roosevelt 145, 146, 178, 203
........................204
Forney, Emanuel 57, 80, 102
Forney, Emanuel E. 105, 106, 145, 146, 176
........................177, 178, 181, 182
Forney, Mrs. Emanuel E. 143
Forney, Emerson 139, 176
Forney, Emma 118, 121, 154
Forney, Emory Owen 128, 163, 194, 195
Forney, Ephraim J. 93
Forney, Ephraim Young 77, 95, 96, 125
........................127, 161
Forney, Ephram Young 96
Forney, Essie 122, 158, 191
Forney, Ester 64
Forney, Ethel 161
Forney, Ethel Lucille 130, 167
Forney, Eva 45, 57, 139
Forney, Eva Mae 174, 202
Forney, Evan Dale 195, 213
Forney, Eve 80
Forney, Evelyn 184, 208
Forney, Everett 160, 161
Forney, Everitt 126
Forney, Fay 161
Forney, Faye 123, 127, 158
Forney, Felix 2
Forney, Florence 174
Forney, Florence A. 202
Forney, Florence Viola 130, 169
Forney, Floyd F. 154
Forney, Floyd W. 167
Forney, Floyd Whitney 130, 166, 197, 198
Forney, Forest 134, 172
Forney, Frances 128, 163
Forney, Francis 151, 186
Forney, Frank 112, 116, 118, 134, 191, 210
.... 72
Forney, Frank B. 100, 135, 174, 175
Forney, Frank C. 173
Forney, Frank Gordon 150, 188
Forney, Frank Gordon, Jr. 188
Forney, Frank R. 151
Forney, Frank S. 188
Forney, Frank Sayers 109, 150
Forney, Frank W. 121
Forney, Franklin 116, 162, 193
Forney, Fred 91
Forney, Fred Freeman 158
Forney, Frederick 63, 74, 76, 93, 94, 102
Forney, Frederick (Philip) 37
Forney, Frederick C. 209
Forney, Fredric Daniel 178, 204, 218
Forney, Fredric Daniel, Jr. 205, 218
Forney, Fredrick 73, 80, 88, 92

Forney, Fredrick Cattell 152, 190
Forney, Gary Kent 191, 209
Forney, Dorothy Gertrude 129
Forney, Genevive 155
Forney, George 57, 67, 73, 77, 82
.... 88, 95, 96, 100, 113
.... 134, 135, 136, 137, 149
.... 174, 185
Forney, George D. 108, 148, 149, 185
Forney, George Douglas 125
Forney, George Franklin 127, 162, 193
Forney, George M. 159
Forney, Georgia Etta 96, 126
Forney, Gerald Arthur 192, 211
Forney, Gerald Lorin 162, 193, 212
Forney, Gerald Lorin, Jr. 194, 212
Forney, Gertrude 134, 172
Forney, Glen 139, 176
Forney, Glen A. 176
Forney, Glen Frederick 190
Forney, Glenn E. 203, 218
Forney, Glenn Frederick 208
Forney, Gilbert 84, 92, 110
Forney, Gilbert Allewelt 127, 162, 193
Forney, Grace 134, 172
Forney, Grace Arline 130, 167
Forney, Grace Edna 118, 156
Forney, Keith George 197
Forney, Hamilton 124
Forney, Hanna 47
Forney, Hannah 66, 73, 86, 87, 88
.... 113, 114, 115
Forney, Harriet 116
Forney, Harriet E. 147
Forney, Harriet (Hattie) E. 105, 146
Forney, Harriet Jeanne 165, 196
Forney, Harrison William Henry 96, 128
Forney, Harry 82, 100
Forney, Harry A. 208
Forney, Harry Alban 152, 190
Forney, Harry I. 116, 151
Forney, Harry I., Jr. 151
Forney, Harry Theodore 129, 165, 197
Forney, Harvey F. 84, 111
Forney, Heddy 73, 89
Forney, Heinrich 59, 70, 71, 72, 73
Forney, Heinrick 90
Forney, Helen 129
Forney, Helena 67
Forney, Helen Darlene 160
Forney, Helen Kathryn 156
Forney, Helen Myrtle 130, 168
Forney, Helen Virginia 190, 209
Forney, Henry 45, 59, 60, 61, 62, 63
.... 70, 73, 81, 96, 101
........................106, 107, 108, 109, 126
.... 127, 138, 139, 175, 206
Forney, Henry, Jr. 59, 72
Forney, Henry Clay 95, 125, 160

Forney, Henry S.	76
Forney, Henry Zebulion	108, 148, 184
Forney, Henry Zebulion, Jr.	148, 184, 208
Forney, Hiram	82, 101, 138
Forney, Howard	147, 154, 184, 208
Forney, Howard Glen	7, 26, 145, 146, 181, 206
Forney, Howard W.	122, 157
Forney, Ida	134
Forney, Ida M.	173
Forney, Ida May	108, 149
Forney, Illa May	151
Forney, Ira Dale	161, 193
Forney, Irene	116, 158
Forney, Isaac	73, 80, 101
Forney, Isaac W.	209
Forney, Isaac William	152, 191
Forney, Isach T.	103, 141
Forney, Isiah	92, 120, 121
Forney, Issac	88, 138, 139, 140, 141
Forney, J. Donovan	159
Forney, J. W.	122
Forney, Jack Lynn	192, 211
Forney, Jackie	162, 193
Forney, Jacob	1, 47, 57, 64, 66, 91, 118, 154
Forney, Jacob (Bush Jake)	56
Forney, Jacob Birchard	118, 156
Forney, Jacob S.	57
Forney, James	85, 113, 176
Forney, James Clark	122, 158
Forney, James F.	116, 154
Forney, James Garfield	119
Forney, James Hamilton	92, 123, 158, 159
Forney, James Henry	77, 96, 127, 128
Forney, James Lawrence	96, 128, 162, 163
Forney, James Lee	192, 211
Forney, James W.	101, 137
Forney, Jana	90
Forney, Janet	191, 209
Forney, Janice	150, 188
Forney, Jasper	92, 125
Forney, Jennie H.	121
Forney, Jennie R.	91, 116
Forney, Jess	116
Forney, Jesse	67, 106
Forney, Jesse Y.	128
Forney, Jesse Young	77, 96, 126
Forney, Jessie	80
Forney, Jessie Shirman	118, 155
Forney, Jessie William	148
Forney, Joann Elaine	181, 206
Forney, Joanne	187
Forney, Joe	118
Forney, Joe W.	156, 157
Forney, Johan	59, 70
Forney, Johann Adam	1, 2, 21, 36, 37, 39, 41, 42, 45, 46, 47, 57, 59, 60,
Forney, Johann Nicholaus	45, 63, 64
Forney, John	57, 59, 63, 67, 70, 71, 74, 80, 81, 82, 86, 89, 91, 92, 93, 101, 102, 103, 118, 119, 120, 121, 122, 123, 124, 125, 137, 140, 141, 142
Forney, John Earl	128, 162, 193, 194
Forney, John Fred	142, 175
Forney, John Joseph	194, 213
Forney, John A.	116, 154
Forney, John Adam	39, 45, 57
Forney, John Christian	56
Forney, John Daniel	56
Forney, John George	100, 134, 172, 173, 174
Forney, John K.	3
Forney, John M.	91, 108, 116
Forney, John Miller	81, 107, 147, 148, 149
Forney, John H.	76, 93
Forney, Gen. John H.	1
Forney, John Henry	135, 202
Forney, John Peter	59, 71
Forney, John Peter Jr.	71, 82
Forney, John R.	159
Forney, John Richard	165, 196, 214
Forney, John S.	30, 76, 125
Forney, John Swope	94
Forney, John V.	158
Forney, John Wayne	95
Forney, John W.	31, 103, 119
Forney, John W., Jr.	158
Forney, Colonel John W.	1
Forney, Col. John Wein	32
Forney, John Wesley	142, 175
Forney, John Wilbur	122, 158
Forney, John William	118, 148, 155, 184, 208
Forney, Joseph	72, 73, 74, 83, 90, 91, 109, 110, 116, 117, 118
Forney, Joseph H.	188
Forney, Joseph Henry	109, 149
Forney, Joseph W.	116
Forney, Josephine	76
Forney, Josephine Louise	127
Forney, Josephus	92, 157
Forney, Josephus W.	119, 120
Forney, Josiah	77, 95, 125
Forney, Josie	121
Forney, Josiphine	108
Forney, Joyce Delaine	181, 206
Forney, Julia	73, 89
Forney, Juliana	57
Forney, Julianna	187
Forney, Julio	100, 136
Forney, Karen Woods	188
Forney, Karle	67
Forney, Karle Herbert	96, 126
Forney, Kate	101, 140
Forney, Kate Ann	118, 155
Forney, Katharine	109

Forney, Kathryn Margaret	152
Forney, Kathy Genel	197, 215
Forney, Kay Cile	192, 210
Forney, Kay Ellen	202
Forney, Keith George	166, 215
Forney, Kenneth	139, 176
Forney, Kenneth Eugene	192, 211
Forney, Kenneth Gillespie	151, 186
Forney, Kevin Joseph	195, 213
Forney, Kimberly	202
Forney, Kitty Bell	115, 152
Forney, Kyle David	195
Forney, Lafayette	92
Forney, Lafayette D.	122, 123, 157, 158
Forney, Lanella Kay	199, 215
Forney, Larry Richard	196, 214
Forney, Larry Wayne	168, 200, 216
Forney, Laura	116
Forney, Laura Dee	151
Forney, Lavina	86
Forney, Lavonne	151
Forney, Lawrence	149, 185
Forney, Leander (Lee)	96
Forney, Leander Edmund	161, 162
Forney, Leander (Lee) Edmund	127
Forney, LeAnne	193
Forney, Lee Junior	162, 193
Forney, Leigh Annette	194
Forney, Leigh (Lee) Clifton	161, 191, 210
Forney, Lelia	155
Forney, Leroy	39
Forney, Leroy Leonard	145, 146, 182, 183
Forney, Leroy M.	151
Forney, Lester Burgess	116
Forney, Lester Wayne	130, 168, 200
Forney, Levi	73, 86, 115, 116
Forney, Levina E.	115
Forney, Lewis Elmer	168, 200
Forney, Lewis S.	45, 64, 103, 142
Forney, Lida	90, 116
Forney, Lidda	73
Forney, Liddy or Leddy	90
Forney, Lillie Frances	96, 126
Forney, Linda Lee	203, 218
Forney, Linder	91
Forney, Linder James	118, 156
Forney, Lisa	188
Forney, Liza	191, 210
Forney, Lois	176
Forney, Lois Maude	130
Forney, Loren Keith	197, 215
Forney, Louis	140, 202, 203
Forney, Louis, Jr.	175, 202
Forney, Louis, Sr.	175
Forney, Louisa	66, 94
Forney, Louisa A.	76
Forney, Louisa Harbater	37
Forney, Louise	84, 111, 129
Forney, Lovice	47, 65
Forney, Lowell Eugene	163, 195, 213
Forney, Lowisa Charlotte	46
Forney, Luanne	200, 216
Forney, Lucy	84, 111
Forney, Luella Young	96, 126
Forney, Lulu May	130, 166
Forney, Luta May	96, 126
Forney, Lydia	57, 64, 119, 157
Forney, Lyle Eugene	195, 213
Forney, Lynette Joy	196, 214
Forney, Lysle M. (Joe)	157
Forney, Mable	139, 175
Forney, Mabel Elizabeth	194
Forney, Madge Marie	175, 203
Forney, Madle Frick	1, 36
Forney, Magdalena	57
Forney, Marce	174, 202
Forney, Margaret	57, 100, 137, 155
Forney, Margaret (Peggy)	80, 105
Forney, Margaret Ann	192, 211
Forney, Margaret Ruth	148, 184
Forney, Margarethe	45, 63
Forney, Margret	82, 100, 104
Forney, Marguerite Louise	166, 198
Forney, Marguerite Lucille	167, 199
Forney, Margureta Ann	128, 163
Forney, Maria	64, 84, 90, 110
Forney, Maria Bertha	37
Forney, Maria Catarina	56
Forney, Maria Eva	46, 56
Forney, Maria Magdalena	64, 70, 71, 72
	73
Forney, Maria Margarethe	59
Forney, Marie	47
Forney, Marie Pearl	161, 192
Forney, Marilyn D.	159
Forney, Marilyn Jean	184, 208
Forney, Marjorie	184, 208
Forney, Marjorie Elaine	163, 194
Forney, Marks	57
Forney, Marlane Duane	165, 197
Forney, Martha	83, 84, 91, 110, 117
Forney, Martha Grace	187
Forney, Marvin D.	151
Forney, Marx	39, 45, 56, 57
Forney, Mary	60, 73, 85, 100, 101, 113
	116, 118, 136, 140, 154
Forney, Mary (Polly)	63, 76, 89
Forney, Mary A.	74, 86, 114
Forney, Mary Alice	192, 211
Forney, Mary Ann	76, 93, 105, 118, 144, 186
Forney, Mary Anne	203, 218
Forney, Mary C.	108
Forney, Mary Catherine	149
Forney, Mary Cathern	149
Forney, Mary Christina	57
Forney, Mary D.	121
Forney, Mary Ella	110
Forney, Mary Ida	84, 111, 112

Forney, Mary L.	103, 142
Forney, Mary Louise	7, 129, 166, 167, 199
Forney, Mary Lucille	168, 199
Forney, Mary M.	81, 109
Forney, Matilda	100, 135
Forney, Matthias	56, 66
Forney, Maude Lois	167
Forney, Maude M.	163
Forney, Maude Mary	128, 162
Forney, Maurice Charles	86, 116, 151
Forney, May	119, 157
Forney, May Edith	135, 174
Forney, Maynard Amiel	161, 192, 211
Forney, Melvin Lee	163, 195, 213
Forney, Merle W.	113
Forney, Merle W., Jr.	153
Forney, Merle W., Sr.	153
Forney, Michael	57
Forney, Mildred	172
Forney, Mildred (Toots)	147, 183
Forney, Mildred Alvina	165
Forney, Millard Chester	161, 192, 211
Forney, Milton M.	84, 111
Forney, Minnie	119, 142
Forney, Minnie Harriet	115, 152
Forney, Minnie Pearl	135, 174
Forney, Miriam Irene	161, 193
Forney, Monroe McKinley	145, 146, 177, 178, 203
Forney, Morgan Thomas	84, 112, 150, 151, 185
Forney, Morrace Lewis	88
Forney, Morris Lewis	73
Forney, Moses	73, 86
Forney, Myrtle	113
Forney, Myrtle Mae	145, 176
Forney, Nancy Jean	196, 214
Forney, Nancy Lee	185
Forney, Nandy	103, 142
Forney, Nelly	142
Forney, Nettie	116
Forney, Nicholas	37, 59, 73, 74, 88, 89, 90
Forney, Nicholaus	45, 46, 59, 63, 64
Forney, Nickel	45
Forney, Nora	119, 134, 157, 173
Forney, Odessa	112, 151
Forney, Olive	124
Forney, Oliver	108
Forney, Oliver Daniel	86, 113, 152, 153
Forney, Ollie	92
Forney, Ora Clifford	127
Forney, Orange A.	85, 112
Forney, Orrie S.	134, 173
Forney, Pamela Sue	195, 214
Forney, Paul Barton	155
Forney, Paul Mossman	150, 186
Forney, Paul Owen	195, 214
Forney, Patrica	188
Forney, Pearle Reiffe	127
Forney, Peter	1, 47, 64, 66, 88
Forney, Sr., Peter	1
Forney, Gen. Peter	1
Forney, Philip	29, 41, 45, 47, 63, 64, 65, 66, 67
Forney, Phillip	44
Forney, Phyllis Eileen	190, 209
Forney, Polly	73, 90
Forney, Rachel	116
Forney, Rachel Cordelia	82, 101
Forney, Raeshelle Jean	199, 215
Forney, Ralph Barton	156
Forney, Raymond	168, 199, 215
Forney, Raymond Frederick	190, 209
Forney, Rebecca	56, 64, 73, 89
Forney, Richard	178, 187, 191
Forney, Richard Alban	152, 189
Forney, Richard Aldrich	160, 191, 209, 210
Forney, Richard Floyd	167, 198, 215
Forney, Richard H.	129
Forney, Richard Larry	191, 209
Forney, Richard Lee	204
Forney, Richard Wayne	198, 215
Forney, Richard Wilcox	210
Forney, Robert	172, 176, 190
Forney, Robert Cranston	196, 214
Forney, Robert Elmore	162, 194, 212
Forney, Robert Eugene	185
Forney, Robert Evans	187
Forney, Robert Hayes	158, 191
Forney, Robert Henry	129, 166, 197
Forney, Robert Kaye	190, 209
Forney, Robert L.	178, 203, 204, 218
Forney, Robert Lafayette	158
Forney, Robert Lester	166, 197, 215
Forney, Robert Philip	194, 212
Forney, Robert Wayne	167, 198, 215
Forney, Roger Franklin	165, 197, 214
Forney, Rohama	101, 139
Forney, Rollin Albion	130, 168, 199, 200
Forney, Ronald	203
Forney, Rosa Nell	121, 157
Forney, Rosanne	202
Forney, Roscoe Calvert	112, 151, 186, 187
Forney, Roscoe Calvert, Jr.	151, 187
Forney, Rose	91, 117
Forney, Rosina	90
Forney, Rosina Margaretha	19
Forney, Roy	134, 172
Forney, Roy Cranston	128, 164, 165, 195, 196, 197
Forney, Rudolph	139, 176
Forney, Russel H.	149, 188
Forney, Russel Henry	188
Forney, Russell	156
Forney, Ruth	113, 124, 125, 152, 153
Forney, Ruth Aileen	165, 196
Forney, Ruth Ellen	176

Name	Pages
Forney, Sally	47
Forney, Salome	47, 57, 67
Forney, Sam'l	88
Forney, Samuel	41, 47, 64, 67, 73, 77, 85, 101, 139, 176
Forney, Samuel Ellsworth	118, 156
Forney, Samuel S.	76
Forney, Samuel Wilcox	125, 160, 191
Forney, Sandra Lee	195, 213
Forney, Sara	84
Forney, Sarah	57, 64, 73, 86, 100, 111, 113, 116, 136
Forney, Sarah A.	103, 141
Forney, Sarah Idella	118, 154
Forney, Sarah P.	73, 87
Forney, Shane	187
Forney, Simon	91, 118
Forney, Soloman	91, 117, 118
Forney, Soloman	74, 91, 92
Forney, Sophia	45, 57, 63, 73, 74, 76, 84, 85, 93, 110
Forney, Stephen	202
Forney, Stephen M.	159
Forney, Steven Lee	195, 213
Forney, Susan	57, 66, 73, 88, 191, 210
Forney, Susan E.	94
Forney, Susan H.	74
Forney, Susan Lynne	205, 218
Forney, Susana	47
Forney, Susanah	101
Forney, Susanna	57, 63, 66, 67, 74, 76, 82, 93, 100, 134
Forney, Susannah	64, 140
Forney, Sylvester	121
Forney, Theresa May	148
Forney, Therese Rose	195, 213
Forney, Thomas	162, 187, 193
Forney, Thomas Millard	192, 211
Forney, Todd Alan	197, 214
Forney, Vada	118
Forney, Verna	161, 192
Forney, Vilet	92, 119
Forney, Viola	92, 124
Forney, Violet Louise (Vicky)	130
Forney, Virgiana	178
Forney, Virginia Lois	152, 190
Forney, Virgiana Louise	204
Forney, Verginia Mae	174, 202
Forney, Virginia May	166, 197
Forney, Volma	142
Forney, Walter	92, 124
Forney, Walter A.	190, 191
Forney, Walter A., Jr.	209
Forney, Walter Alban	115, 152
Forney, Walter Alban, Jr.	152, 190
Forney, Walter Lee	191
Forney, Wayne Irving	130, 167, 198, 199
Forney, Wendy Lee	197, 214
Forney, Colonel Wien	1
Forney, Wilbur	116, 189
Forney, Wilbur Dean	114, 153
Forney, Wilfred Guy	151, 187
Forney, Will	91
Forney, William	172
Forney, William C.	108
Forney, William Dwight	160, 191, 210
Forney, William Earl	135, 175
Forney, William Ed.	134, 172
Forney, William H.	83, 109, 110, 149, 150, 188, 189
Forney, Gen. William H.	1, 30
Forney, William Hamilton, Jr.	185
Forney, William Harrison	109, 150
Forney, William Harrison, Jr.	150, 189
Forney, William Henry	100, 134
Forney, William S.	95, 125
Forney, Wilson	84, 85, 111, 113
Forni, Anna	11, 12, 14, 15
Forni, Barbli	15
Forni, Cathrin	15
Forni, Christ.	12
Forni, Christen	11, 12, 14
Forni, Hans	11, 12, 14
Forni, Jacob	14
Forni, Margareta	15
Forni, Margret	15
Forni, Michel	11, 12, 14
Forni, Peter	11, 14, 15
Forni, Steffan	14
Forni, Uli	12
Forni, Ulrich	14
Forni, Verena	12, 15
Fornic, Christian	21
Fornich, Christian	20, 21, 22, 26
Fornich, Hans Adam	22
Fornich, Johann Adam	26
Fornich, Johannes Adam	26
Fornick, Christian	19, 20
Fornick, Elisabeth Louisa	20
Fornick, Hans Adam	21, 19
Fornick, Johann Adam	20, 19
Fornick, Louisa Charlotte	20
Fornick, Maria Christina	19
Fornick, Marx	19
Fornick, Nickl	20
Fornick, Niclas	20
Fornickin, Maria	19
Fornig, Anna Christina	19
Fornig, Christian	19
Forny, Anna	9, 15
Forny, Anni	10
Forny, Christian	19
Forny, Christina	19
Forny, Steffan	10
Foss, Adeline	155
Foutz, Effie	155
Freudenreich, Pastor Johannes Jacob	9
Frey, Anna	12

Name	Page(s)
Frey, Hans	15
Franklin, Ben	29
Frick, Madelena	10
Frick, Madle	1, 10, 11, 14, 23
Frick, Magdalena	12
Frutiger,	9
Fucher, Nicolaus	10
Fuller, Zuma Ella	148
Fullerman, Mary Elizabeth	185, 148
Furhman, Catharine	144, 143, 105, 145, 146
Furney, Adam	52
Furney, Mark	52
Galli, Niehaus	15
Garand, John C.	5
Garfield, President James A.	5
Gautschin, Barbara	59
Gayger, Anna	20
Gayger, Hans	20
Geiersberg, Fraulein	20, 26
Geis, Estella	106
Geis, Wm.	106
Gelwicks, Eva Cathrine	56
Gelwicks, Georg Carl	56
Gerber, Cathrie	11
Gerber, Madelen	10
Gerber, Madle	10, 11
Gerber, Magdalena	14
Gerber, Nicolaus	16
Gerber, Peter	10
Gerber, Uli	11, 12, 15
Gerber, Ulrich	16
Gerber, Valentin	15
Gerber, Vernena	10
Gerger, Trini	11
German, Lottie	175
Gibbs, Bernice Edna	196, 214
Gillespie, Julia	151, 186, 187
Gissler, Anna	10
Glas, Elizabeth	85
Glauren, Madlen	10
Glenn, Jean	149
Gluckner, Mary	148, 185
Gould, Jay	32
Grasser, Donna	197, 214
Graves, Viola	130, 168, 169
Green, Ruth	162, 193
Grove, Catharine Susanna	67
Grove, Elizabeth Margaretta	67
Grove, Jacob Forney	67
Grove, Stephen	67
Guinn, Mr.	157
Gundy, Fanny	71, 82
Gurther, Mari	10, 14
Gurtner, Christen	15
Gurtner, Hans	15
Gutshall, Christine Ann	192
Gutshall, James Merlin	192
Gutshall, Merlin James	192
Gutshall, Michael Glenn	192
Gutzmer, Jayne Lynette	200
Gutzmer, Katherine Louise	200
Gutzmer, Marvin J.	200
Haefke, Isabelle	203, 218
Haffer, Ella	139, 176
Hagg, Maria	12, 14
Hague, Floyd A.	162
Hague, Jack	162
Hague, Loraine	162
Hallett, Mr.	190
Hamersley, Charlotte	154
Hamilton, Eliza J.	121
Hammersley, Cleo	124
Hammersley, Harry	124
Hammersley, Mary	124
Hammersley, Stella	124
Hamsch, Maria Magdalena	25
Handwork, John	89
Handwork, Polly	73
Haney, Lewis M.	211
Harris, Deborah	76, 93, 94
Harris, J.	63
Harris, Noah	140
Hart, Clay Dunham	127
Hart, Cora	127
Hart, Henry	127
Hart, John	127
Hart, Joseph	127
Hart, Leroy	127
Hart, Mabel	127
Hart, Mayme	127
Hart, Mina	127
Hart, Ruby	127
Hasler, Al.	167
Hasselbacker, Lloyd	162, 163
Hasselbacker, Margaret	162
Hassler, Eva	26
Hassler, Maria Eva	20
Hassler, Matthias	20, 26
Hasslers, Apollonia	19
Hasslers, Mattias	19
Hatfield, Mr.	157
Haughelin, William	60
Hawk, Mr.	89
Hawk, Rebecca	73
Haydu, John J., Jr.	206
Haydu, Karen Jean	206
Haydu, Nancy Ann	206
Hays, Isaac Reed	174
Hays, Isaac Reed, Jr.	174
Hayward, Burt Forney	128
Hayward, Edna	128
Hayward, Hazel	128
Hayward, William Lincoln	128
Heald, William	63
Hegg, Mari	12
Heines, Nellie	192, 210

Helmick, Birchard	156
Helmick, Clyde David	156
Helmick, Harlan	156
Helmick, Jessie Howard	156
Helmick, Joe	156
Helmick, Ralph	156
Helmick, Roland	156
Helmick, Sheldon	155
Helsel, Mary Ellen	134, 172, 173, 174
Hempeler, Ulrich	16
Henderson, Ernest James	160
Henderson, Helen Edmona	160
Henderson, James Forney	160
Henry, Ametta	136
Henry, Charles	136
Henry, Grace	136
Henry, Jennie	136
Henry, John	136
Henry, Mary	136
Hensel, Abigial	118, 155, 156
Henshe, Walter Wm.	198
Hewitt, Henrietta	130, 168
Hewitt, Shirley Ann	199, 215
Hiesing, Andreas	15
Hiet, Isabel May	184
Hiet, John	184
Hisey, Avis	115
Hisey, Elmer	115
Hisey, Irene	115
Hisey, Marsella	115
Hoffert, Thomas	73
Hoffman, Christina	57
Hoffman, Henry	57
Hoffman, Maria	57
Hofmeister, Harry	184
Hofmeister, Helen	184
Hofmeister, Helen M.	208
Hofstetter, Abraham	15
Holbrook, Willie	184, 208
Hooper, Issac	141
Hough, Hannah	153
Hoyle, Ford	173
Hoyle, Maud L.	173
Hunslman, Elizabeth	90
Hunt, Janette	138
Hurd, David Allen	202
Hurd, John Keith	202
Hurd, Max G.	202
Hurrah, William	62
Hutcheson, Clark	175
Huxley, Dan	206
Huxley, Jared	206
Huxley, LaVerne	181, 206
Isti, Barbara	14
Jacobs, Amelia	155
Jellisen, William	80
Jenner, Anna	14
Jensen, Leonard	166
Jensen, Marvin Leonard	166
Jensen, Shirley Ilene	166
Johnson, Ephraim	93
Johnson, Margaret R.	148, 184
Johnson, Marie	149, 188
Johnson, Nancy	93
Johnston, Felton M.	32
Jones, Ada Lorene	197, 215
Jordening, Joel	200
Kahl, Nelda	198, 215
Kale, Adda	173
Kale, Heddy	73
Kale, Mr.	89
Karle, George Adam	67
Karle, Susanna	67, 77
Karnaghan, Annie	126, 160
Kasza, Anna Keck	182
Kasza, Harold	182
Kauffman, Mr. Robert D.	42
Kauffman, Mrs. Robert D.	42
Kaufman, David Spangler	33
Kaufmann, Adam	16
Kelly, W. A.	30
Keyser, Doris	175
Keyser, Earl	175
Keyser, Robert	175
Kiefauber, Anna Margaretha	56
Kiefauber, Conrad	56
Kiefauber, Johann Nicolaus	56
Kiefauber, Maria Catarina	56
Kiefauber, Nicholas	56
Kiefauber, Peter	56
Kincaid, Tom	136
King, Mary (Polly)	84
King, Polly	110, 111, 112
King, Thomas	84
King, William P.	33
Kingdom, Bernice Eileen	163
Kingdom, John Francis	163
Kingdom, Raymond	163
Knisely, Jesse Clyde	116
Knisely, Joseph	116
Knisely, Perry C.	116
Knisely, Ralph	116
Koch, Joyce	195, 214
Kolb, Hans	10
Kraff, Hans	16
Krafft, Elsbeth	12
Krueger, Cheryl Ann	199
Krueger, Hilmar Fred	199
Krueger, Shiela Marie	199
Kunkle, Lazarus	100
Kunkle, Sarah	101
Kunkle, Sarah A.	138
Lafayette, Marquis de	5
Lambright, H. M.	138

Name	Page
Lambright, Rosemary	138
Lammot, Daniel	65
Lammot, Elizabeth	65
Lammot, Margaretta Elizabeth	65
LaMotte, Jean Henri	65
LaMotte, John	66
LaMotte, John Henry	66
Lanning, Arminda	122, 157, 158
Law, Jacob W.	115
Lawson, Olga	185
Lawson, Rena	185
Layman, Virgiana	202
Lease, George	65
Lease, Leonard	65
Lebengood, Geo.	117
Lehman, Elizabeth	103, 140, 141, 142
Lemann, Christen	15
Lemann, Hans	15
L'Enfant, Charles	5
Lesher, Sabastian	146
Lesher, Viola L.	145, 146, 176, 177, 178, 181, 182
Lewis, Anna	147, 183, 184
Lewis, Arthur, W.	173
Lewis, Will	136
Liebert, Jacob	63
Long, David	149
Long, Martha	191, 209
Longfellow, Henry Wadsworth	5
Lower, Mathias	62
Luscher, Christiana	13
Maasovis, Barb.	10
Mackintosh, Mr.	172
Magel, Margaret	191, 209, 210
Maholm, John	63
Mansell, Aubrey	136
Manypenny, Ruth	193, 212
Marino, Peter	185
Marvin, Susanna H.	83
Mason, Bette	159
Mason, Charles	38
Mathews, Mary	125
Mathisen, Barbara	10
Mathisen, Barblen	10
Metler, Elsbeth	14
May, Polly	84
May, Sarah	73, 84, 85, 86, 87, 88
May, Sophia	85
May, William	84, 85
May, Yacob	85
Mayer, Theobalth	23
McClintook, LaVern	197, 215
McDonald, Tressa	128, 162, 163
McFarland, Eliza	107
McGuire, Evelyn	162, 194
McKown, Gail	192, 211
McLeod, Peggy Jean	198, 215
Meier, Christoffel	16
Meier, Michel	15
Meinor, Elizabeth	73
Meinor, Julia	73
Mellinger, Melchor	110
Melsheimer, John Adam	39
Melton, Donald George	168
Melton, Martin Luther	168
Mettler, Cathrin	14
Mettler, Elsbeth	10
Mettler, Madlen	13
Meyer, Anna Margarethe	57
Meyer, Mrs. H. G.	142
Meyer, Mr.	57
Meyteler, Dichtla	9
Milar, J. Calvin	155
Milar, J. Thurman	155
Miller, Bernice	161
Miller, Elta	177, 203
Miller, Jessie	135
Miller, Joanne	161
Miller, Louise	135
Miller, Murry	161
Miller, Paul L., Jr.	188
Miller, Pearl	135
Miller, Peter	110
Miller, Raymond	135
Miller, Sam	134
Miller, Walter	161
Minard, James B. Jr.	109
Minard, Katharine	83
Miner, Andrew	137
Minner, William Richard	113
Minor, Mr.	89
Miskimen, James	91
Miskimen, Susan	91, 116
Modisette, Helena Beatrice	166, 167, 197, 198
Monteverce, Richard	198
Morris, Jennie Luella	153, 189
Mossman, Elizabeth	112, 150, 151
Mowen, Susanna H.	83
Mudry, John Paul	197
Muhrer, Hans Jerg	27
Muller, Verena	12, 14
Mullins, Priscilla	5
Mulvaney, Maude	162, 193, 194
Mundry, Carolyn Jeanne	197
Murer, Barbara	15
Murer, Christen	15
Murnan, Pearl Irene	161, 192
Murphy, Ira	158
Musser, Cathorine	81, 106, 107, 108, 109
Musser, Peter	63, 81
Musser, Susannah	86, 115, 116
Muttersbaugh, Henretta	142, 175
Myers, Catherine	66
Nace, Louisa	66
Nace, Matthias	66
Nagel, Abraham	85

Name	Pages
Neises, Rita	194, 212, 213
Nicely, Minnie	134, 172
Nichol, John	70, 72, 73, 74
Nicholson, Col. John P.	30
Nolan, Lois	140
Noll, Henry	193
Noll, Jack Lee	193
Noll, James C.	193
Noll, Judy	193
Norton, Robert H.	192
Norton, Rose Marie	192
Oberle, Marx	20, 37
Oberli, Marx	26
Oberly, Elisabetha Johannis	19
Oppliger, Hans	10
Otrick, Marie	175
Overstreet, Mary	162, 193
Owing, Robert	40
Palkovich, Joe Martin	198
Palkovich, Jo Linda	198
Patton, Judy	193
Payne, Mr.	109
Penn, John	52
Penn, Richard	52
Penn, Thomas	52
Penn, W.	42, 47
Peterman, Mary Elizabeth	91, 116, 117, 118
Peterson, Donald	199
Pelz, David Randall	194
Pelz, Lori Susan	194
Piper, Sara	62
Piper, William	62
Pirri, Hans	10
Plunkett, Charlotte	187
Prime, Mildred Amelia	174, 202
Pritchard, John	63
Rabe, Susannah	62
Rakai, Helen	194, 212
Rakestraw, Oscar	174
Rakestraw, Pearl	174
Ramsey, John	70
Ramseyer, Mr.	154
Rantz, Issac	111
Read, William	61
Reebel, Jacob	136
Reed, William H.	185
Reese, George	202
Reeves, Mary	188
Regan, John H.	33
Rettinger, Georg Peter	21
Rettinger, Peter	23
Reuber, Barbara	10
Reuber, Hans	11
Reuber, Josef	11
Reusser, Babi	11, 12
Reusser, Baby	10
Reusser, Barbara	12
Reusser, Elesbeth	13
Reusser, Elsbeth	12, 13, 14
Reusser, Josef	15
Reusser, Ulrich	16
Reutiger,	9
Revere, Paul	5
Reynolds, Charles	106
Rice, Lory Earl	165
Rice, Richard Bertram	165
Rice, Robert Allen	165
Rice, William Forney	165
Ricks, Margaret May	149
Rife, Abraham	95
Rife, Ephraim Forney	95
Rife, Helen, Elizabeth	95
Ritchie, Celicia	113
Ritschel, Henry	195
Ritschel, Lisa	195, 213
Robbins, Harriet	164, 165, 195, 196, 197
Robinson, Elizabeth	161, 162
Robison, Celina Allie	135, 174, 175
Robison, Donald Keith	202
Robison, Gerald Glen	202
Robison, Glen M.	202
Robison, James Lee	202
Robison, John William	202
Rodgers, Ann Marie	196
Rodgers, Elizabeth Jeanne	196
Rodgers, James Cranston	196
Rodgers, John Wallace	196
Roe, Josie	157
Rohrbach, Christine	70, 80, 81, 82
Roht, Verena	14
Roosevelt, President Franklin D.	5
Roosevelt, President Theodore	5
Root, Leland	199
Rorer, Hattie	155
Rosenbloom, Richard John	210
Rot, Christina	14
Rot, Margret	14
Rot, Uli	15
Rotach, Molitor	10
Roth, Christen	10
Roth, Christine	10
Roth, Elsbeth	10, 14
Roth, Elsi	11, 12
Roth, Froni	11
Roth, Margret	10
Routan, Abrahm	59
Ruch, Armenus	110
Ruchti, Christen	15
Rudysill, Jacob	63
Rukenbrod, Laura V.	111
Rummel, Ann	83
Rummel, John	83
Rummel, Mary	83
Rummel, Samuel	83
Rummel, Sarah	83, 100

Name	Pages
Rupp, Cathrin	13, 15
Rupp, Christine	13
Rupp, Hans	15
Rupp, Margret	11
Russer, Baby	11
Russer, Barb.	11, 14
Russer, Uli	10
Ruxegger, Cath.	12
Ruxegger, Cathie	10, 23
Ruxegger, Cathrin	11
Ruxegger, Hans	11
Ruxegger, Peter	11
Sallie, Tamanie	187
Sansenbacher, Chas.	172
Sayers, Frank	110
Sayers, Mary	109, 110, 149, 150
Schaeffer, Christiana L.	152, 190, 191
Schappaugh, Hattie	130
Scheer, Lena May	165, 197
Schenk, Anna	14
Schenk, Barbara	12, 14
Schluen, Maria	9
Schmid, Anni	14
Schneeberg, Froni	11, 14
Schneiter, Anna	12
Schneiter, Christen	15, 16
Schonenberg	14
Schreiber, Anne	10
Schultz, Della	168
Schwaar, Elsbeth	11, 12, 14
Schwaar, Elsi	11
Schwab, Nora L.	156
Schwoope, Micheal	29
Seiter, Maud	184
Sell, Abraham	46
Sempach, Hans	16
Sentz, Laura	125, 160
Shambrook, Fanny	127
Shane, Ella E.	127, 161
Shaw, Inez	174, 202
Shaw, Maria	116
Sheets, Harriet E.	152
Sheets, Harriet Emeline	115
Sheline, Bertha	154
Shell, Lloyd T.	183
Shellhouse, John	106
Shelton, Mae	191, 210
Shemmell, Geo.	70
Shepler, Susan	73
Sherz, Elizabeth	47, 64, 65, 66, 67
Shields, Juanita	190, 209
Shiley, Jacob W.	149
Shriver, David	64
Shriver, Ludwig	64
Shriver, Mary	94, 125
Shriver, Rachel	64, 76
Shriver, Susanna	72
Shrum, Peter	81
Shultz, Della	200
Schultz, John	100, 101
Schultz, Mary E.	82, 100, 101
Simmons, Irene	161
Simmons, Lydia	100, 134, 135, 136, 137
Simmons, Wilbur	161
Simons, Margaret	100
Simons, Peter	100
Sitler, Elma or Ema	111
Sittler, Martin	70
Slagle, Col. Henry	56
Slater, Agnes	186
Slutts, Jane	116
Smeltzley, Mr.	117
Smith, Martha	83, 109, 110
Smylie, James	63
Smyser, Sabina	57
Snow, Donald Leroy	210
Sousa, John Philip	163
Spandauer, Robert Lee	208
Spandauer, Susan Lee	208
Spandauer, Terri Lee	208
Spear, Renee Elizabeth	194
Spear, Ronald	194
Sponsailer, Elizabeth	73, 88, 89, 90
Sproules, Alan Carl	198
Sproules, Alfred N.	198
Sproules, Diane Kristine	198
Stackhouse, Alta Mae	176
Stackhouse, Gertrude	176
Stackhouse, Helen	176
Stackhouse, Homer	176
Stackhouse, Myrtle	146
Stallsmith, Elizabeth	114, 153
Stallsmith, Esther	114
Stallsmith, George	114
Stamp, Alice	148
Standish, Miles	5
Starr, Magdal.	14
Starr, Magdalena	12, 13
Stauffer, Christen	15
Stauffer, Verena	14
Stauffer, Vincentz	15
Steiner, Ulrich	15
Stemnerich, Julia	150
Sterno, Anna	12
Sterno, Uli	15
Stough, Rev. John	73
Strock, Chester Earl	110
Strock, Ella	83
Strock, Lorenzo Dow	110
Strock, Olga	110
Stucker, Uli	11
Stutz, Jacob	16
Stutzmann, Anna	14
Stutzmann, Hans	15
Sutor, Hans	15
Sutterin, Anna	14
Swank, Catherine	101, 137, 138

Switzer, Elizabeth E.	95, 96, 125
Swope, Eliza	76
Tagg, Rev.	152
Tallyn, Carrie Susanna	128, 163, 164
Taylor, Col.	120
Taylor, James	63
Taylor, Mary M.	134, 172
Taylor, Mrs. Robert H.	138
Taylor, Sarah	116
Thomas, George	52
Thomson, Craig Westley	198
Thomson, Ford Wesley	198
Timmons, Charles	76
Timmons, Polly	63
Tipton, Jean	124
Tipton, Mildred	124
Tipton, William	124
Tochter, Hansen	10
Tochter, Peter	11
Townsend, Louise	175
Trott, Walter	158
Tschiener, Elsbeth	14
Tschiner, Anna	14
Tustherr, Barbli	10
Tyler, President John	5
Uhl, Mr.	117
Uli, Cahrin	9, 12
Uli, Cathie	11
Uli, Cathrie	12, 14
Uli, Matthaus	12
Ulrich, Emilie	160, 161
Ulrich, Matthew	38
Usinger, Eva	11
Uziger, Eva	14
Vanarsdale, Simon	60
Varni, Hans	13, 14
Varni, Verena	15
Varny, Anna	15
Voltaire, Francois Marie Arouet	6
von Blarer, Fraulein	20, 26
von Farne, Agens	9
von Farne, Christian	9
von Farne, Nicholaus	9
von Farne, Uli	9
Vorce, Frank	167
Vorce, Goldie May	167, 198, 199
Vornick, Christian	19
Vornick, Christina	19
Vornick, Elisabeth	19
Wahrung, Anna Eva	25
Wakefield, Hazel V.	190, 209
Walker, Ellen	92, 124, 125
Walker, William	60
Ward, Earl Winston	168
Ward, Linda Kay	168
Watters, George L.	168
Wegle, Mr.	154
Weib, Christen	10
Weib, Matthys Zonggs	11
Weibel, Fenner	15
Wellendorf, Margaret M.	203, 218
Wenger, Anna	14
Wenger, Margaretha	14
Wertmuller, Christen	10, 28
Westenbarger, Cora	139, 175, 176
Widmann, Maria	10
Wilcox, Carrie Edmona	125, 160
Wilkinson, Nell	150, 188
Will, Delmer	208
Willener, Margret	14
Wilson, Eliza J.	92, 119, 120, 121, 122, 123
Wilson, Mr.	157
Winsper, Mrs. Anna	155
Winsper, Cora	156
Winter, Charles Ross	202
Witherspoon, Albertha	112
Wittwer, Hans	15
Wolf, Lelia Floyd	130
Wolfe, Arline	166
Wolfe, Elaine	166
Wolfe, Lelia F.	166, 167, 168
Wolfe, Marion A.	166
Woods, Helen	188
Wright, Asenith Irene Courtney	113, 152, 153
Wright, Cashmere	141
Wright, Dora	141
Wright, Fanny	141
Wright, George	141
Wright, Mandy	141
Wright, Perry	141
Wright, Will	141
Wyss, Christen	15
Young, Edward P.	85
Young, Elizabeth	77, 95, 96
Young, Henry	77
Young, Martha A.	85
Young, Thomas P.	85
Zarich, Johann Peter	40
Zeigler, Chauncey	113
Zeigler, Maude	113
Zeigler, Elizabeth	57
Zimmerman, Jakob	21
Zimmermann, Anna	11
Zimmermann, Christen	8
Zimmermann, Christian	23
Zimmermann, Christien	10
Zimmermann, Hans	11
Zimmermann, Magdalena	12
Zimmermann, Peter	15, 26
Zimmermann, Uli	10
Zimmermanns, Peter	19
Zimmermanns, Rosina Margaretha	19

Zolikhoffer, Anna Margaretha 24
Zongg, Christine 11
Zuber, Matthys 15
Zunor, Peter 10
Zuomin, Anna 14

www.ingramcontent.com/pod-product-compliance
Lightning Source LLC
Chambersburg PA
CBHW062109160426
42814CB00043B/215